# The Parable of the Knocker

## The True Crime Story of a Prosecutor's Fight to Bring a Serial Killer to Justice

Bryan Porter

WALDORF PUBLISHING

Published by Waldorf Publishing
2140 Hall Johnson Road
#102-345
Grapevine, Texas 76051
www.WaldorfPublishing.com

The Parable of the Knocker
The True Crime Story of a Prosecutor's Fight
to Bring a Serial Killer to Justice

ISBN: 978-1-64316-598-1
Library of Congress Control Number: 2018943887

## Dedication

To my beautiful wife, Karin, to my mom and dad, to
Scott and Laura and to Maggie.
Thank you for helping me find my way.
Words can never express my appreciation for the kind-
ness you showed me in those dark days.
Rest assured that because of the journey, and because of
your love, I am a better man.

## *AUTHOR'S NOTE*

Two months after the conclusion of the serial murder trial that is the subject of this book, I received a call from a local author. During the ensuing conversation, the author informed me that he wanted to write a true crime book about our case. He asked if I would be willing to give him access to evidence, photographs and documents. He envisioned interviewing me in detail about the investigation and the trial.

I was flattered an established author was interested in the case and I said I would consider his proposal. Internet research revealed he was respected and well-credentialed, with several popular non-fiction titles to his name. I believed he would do a good job writing the book.

But he had not lived and breathed the case as I had. He had not met the families of the victims. He had not been brought to tears by their grief or awed by their resilience. He had not felt the stress of putting the trial together or the concomitant fear of failure. He had not lain awake at night wondering whether he was up to the task.

There was only one way to make sure the story was told correctly.

I would write it myself.

****

I elected to share the story of the investigation and trial of Charles Severance for a variety of reasons. For starters, the case was a significant personal challenge. I had just started my first term as the elected prosecutor when Severance killed his second and third victims. I was unprepared for both the intense media attention the case received and the complexity of the investigation.

When I began to write this Author's Note, I recalled the sleepless nights and tremendous stress I labored under. I realized that, with the help of a countless number of people, I had grown as a person and as a lawyer. Committing the journey of personal growth to paper was difficult but ultimately cathartic. I hope the things I learned through my trial-by-fire may be useful to others facing challenges: trust your gut, seek the help of others and believe in your team.

For readers who happen to investigate or prosecute violent crimes, several specific lessons are evident. Law enforcement officers must always remember that homicide is an offense against the victim *and* their surviving friends and family. Prosecutors and detectives have a sacred obligation to honor the memory of a murder victim since they cannot speak for themselves. The victim survivors demand and deserve the appropriate level of time, concern and sensitivity. Even in jurisdictions that suffer a significant amount of violence, a murder is never "just another case." Murders are grievous, violent assaults on the rule of law and must always be treated as such.

Every human society since time immemorial has recognized that killing another human being is morally opprobrious. While ancient societies carved out categories of "justified" killings such as human sacrifice and frequent capital punishment, no group of humans has ever encouraged the indiscriminate killing of culturally homogenous people as a social more. Humans are naturally averse to homicide because it tears at the ties that bind society together.

More mundane lessons can be gleaned: homicide cases must be given priority and investigated thoroughly. All leads must be "run down" and all potential evidence analyzed. Cops and D.A.s must beware the specter of confirmation bias, a topic I discuss at length in this book. Above all else, governmental agencies must inculcate a sense of fair play and a dedication to the relevant rules of ethics.

For society at large, the Severance case provides a chilling illustration of the intersection of guns, violence and mental health. This is a crucial issue, one that grows more pressing with every mass shooting or serial killer case reported on the news. The same combination of anger, resentment and isolation from mainstream society that drove Charles Severance to murder fuels mass shooters. Much more attention needs to be focused on addressing and hopefully preventing these needless crimes.

One of the surprising points about Severance is that he was not criminally insane. He did not hear voices or receive commands from his neighbors' dog. He knew what he wanted to do and planned his crimes methodically. He understood right from wrong. He did not want to be caught. Severance was not schizophrenic and, therefore, did not fit neatly into the stereotype of a "crazed serial killer."

Severance did suffer from serious mental illness, namely at least two personality disorders, and his diagnosis definitely contributed to his crimes. But Severance's rationality and intelligence rendered him capable of avoiding the attention of the mental health system. He was never hospitalized or identified as a potential threat to the public. He was crafty enough to fly under the radar. The same is true of many of the mass shooters plaguing our nation. Most have never received mental health treatment or been identified as a risk to others before resorting to violence.

While their numbers are few, other Charles Severances unfortunately walk among us. Relying on the "mental health system" to identify and stop all of them before they kill is naïve. Mental health evaluation and treatment are necessary parts of the response to be sure; so is a comprehensive review of how the American legal system responds to mentally ill persons in both civil and criminal contexts. More difficult to achieve in the current political climate, but just as significant, are reasonable restrictions on firearms. One of my main reasons for writing is to provide my thoughts on these matters. I share some concrete proposals for dealing with the intersection of guns and mental health in the afterword.

The unrealistic way criminal investigations are depicted in popular culture also inspired me to write. Television shows and movies usually omit the humanity of prosecutors and police detectives. Public servants are shown as automatons who focus laser-like on finding a killer and who have no second thoughts. Nor do they have a personal life. In the 44 minutes of a televised crime drama there is little time for families or the immense stress that accompanies a significant case.

The dedicated team of detectives and agents who worked the Severance investigation did so with commitment, professionalism and personal sacrifice. They are outstanding public servants who should be praised for their diligence. They deserve to be recognized and I write in part to do so.

Television tremendously simplifies the investigative process, a dramatic convention that impacts real-life murder cases. Jurors inured to fictional cases have unrealistic expectations about how detectives should go about their jobs. They may expect inculpatory forensics such as DNA to exist in every trial, unaware that it is, in fact, exceptionally rare for detectives to locate such evidence at a crime scene. Jurors might remember an outlandish investigative technique that proved success-ful on their favorite police procedural and then question why the real-world detectives did not mention it in court. Most citizens have been conditioned to believe the phrase "circumstantial evidence" is a synonym for "weak case." This is neither legally nor factually true. The very nature of murder cases, in which the best witness is necessarily deceased, makes it almost certain the prosecution will have to rely on circumstantial evidence.

In my business, we have a name for the phenome-non of jurors bringing unrealistic expectations with them into the courtroom: the "CSI Effect," a reference to the eponymous prime-time drama. I write in part to explain how things work in the real world.

Finally, Severance's first offense was the 2003 kill-ing of Nancy Dunning. Nancy's death remained an un-solved mystery for over a decade. During that decade, suspicion unfairly descended on her husband, Jim. Even now, years after the trial, I occasionally have someone tell me "Jim *must* have been involved." Such unjustified speculation makes my blood boil, particularly since Jim passed away before Nancy's killer was identified and ar-rested.

No one who watched the Severance trial could har-bor any belief that Jim was culpable in his wife's death. I fervently hope this book establishes, once and for all, that Jim Dunning was an innocent man.

\*\*\*\*

Another topic urged me to write. In recent years, prosecutors have received a significant amount of negative attention in the public arena. This is understandable given the authority inherent in the job. In many cases the criticism is justified. DAs are human and in any large population of people there will be some bad actors. A prosecutor who abuses the power inherent in his office should be exposed and taken to task.

It is rare for the media to report on a prosecutor doing a good job. As one writer explained: "A headline reading 'Government wins Big Murder Case!' doesn't sell advertising." That may be true and railing against an unfair world won't accomplish much. But when members of the general public only hear about corrupt district attorneys it begins to believe the exceptions are the rule. DAs are stereotyped as egotistical climbers who thrive on putting people in prison. I write in an effort to push back on these negative views of my chosen profession.

A prosecutor's duty is not to "get a conviction at all costs." Likewise, it is not our job to "put people in jail." Our responsibility is to hold offenders accountable for their actions by obtaining just results. Holding someone accountable does not necessarily require jail time. Non-violent offenders usually merit a helping hand as opposed to a heavy one. A forward-thinking prosecutor understands that the goal is to help the offender learn from his mistakes and become a contributing part of society. A just result can often be accomplished through a combination of probation, treatment for underlying issues and community service. Diversion programs that allow citizens to avoid the stigma of a criminal conviction can help reduce recidivism. As Supreme Court Justice Robert Jackson, the lead prosecutor in the Nuremburg trials, once said in a famous speech: the successful prosecutor is expected to temper her prosecutorial "zeal with human kindness."

As a new paradigm prosecutor, I am constantly on the lookout for smarter ways to address anti-social behavior and crime. I strive to be forward-thinking and am always willing to consider whether our approach is the right one. In my opinion, the worst justification for a decision is "that's the way we've always done it." I sincerely believe I have a duty to be innovative and thoughtful in my approach to the responsibilities of my office.

****

I have never seen a prosecutor's role as a protector of civil liberties accurately described. When I took office, I swore an oath to uphold the Constitution, and I don't take oaths lightly. My job is to defend the Constitution, and that means knowing what it says and how appellate courts have interpreted those words.

The very first thing my assistants do when they catch a case is "issue spot," scouring the file for legal issues such as warrantless searches and custodial interviews of suspects. Where they find police mistakes, they take action. A huge part of a prosecutor's job is to provide instruction to law enforcement, pointing out where errors were made and how to avoid them in the future.

I have spent a career teaching law enforcement officers and prosecutors to uphold the Constitution they swore an oath to defend. Over the years I have taught literally thousands of police officers the law of search and seizure. I have traveled all over Virginia to provide this crucial instruction and have presented in states as varied as Maine, Nevada, Maryland and Georgia. I always emphasize the courts' preference for search warrants, telling cops that warrantless searches are presumed to be illegal. I stress that citizens have the right to refuse a request for police consent to search and that deciding to not answer the questions of a detective is never a crime.

I routinely present the same class to private citizens. The public has a right to know where the line between civil liberty and police intrusions has been drawn by the courts. The citizen who does not know his rights is powerless to preserve them. I am proud to provide this crucial public service.

If there is a threat to civil liberties it comes from the "big data" private corporations. I pose a simple question: who is a social media website's customer? Is it a person who opens an account or posts photos? Of course not, because social media websites do not charge for their service. The real "customers" are other companies seeking to obtain entrée to the website's users. "Big data" corporations monetize the personal information of their users, providing it to others who seek to hone their advertising. Worse yet, there is almost no judicial oversight of these practices.

****

The vast majority of people charged with crimes are not violent recidivists. To the contrary, the vast majority of crimes under my office's responsibility are non-violent misdemeanors. Over the years I have become convinced that two factors, above all others, account for a disproportionate amount of criminal behavior: mental health issues and substance abuse. In many offenders both problems are present.

A prosecutor who uses the threat of jail as a "one size fits all" response will never increase the collective felicity of his constituency. Innovative programs must be introduced to confront the dual specters of mental health and substance abuse.

In Alexandria, we have adopted two such programs. In early 2017, my office introduced a Mental Health Initiative (MHI). A senior prosecutor is assigned to run the MHI. She adopts cases from other assistants in the office in which mental health issues significantly contributed to the underlying crime. The MHI is designed to provide the offender with a host of services and treatment in an effort to address the root cause of their issues and get them on the right track. In many cases, a criminal conviction is avoided altogether. As a "new paradigm" program, MHI requires my office to go beyond the threat of jail time and liaise with a host of City agencies such as probation and the Department of Community and Human Services.

In another example of inter-agency cooperation, Alexandria has recently adopted and initiated a Substance Abuse Treatment Court. This comprehensive program provides drug and alcohol treatment and compliance monitoring to help offenders break the cycle of addiction. If the substance abuse proves to be an attempt to self-medicate an undiagnosed mental illness, mental health professionals stand by to assist. Importantly, the program requires the agreement of the person charged; they must truly want assistance and must agree to abide by the terms of the program. This "buy-in" component significantly increases the chance of success.

In my brief stint as the elected prosecutor I have adopted other progressive policies. My office does not "stack charges," indicting as many counts as possible in an effort to force a defendant to plead guilty. I have prohibited my assistants from requesting cash bail for low-level offenses; it is unconscionable that a person would remain in jail before trial for want of $100 to secure a bond. I have recently expanded our diversion program, allowing certain non-violent offenders to avoid damaging their future by incurring a criminal conviction. It is my policy to expeditiously approve every expungement request that complies with the Code.

\*\*\*\*

Courts repeatedly remind prosecutors that we are "ministers of justice" whose duty is to ensure a just result is reached in every case. If a prosecutor is personally convinced a suspect is innocent, then she cannot ethically prosecute the case and must dismiss it. This obligation to seek justice means a prosecutor's "conviction rate" is not the right way of evaluating her performance. In many cases, a prosecutor's duty to obtain a just result will dictate she dismiss a case for lack of evidence. If intentionally "losing" a case is often the just result, it follows that keeping track of "wins and losses" is lower-level thinking that does not accurately measure how a prosecutor does her job.

In my office, I do not compile "won-loss" records or "conviction rate" statistics for my assistants. To the contrary, I evaluate them on their adherence to the rules of ethics and their professional judgment. Indeed, I consider adherence to the rules of ethics applicable to prosecutors—which I discuss at several points later on in this book—to be the "Prime Directive" for my assistants.

**** 

Violent crime is another matter. The prosecutor has sworn an oath to protect the community from violence. Once the DA has weighed the evidence and decided to formally charge someone with murdering another human being, the "just result" from her perspective will be to secure a conviction so as to protect the citizenry. The stakes are high in a murder case; if the defendant is acquitted, the victim and his family have no justice and a killer walks free empowered to act with impunity in the future. Someone who maliciously kills another human being must expect stringent punishment.

Prosecutors must remain cognizant of their responsibility to address the needs and concerns of those who have been victimized by violent acts and must sincerely weigh the wishes of victims about the conduct of a case. In Virginia, the legislature has enacted a "Victim's Bill of Rights" which statutorily requires the DA to solicit and consider a victim's wishes and to keep the victim apprised of the progress of the case. I fear that the rights of victims, particularly survivors of murder victims, may be misunderstood or overlooked by the general public.

****

In writing this book, I have tried not to sensationalize. The unvarnished facts are sufficiently compelling and I did my best to stick to them, relying on trial transcripts and investigative reports to ensure accuracy. Where possible I used direct quotes. I believe I avoided veering too far into speculation although, since Severance never gave his side of the story, I have indulged in a few inferences about his motivations and methods. I have tried to clearly identify those passages where I was forced to resort to conjecture.

For obvious reasons, I strived to honor the privacy of the huge number of people affected by Severance's rampage. That group obviously includes the surviving victims and their friends and families, but other reluctant people were involved. I estimate that over 50 individuals connected to this narrative satisfy the Virginia Code's definition of "victim." With that large number comes an equally large number of reactions to the tragedy. For example, some of the victims have become public advocates for reasonable restrictions on guns, while others have studiously avoided the glare of the public's eye.

My best course with regards to respecting the privacy of those affected was to omit names and identifying information wherever doing so was possible. Where I have found it necessary to name specific people, I have tried to do so in the briefest fashion possible. I also studiously avoided speculating about how the surviving victims felt or were impacted by the crimes. My goal was to tell my story and narrate from my viewpoint, focusing on the police investigation and trial. If a reader wonders why a particular person is not named, or why a specific twist in the investigation is dealt with summarily, rest assured it is an effort to protect someone who was affected by this case.

There were an immense number of individuals who worked on the investigation, so many it is impossible to name them all or detail their contributions. By necessity, I focus on the four detectives and the three prosecutors who, along with me, formed the core trial team. There are dozens of others just as deserving of mention. I hope the reader will forgive the constraints of the written word and understand those who are mentioned are surrogates for a host of others.

The epigrams, displayed in bold at the beginning of each chapter, are Severance's words, quoted directly from the collection of his writings recovered by police. At trial, I would refer to this collection of horrifying documents as the "Manifesto of Hate."

## *PROLOGUE*

### <u>January 1997</u>

"I think that asshole just stole a can of soup from a shopping cart!"

The rookie police officer looked up from the report he was writing and glanced to his right. The eerie red glow from the police car's interior dome light—customized to allow an officer to write while not ruining his night vision—washed his training officer's face with crimson. The January air outside their parked police car was clear and crisp. The rookie followed his training officer's eyes as she stared toward the neon-lit façade of a nearby supermarket and a man standing just outside of the store entrance.

After finishing their classroom instruction at the police academy new police officers were assigned to ride with an experienced cop known as a Field Training Officer (FTO). This rookie had won the lottery by being assigned to FTO Adrienne Miller. Miller was small of stature, but fearless. She was also tough and no-nonsense; necessary qualities if she were going to teach the rookie how to stay safe in the always-dangerous world of policing.

The rookie had stopped his police cruiser in the parking lot of a nondescript strip mall. It seemed like a quiet spot, perfect for finishing the police report from an earlier call for service. At Miller's direction the rookie had backed into a parking space and left the engine running. If the pair received a hot radio run the rookie could drop the transmission into drive, flip the switch for the emergency lights and be moving forward within seconds.

The rookie had been riding with Miller for the past three weeks. Throughout that time, the frigid January weather made it difficult to get out of the police car. Miller used the ample down time to teach the little things cops need to know: always look for expired registration stickers on license plates, always sit with your back to the wall when eating in a restaurant and always wear your watch with the face on the inside of your wrist to add a little protection to blood vessels if you're in a knife fight.

Before the rookie could even put pen to paper—in 1997, police officers still wrote reports by hand—Miller had noticed a white male in his late 30s who walked, slightly stooped over, out of the supermarket. He was wearing a black leather bomber jacket. The man wore no hat or gloves despite the freezing temperature. Of average height and weight, the man's dark hair was receding and featured a prominent widow's peak jutting out from his high forehead. Though his face was gaunt with thin cheeks and lips most women would have considered him handsome.

The intensity of the man's stare was striking. As he walked out of the grocery store his eyes locked on the police car like two pieces of iron drawn to a magnet. He stood stone-still with tendrils of smoky breath emanating from his nostrils as he exhaled. Something about him caused Miller's "spider sense" to tingle.

Miller assumed that, at this distance, the man could not see into the police car. After 20 seconds of standing and staring, he seemed satisfied the officers posed no threat and began to walk away from the front of the store. As he did, the man passed a parked shopping cart full of canned goods. A large sign stood next to it proudly proclaiming: "Christmas Campaign to Help the Homeless." Miller watched as the man stopped near the sign and scanned the area, trying to determine if anyone was watching. With no warning his right hand flashed into the cart. The man helped himself to several cans of food, placing them in the large pockets of his leather jacket. After casting a sidelong glance back at the police car, he walked to a decrepit Ford pickup truck and got into the driver's seat. First the tail lights came on—at least the left one did, as the right was cracked and burned out—and then the engine roared to life, discharging a puff of black smoke from the exhaust.

Like most cops, Miller had a distinct sense of right and wrong and stealing canned goods destined for the homeless offended it. As she watched the man get into his pickup truck and start to drive off she looked over at the rookie: "That guy just stole from a homeless food drive. Get behind him and pull him over."

"You heard me, light him up."

**** 

The rookie put the cruiser into drive, activated the overhead emergency lights and pulled in behind the pickup. The truck slowly drove on for about 100 yards, meandering about the parking lot as though the driver was thinking about gunning the engine and making a run for it. After the rookie squelched the siren for a second or two the truck finally stopped in front of a video rental store. The rookie grabbed the microphone and marked out: "Unit 331, we'll be out on traffic in the 3600 block of King Street." As he awaited the dispatcher's reply the rookie could see the man intently watching him in the reflection of the rearview mirror. Just as Miller had taught him to do, the rookie trained the police car's bright white spotlight on the parked truck. The light had trouble penetrating the haze belching from the pickup's exhaust pipe.

The two police officers exited and walked toward the truck with the rookie on the driver's side. They noticed the man in the truck was using a large external mirror mounted on the driver's door to watch them as they approached. The driver's window was down and the rookie could hear the gentle twang of country music playing on the radio.

"Sir, may I see your license and registration?" the rookie said as he reached the window. The man in the truck stared straight ahead with both of his hands clenching the steering wheel so tightly the rookie thought the wheel might crack. The man did not answer and made no move to retrieve his wallet. The rookie again asked for the license.

The driver replied in a loud, clear voice: "I am a proud citizen of this City. I will have you know I recently ran for mayor of Alexandria."

Then, even louder: "I do not play by your rules!"

****

This was the most unusual traffic stop the young police officer had made in his brief career. He ignored the odd response to his request for identification and tried again, this time more forcefully: "Sir, we are investigating a larceny of canned goods from the grocery store over there. Please hand over your license."

The driver did not respond. Just as the rookie was about to open the door and locate the license himself, the driver reached into the inner pocket of his jacket and retrieved his wallet. He handed the entire billfold to the rookie with one hand, grasping the steering wheel with the other and continuing to look straight ahead.

The rookie opened the billfold and discovered it was filled with scraps of paper covered in scrawling handwriting. He located the license and pulled it out. The driver's name was Charles Stanard Severance, 36 years of age, with an address on Gunston Road in Alexandria—about a mile from the site of the traffic stop. The rookie had grown up in Alexandria and knew Gunston Road was on the outskirts of a neighborhood known as Del Ray.

Still looking straight ahead, Severance blurted out in an angry voice: "I am a proud homeowner and taxpayer. I ran for mayor and received 10 percent of the vote in the last election! I demand you release me immediately!"

Severance's refusal to look at him and unusual anger made the rookie very apprehensive. Not for the last time, he thought there was something not quite right about Charles Severance.

As the rookie contemplated his next move, Miller leapt from her station on the passenger's side of the truck. She noticed her door was unlocked and could see two cans of food resting on the bench seat. Opening the door, she grabbed the cans and told Severance she had seen him steal them from the shopping cart. Severance now released his death grip on the wheel and reacted, angrily pointing at Miller and yelling "you need a warrant for that!" He pawed at the cans, knocking one of them out of Miller's hand.

Miller ordered Severance not to move and walked around to the driver's side. She told the rookie she was going to go back to the grocery store to see if the management was willing to prosecute Severance for the theft. Given the freezing weather, the rookie told Severance to stay in the truck and then went back to his police cruiser.

From this vantage point the rookie could see Severance was "acting hinky," a police catch-all term for someone who is thinking about fighting or fleeing. Severance continued to stare into the rearview mirror of his truck. Once or twice, he broke eye contact with the police car and moved his hands under the driver's seat.

A few minutes later, Miller returned to the cruiser and informed the rookie she planned on arresting Severance on two charges: misdemeanor larceny and obstruction of justice for knocking the can from her hands. Miller explained she had a "really bad feeling" about Severance and felt he was likely to resist.

The rookie approached the pickup again and said: "Mr. Severance, I need you to step out of the truck. You're under arrest."

Severance immediately raised his voice, shouting: "I am a proud citizen of this City and I will not suffer this lunacy!" He made a quick move to go under the driver's seat with both of his hands. This unexpected movement prodded the rookie to action. He threw open the driver's side door and grabbed Severance's left arm. The rookie could see an object under the driver's seat that seemed to be the focus of Severance's attention. Concerned it might be a weapon, the rookie placed his other hand on Severance's right shoulder and started to drag him out of the truck. Severance forcefully tried to pull away from the rookie and continued to grab for the object under the front seat.

Miller ran around from the passenger side and joined the struggle. Severance did not give up easily, ignoring repeated commands to "Stop resisting!" Finally, with their combined efforts, the two officers were able to pull Severance from the vehicle, get him up against the truck and handcuff him. As he continued to scream about "law enforcement lunacy" the officers half-dragged Severance to the police cruiser and secured him in the rear seat.

The rookie then returned to the pickup truck to search it. Under the driver's seat, directly where Severance had been reaching, the rookie could see a black piece of canvas cloth. He pulled the cloth away, revealing a small handgun. The gun, a .380 Czech-made semi-automatic pistol, was fully loaded with a round in the chamber. To fire it, all Severance would have needed to do was point it and pull the trigger.

For the first time in his brief police career the rookie realized a person with whom he was dealing could easily have killed him. Throughout the time Miller was talking with the supermarket manager, Severance sat in his truck with a loaded pistol beneath his seat and within easy reach. Had Severance decided to grab the gun and shoot his way out of the encounter the rookie would not have stood a chance.

The realization he could have easily been killed made a forceful impression on the young officer.

**\*\*\*\***

On January 23, 1997, Charles Severance was charged with three misdemeanors: Petit Larceny, Obstruction of Justice and Carrying a Concealed Weapon. Three months later, the Larceny and Obstruction charges were dismissed after Severance pleaded guilty to the Concealed Weapon count. He was sentenced to serve 10 days in the Alexandria jail.

At the time Severance began his brief jail sentence the elected Sheriff for the City of Alexandria was James "Jim" Dunning. Sheriff Dunning's deputies booked Severance into the jail and guarded him for his stay in what Severance would dub the "rebar motel." Jim Dunning's name was on the warrants charging Severance with his crimes and Jim Dunning's photo hung on the wall of the booking station where incoming inmates were processed.

****

The rookie didn't know it at the time, but this chance 1997 parking lot encounter with Charles Severance was the first in a series of events that would culminate in the cold-blooded assassinations of three Alexandria citizens.

---

## PART I - MODUS OPERANDI

---

### Chapter One

*"Local law enforcement lunatics parade around as though they are exempt from family violence. They are not exempt. They are weak and prone to attack. An effective predator knows."*

Alexandria, Virginia, is a historic city nestled on the banks of the Potomac River. From its vibrant waterfront a visitor can see the Washington Monument. Founded in 1749, the City's 170,000 residents are never afraid to cite the huge number of "George Washington Slept Here" plaques hanging on buildings in the City's quaint Old Town section. One of Alexandria's oldest edifices is Gadsby's Tavern, a colonial inn and alehouse in which the docents dress up in period garb, curtsy and shout "huzzah" as they nuzzle pewter tankards.

Real estate prices and net incomes are high in Alexandria and violent crime is routinely low. It is unusual for the City to clock more than five murders in a calendar year and one year in recent history there were none. Like any urban area, Alexandria has problems with mundane crime: petty theft, drunk driving and domestic assault. But Alexandrians are far more used to watching smoke curl from the chimneys of ancient homes than from the barrel of a discharged firearm.

If Alexandria is an idyllic city, then Del Ray is its

most idyllic neighborhood; quiet streets with quiet homes made of dimpled bricks and with children playing in quiet front yards. Most Del Ray homes are large enough for prospective buyers to get momentarily lost inside during an open house. The large houses boast even larger purchase prices.

In December 2003, Nancy Dunning, a successful real estate agent and a devoted mom, lived on Mount Ida Avenue right in the heart of that idyllic neighborhood. Nancy had been unofficially crowned the "Queen of Del Ray" for her connection to the community. Nancy resided in a beautiful brick home with her husband, Jim, the City's elected Sheriff. The center-stairway colonial provided the perfect home base for the couple to raise their two children.

Living in ideal homes in the ideal neighborhood of an ideal city, Nancy and her neighbors slumbered soundly in their beds at night, focused on the things the American Dream told them to worry about: the promotion at work, buying an "entry-level" luxury sedan and their children's soccer games.

While Nancy and her neighbors slumbered the Alexandria Assassin seethed.

The illusion of security enjoyed by the "elite law enforcement class" enraged him.

He would "increase uncertainty" among the elites.

He would "introduce murder" into their "safe and secure neighborhood."

He would watch that neighborhood "shudder with horror."

He would do so "Again. And Again. And Again."

\*\*\*\*

It was just weeks before Christmas 2003 and 56-year old Nancy Dunning had some shopping to do. Not for her family—she had finished buying presents for them weeks ago. Instead, she needed some smaller items to donate to her favorite charity's Christmas drive. She planned on going to the local Target store, located right outside of Del Ray and about 10 minutes from her home.

On the morning of December 3, as Nancy was getting dressed to head out to Target, she saw her husband preparing to go to work. Jim asked Nancy if she could meet him and their adult son, Chris, for lunch. Nancy readily agreed to the lunch date, setting the time at 11:30 a.m. at the family's favorite restaurant. By coincidence, the restaurant was situated in the same strip mall where the rookie officer arrested Charles Severance in 1997.

Nancy gathered her purse and her flip-style cell-phone and headed to her car. She drove a gray Toyota which bore both a Sheriff's license plate replete with a badge and a "Jim Dunning for Sheriff" bumper sticker. The plate and sticker loudly proclaimed the identity of the car's owner to anyone interested, but those who live in idyllic neighborhoods need not worry about being followed by an urban assassin.

Nancy made the short drive to Target and parked. She entered the store at about 9:30 a.m., shuttling a shopping cart and spending about an hour inside. As she walked around the store, Nancy was intently focused on her prospective purchases. So focused she did not notice the clean-cut young man who entered the store about 30 minutes after her. She did not see that he walked slightly stooped over and wore a black leather bomber jacket. She did not notice his receding hairline or the prominent widow's peak in the middle of his forehead.

By coincidence Nancy was walking directly toward the man as he entered the Target. She failed to register the surprise in the man's eyes as she passed within feet of him. Nor did she see him cough, pretend to make a call on his cellphone and bend down to avoid her seeing his face. Nancy did not notice as he stood up and begin to shadow her movements for the next 30 minutes. She didn't observe the man leaving the store directly behind her, buying nothing and saying nothing to anyone inside.

The kind and gentle Queen of Del Ray did not see the roiling anger flashing behind his dark eyes.

*　　*　　*　　*

Unknown to both Nancy Dunning and the man who followed her around the store was the fact that their movements were captured by the Target video system. In the days after Nancy's murder police detectives learned Nancy had been at Target immediately before her death. They responded to the store and obtained copies of the VHS tapes containing the surveillance feed from the morning of the crime.

The video itself was of poor quality but the detectives were able to locate Nancy as she entered. She remained in sight of one of the many Target security cameras for most of the next hour, walking around the store and selecting items to purchase.

The footage also captured the young man who came into the store after Nancy. It caught him as he literally almost ran into her. It taped him quickly bend to tie his shoe. Although the blurry camera made his features difficult to discern, the camera clearly displayed his widow's peak and leather jacket. The detectives reviewing the video were suspicious of the man's movements because he seemed to follow Nancy around as she shopped. He also walked out of the store immediately behind her after making no effort to buy anything. Police released still images of the man to the media in an effort to generate tips.

Due to the poor quality of the video images no leads were ever developed from the Target video. The tape sat in the police property room collecting dust for over a decade until the Alexandria Assassin killed two more prominent Alexandrians.

Once detectives identified Charles Severance as a suspect in those murders they learned striking facts about him: in 2015, Charles Severance had long, grey hair and an unkempt beard, matching a composite sketch created by a surviving victim. In 2003, he wore his dark hair short, revealing a prominent widow's peak, just like the man depicted in the Target video.

If the same person committed all three murders, the killer had aged and changed appearance in the exact same manner as Charles Severance.

*     *     *     *

Nancy left Target and drove directly home. She parked her Toyota in her garage, leaving the overhead accordion door open. The garage was attached to the house and communicated directly with the kitchen. Nancy went inside and placed the items she had purchased on a nearby counter. She opened her cellphone and dialed a friend's number, receiving no answer. She didn't leave a message. Detectives subsequently reviewing Nancy's phone records determined she made this call at 10:54 a.m.

As Nancy flipped her phone closed, she heard a

knock on the front door. Nancy wasn't expecting anyone, but the knocks did not cause her any alarm. It was daylight in an idyllic neighborhood. Perhaps it was a delivery person dropping off an early Christmas package.

She opened the front door. Directly in front of her stood a young man with close-cropped hair, a leather jacket and a distinctive widow's peak. She had never seen the man before and had no clue who he was or what he was about to do.

Nancy could not see he was wearing latex gloves. She could not see the small, silver revolver cradled in his right hand.

Nancy asked: "Can I help you?"

The man at the door coolly responded: "I ask the questions."

He raised his right hand and fired.

****

No one knows what Nancy's assailant said before he fired. In another related homicide that occurred a decade later a surviving witness was able to confirm the killer briefly spoke to his victim when she opened her front door. However, the witness was not close enough to make out exactly what was said.

After that subsequent murder Charles Severance was identified as a suspect and arrested. When he was taken into custody, a large cache of his angry writings was recovered. These documents, which will collectively be referred to as the "Manifesto of Hate" for reasons that will soon be apparent, contained the handwritten words "I ask the questions" a number of times. This terse statement was employed in a sarcastic manner and used to flaunt Severance's personal belief in his superiority over those he considered members of the "law enforce-ment elite."

Given Severance's proclivity to use the phrase, it is reasonable to surmise he uttered it, or a similar sarcastic remark, when greeted at the front door. He would have gained satisfaction by expressing his control of the situa-tion, particularly if he did so in a mocking tone. It would have pleased him to see the uncertainty in his victim's eyes just before he raised his five-shot mini-revolver and pulled the trigger.

****

The first round hit Nancy directly in the chest. It probably would have been fatal on its own. Nancy re-treated into her home. The killer fired again. This time Nancy was able to get her arm up in a defensive posture. The bullet went through her arm and hit her chest but did not penetrate. Nancy stumbled into a nearby table, knocking over several family photos.

As she lost consciousness, Nancy fell onto her back near the bottom of the home's main staircase. The killer walked over to her and placed the revolver behind her left ear. He fired again, killing her instantly. Crime scene investigators would confirm all three bullets were very small .22LR rounds. No spent cartridge cases from fired bullets were left behind, suggesting the killer used a re-volver.

The entire attack was over within seconds.

The killer did not touch anything in the home or steal anything. He was not a petty thief. He was an as-sassin, free from the oppressive laws of the "government elites." He was a "proud patriarch" and a "noble savage" who was justified in killing whomever he pleased as a matter of "duty to his class."

The Alexandria Assassin blamed Sheriff Jim Dunning for a court's decision to deny him custody of his infant son. As he wrote in his Manifesto, his calculus was simple:

**"They kidnap and they die."**

\*\*\*\*

Father James Walsh was the principal celebrant at Nancy's funeral mass. Struggling to find the words to describe a paragon of the community, Father Walsh extolled Nancy's kindness, her civic virtue and her love of family. He gave a stirring homily in which he urged Nancy's friends and family to find hope through their faith.

"We have all died this death," Father Walsh said. "Nancy was a gift, directly or indirectly, to each of us here today. As the pain recedes, we will feel her life as a gift." Father Walsh continued, telling those assembled all of God's servants "must entertain grief and anger. But when the grief and anger come knocking at the door… it is not all that is there. We can also listen for the voice of hope."

As he gave his homily, Father Walsh had no idea what had transpired during Nancy's murder. His chosen metaphor of "grief… knocking on the door" is, therefore, striking. Grief and anger had indeed come knocking on Nancy Dunning's door. But no one knew who the Knocker was or why he knocked.

The Manifesto of Hate contains a poem entitled the "Parable of the Knocker." This disturbing document explains in cryptic words why the Alexandria Assassin decided to kill.

It would take 12 years, the assassination of two

more people and a team of dedicated police detectives and prosecutors to decipher the "Parable of the Knocker."

**\*\*\*\***

Quick: how many states are there in the Union?

The answer isn't 50. There are 46—and four Commonwealths. The difference boils down to the type of land grants the King of England bestowed back when we were his wayward colonies. For almost everyone, this is a distinction without a difference. But it matters to me, because I am the elected Commonwealth's Attorney for the City of Alexandria.

The reader might say: "That's great. But what's a Commonwealth's Attorney?" If I used the more common term State's Attorney, I would get more recognition. But the Commonwealth of Virginia loves tradition and elected prosecutors in Virginia carry an anachronistic title.

In other words, I am Jack McCoy from Law and Order, only not as handsome and definitely not as good at trial. McCoy is so good at closing argument I sometimes suspect his lines are scripted.

I began my career in law enforcement in 1995 as a police officer with the Metro Transit Police, transferring to the Alexandria Police Department in late 1996. I went to law school in the evenings at George Mason University while working the midnight shift as a cop.

I immediately made the jump to prosecutor after passing the bar exam, starting as an Assistant Commonwealth's Attorney in Alexandria in October 2001. As I gained experience, most of my time was spent prosecuting felonious assaults: shootings and stabbings with the odd screwdriver or stomping attack thrown in for good measure. By 2012, I had about 10 murder cases under my belt.

In 2013, my boss and predecessor in office, Randy Sengel, decided he was retiring. In many ways, running to succeed Randy as Commonwealth's Attorney made sense. I was born and raised in Alexandria and had lived there most of my life. My mother had been a beloved teacher at a local private school for over 30 years and my father had a lengthy career in the City public school system, retiring as deputy superintendent, so my last name was well-known. If I ever were going to win a political race, it would be this one.

On November 5, 2013, I was elected to my first term. My wife Karin and I celebrated the victory with a well-deserved vacation. We flew to Grenada and climbed aboard a 40-foot sailboat for a week-long adventure. I looked forward to the rest of the trip and then to getting back to the office so I could start on the many administrative changes I planned on implementing.

While I was thinking these thoughts, sailing through a stiff wind on four-foot swells, the Alexandria Assassin was planning on implementing some changes of his own.

\*\*\*\*

Ron Kirby lived on a quiet, tree-lined lane appropriately named Elm Street. His house, situated about halfway up the northern slope of a local prominence called Shuter's Hill, was tucked into the same neighborhood as Nancy Dunning's. Native Alexandrians might insist the two homes were in different sub-neighborhoods, Mount Ida and Rosemont, but only a mile separated them. That distance was cut in half by a suburban thoroughfare, Braddock Road, which runs east-west through Del Ray.

The Kirby home was a well-maintained brick bungalow, replete with a large front porch running the width of the house. Elm Street was exceptionally quiet and many of Ron's neighbors were empty nesters. To find Ron's house, a visitor would have to drive through a warren of short roads and make a number of right-angle turns. Elm Street was even more isolated and serene than Mount Ida Avenue.

Ron shared the home with his wife, a devoted volunteer to liberal causes. Ironically, one of the issues she was most passionate about was gun control. He was close with his two adult children from his first marriage and both were frequent visitors to the Elm Street home.

At 69, Kirby was nearing retirement age. His senior position with the Council of Governments, a non-profit association usually referred to as COG, allowed him a little schedule flexibility. The Washington area is a hodgepodge of jurisdictions split between the federal enclave of D.C., Virginia and Maryland. COG brings together representatives from the different governments to develop solutions to the region's major challenges. Ron had served as COG's director of transportation planning for almost 27 years. Beloved by his COG coworkers, his friends and his family, Ron had absolutely no enemies.

In the late 1990s, Ron had been a moving force behind the planning and construction of the new Woodrow Wilson Bridge in southern Alexandria. That span, connecting Virginia and Maryland, was a complicated, multi-jurisdictional project illustrative of Ron's ability to bring groups with diverse interests together.

Ron Kirby had made a career out of building bridges, both metaphorically and literally.

On the morning of Monday, November 11, 2013, Ron was focused on a more mundane project involving water: repairing his kitchen sink.

Ron had decided to work from home. A couple of nights before, he had been looking for a trash bag when he noticed a slow leak from a pipe. Ron unsuccessfully tried to fix it and concluded it was beyond his ability to repair. Ron called a plumber and took the earliest time slot available for a house call: 11:30 a.m. on November 11.

At a little after 9:00 a.m., Ron's wife kissed him goodbye and walked out to her car. She had a doctor's appointment that morning and thereafter was attending a meeting at one of the many organizations for which she volunteered. As she left, Ron poured himself a cup of coffee and sat down, putting on his glasses and opening the newspaper. The front windows of the home, exposed to the northeast, admitted the bright rays of the sun into his living room.

Ron Kirby had just about two hours to live.

****

At 11:32 a.m., the plumber called Ron's cellphone to say he was running slightly late for the appointment. He briefly spoke to Ron during this call, establishing that Ron was still alive. Phone records subsequently confirmed the time of this conversation.

At 11:42, the plumber arrived at the Elm Street house. He called Ron's cellphone, but no one answered. After a brief delay, the plumber walked up to the Kirby's front door. He rang the doorbell, received no response and returned to his truck.

At 11:46, the plumber called Ron again and received no answer. He waited 15 minutes and, after a third unanswered call, decided to leave for another repair call. Given Ron was alive and answering the phone at 11:32 but did not answer at 11:42, it can be inferred he was killed in the intervening 10 minutes.

****

Around noon that morning, Alexandria Police Detective Sean Casey was dispatched to respond to the Kirby home for the call of a possible homicide. Having grown up in Alexandria, Casey immediately recognized how unusual it was for a violent crime to have occurred on secluded Elm Street. Casey's mind raced as he approached the Kirby residence.

Quiet, intelligent and focused, Casey was young for a detective and an Alexandria native. His superiors had recognized the potential of this hometown kid early on and quickly promoted him to criminal investigations.

Casey soon learned serving as a detective was far different than being on uniformed patrol. Patrol officers were conditioned to respond to an emergency, handle it and go back in service. Detective work required a more thorough approach. Complicated cases demand months of follow-up work: interviews, following leads and waiting for the back-logged lab to finish with the forensic analysis of evidence. A good detective has to have determination, an ability to talk to people and a sense of obligation to the community. Sean Casey possessed all three qualities in abundance.

A patrol sergeant approached and informed him the first uniformed officers to respond had observed no signs of forced entry. Casey learned Ron's wallet had been located with $60 cash in it, eliminating theft as a motive. It appeared someone had ambushed Ron, attacking with little or no warning.

Casey entered the house and met with crime scene investigators. They surmised Ron had been sitting in his living room, reading, when he heard a knock at the front door. Ron had stood up to answer, taking off his reading glasses and holding them in his hand as he walked the short distance to the door. Ron was holding his glasses when his attacker started shooting. One of the rounds struck the glasses and shattered a lens.

The location of Ron's body, coupled with the location of the fired ammunition recovered from the living room, established Ron was shot immediately after he opened the front door. Two small caliber rounds were fired into his chest from extremely close range. The medical examiner would determine these rounds, identified as .22LR bullets, struck major blood vessels and would have proved fatal within minutes.

Given Ron's size and good health, he did not immediately collapse after being shot, instead retreating back into the living room in an effort to flee his assailant. The shooter stepped into the foyer and then continued to the foyer's threshold with the living room, firing three more .22LR rounds and striking Ron in the hip with one of the shots. The rapid loss of blood from the shots to the chest brought Ron to the floor of the living room. This is where he was found by a family member.

One fired .22LR bullet was located inside of a piano in the living room. The piano had been behind Ron as he retreated from the gunfire; the gunman had missed Ron with this round. Investigators also recovered another .22LR bullet from the floor behind Ron. This round had also missed and struck a cast-iron radiator.

There were no fired cartridge cases recovered from the scene, implying a revolver was used. The detective did some simple math and arrived at the total number of rounds fired during the attack. Three bullets from Ron's body plus two recovered from the living room meant the assassin had pulled the trigger five times.

Casey did not know it yet, but there was only one five-shot .22LR mini-revolver produced in America.

Charles Severance was obsessed with that exact firearm.

\*\*\*\*

On November 11, 2013, as Ron Kirby was murdered in his Del Ray home, my wife and I were sailing between Bequia and Grenada in the Windward Islands. When we got back to port I had an email about the case in my inbox. I had no inkling at that point the same man had murdered both Ron Kirby and Nancy Dunning.

We returned home on November 15 and soon thereafter I met with Detective Casey to be briefed on Ron's murder. Casey recounted the evidence and explained Kirby had been shot in broad daylight as he answered a knock at his front door. He had no witnesses and no real leads. I've always known Casey to be direct and he made it clear he did not have a lot to work with. Ron Kirby's murderer had struck without warning and had apparently disappeared without a trace.

When a person with no known enemies meets a violent demise, it is standard practice for the police to investigate whether a family member was involved. Beginning with when Cain slew Abel, a review of the vagaries of human existence establishes familiarity often breeds contempt. When no obvious leads are presented at a murder scene, the first page in a detective's playbook is to determine whether any close friends or relatives had an axe to grind.

I asked whether Casey had considered the possibility that someone close to Ron had been involved in his death. He shot me a look that shouted: "Of course I have, Porter," explaining he had already eliminated the family as suspects. Casey had corroborated their whereabouts, interviewing witnesses and obtaining video footage that proved Ron's loved ones had nothing to do with the crime.

As Casey left, I focused on a more immediate worry: my parents. At the time, my mother and father lived in the Kirby neighborhood. Worse yet, they had a penchant for keeping the front door of their home open with nothing but an unlocked storm door between them and the world. Their dog Maggie liked to sit at the door and watch the world go by. I called my father and told him he needed to start closing and locking the door. He has ever since.

My dad heard a rumor floating around that "someone close to Ron" might have killed him. I encountered this rumor as well, but I knew there was absolutely no evidence to support it. Rumors, like maggots in an eighteenth-century laboratory, seem to spontaneously generate. I was direct with my dad, making it clear that the evidence suggested it was a random attack.

How rumors start, I'm not certain. But they quickly get repeated—and believed—by people trying to rationalize random violence. If you can explain why a murder happened—if there is an "angry brother" or a "nutty former business partner"—then you can dispel the horror a little bit. An explanation means "it couldn't possibly happen to me." No one wants to think that death could unexpectedly darken their door.

Like everyone else, my parents wanted to feel safe. They wanted a plausible explanation for the Kirby murder. They wanted to keep the front door open and the storm door unlocked. They wanted Maggie to lay down at the front door and watch the world go by.

In a perfect world the door could be kept unlocked.

But the world is filled with imperfect creatures.

\*\*\*\*

On the morning of Thursday, February 6, 2014, I was conducting a sentencing hearing on the most high-profile homicide case I had prosecuted to that point. An off-duty law enforcement officer from another jurisdiction had gotten into an altercation and had shot and killed a young man who showed a great deal of promise. Although the officer wasn't in uniform, he asserted he was trying to arrest the victim during the incident. Therefore, the community and the press considered it a law enforcement shooting and the case received significant media attention. After an extremely hard-fought murder trial, the jury compromised and convicted the officer of the lesser charge of manslaughter.

In the week before the hearing I prepared a lengthy sentencing argument. As the judge took the bench, I nervously surveyed the courtroom and observed a gaggle of local reporters sitting in the courtroom pews.

The sentencing hearing began at 10:00 a.m. The judge heard my argument first and then that of the defense attorney, Chris Leibig. Neither of us were aware we would be locking horns again on another significant case within a matter of months.

The sentencing hearing was over around 11:50 a.m.

That was about twenty minutes after Ruthanne Lodato was shot.

****

As the judge left the bench, the courtroom deputies yelled out "Court is in recess!" One approached me and whispered: "There's been another shooting in Sector Two. It's bad. You need to get out there."

The Alexandria Police Department splits up the City into three sectors, with Del Ray in Sector Two. Something about the urgency in the deputy's voice caused me to feel uneasy. I'm not one who really believes in "extra-sensory perception" but as I walked toward my office, I felt a heavy, looming dread.

The best way I can explain it is to liken it to a tsunami. When a tsunami is about to hit, the physics of the event cause the water close to shore to recede significantly shortly before the wave crashes. To eyewitnesses, this effect seems almost supernatural. The sea floor is quickly exposed for hundreds of yards with fish flopping and seaweed exposed to the sun.

The phenomenon often causes an additional problem. Unsuspecting tourists walk out onto the exposed sea floor because of the novelty of it, unaware of the danger of the water returning in the form of a tidal wave. They don't know that in a matter of minutes a literal wall will come crashing down upon them.

That's how I felt. The waters had receded, exposing a strange and a previously unexamined landscape.

But I vaguely sensed a wall of water on its way.

**\*\*\*\***

Ruthanne Lodato grew up in Del Ray, on Ridge Road Drive. In her home just off of busy Braddock Road, Ruthanne, now 59-years old, lived the quintessential American life. Her close-knit family was a fixture of the Alexandria community.

Born into the Giammittorio clan, Ruthanne's father and brother were both Alexandria judges known for their judicial wisdom. I was too young to practice law before Ruthanne's father, the late Hon. George Giammittorio, but as a new prosecutor, I appeared in front of her brother, Hon. E. Robert Giammittorio, in misdemeanor criminal court almost every day. Judge "G" possessed a great sense of humor and was not afraid of using a dose of sarcasm to emphasize a point, such as scolding a young prosecutor who was late to court.

Ruthanne came from a devoutly Catholic family and she remained connected to her church throughout her life. She attended a series of Alexandria Catholic schools and then Catholic University in Washington, D.C. She met her future husband, Norm Lodato, while both were in elementary school and attending the same church.

Norm and Ruthanne were married in 1977 and they bought their home on Ridge Road Drive two years later. The Lodato home was right across the street from Ruthanne's childhood residence. The Lodatos soon had three beautiful daughters whom they taught to focus on faith, family and community. Ruthanne served as an organist at her church, Blessed Sacrament, occasionally playing at weddings.

After Ruthanne's father passed away, her mother, Mary Lucy, moved into Norm and Ruthanne's house. They built an addition on the back of the home so Mary

Lucy would have sufficient space in which to live and they employed a home health aide, Jeanette, to assist her.

Norm worked for the state government and Ruthanne ran a small business out of her home. That business, Music Together, was centered on teaching young children basic musical and social skills. Ruthanne taught music to hundreds of young Alexandrians over the decades. She doted on every child she taught and her love and attention impacted each of her student's lives. It is impossible to mathematically gauge Ruthanne's good work but there was no doubt she was the best Alexandria had to offer.

It would be hard to live a more modest and loving life than that of Ruthanne Lodato. Of course, she had no enemies. Who on earth could wish to harm such a caring and compassionate person?

\*\*\*\*

The morning of Thursday, February 6, 2014, began as normal for Ruthanne. She worked from home and her student appointments were scheduled for the afternoon and evenings. This gave her the time to tweak her lesson plans or to call her daughters to catch up on their busy lives.

Norm left the house early that morning, sometime around 8 a.m. He was going to a doctor's appointment in Fairfax and wanted to beat the traffic. Ruthanne had a meeting scheduled at noon but her morning was free. After breakfast, she began to work while seated at a small desk in the dining room of the house, not far from the front door. Jeanette, the home healthcare aide, arrived about 8:30 to help Mary Lucy with her morning routine.

At about 11:30 a.m., the doorbell rang once. Ruthanne was not expecting company, but it was lunchtime on a sunlit day. Ruthanne lived in a safe and secure neighborhood. Maybe it was a neighbor dropping by. At worst, it was a salesman soliciting door-to-door.

Ruthanne walked to the door and opened it.

The Alexandria Assassin said something and then fired twice without warning.

**** 

Ruthanne suffered two gunshot wounds, one to the chest and one to the left arm. The fatal first shot was in the direct center of her chest. The second shot traveled through her left arm and exited, continuing on to strike her left chest.

Ruthanne screamed and staggered away from the door, retreating into her home. As she reached the family room, she fell to the floor. The shooter entered the foyer of the home and started to walk toward Ruthanne as she lay supine. He raised his revolver and prepared to fire again but was interrupted as Jeanette walked out of the kitchen and into the foyer, which communicated directly with the family room.

Jeanette had heard the doorbell ring. She recognized Ruthanne opening the door and then heard a male voice say something, although she could not make out what was said. Soon thereafter, Jeanette heard Ruthanne scream and went to check on her. Jeanette was not prepared for the hellish scene into which she stumbled. As she walked out from the kitchen into the front of the house, she saw Ruthanne laying on the floor, fighting for life.

She also saw a gaunt, middle-aged man in the foyer of the home. Absolutely terrified, Jeanette collapsed to the ground. She watched as the man stopped and turned his attention to her. She saw his beard. She saw a "black circle" concealed in the sleeve of the light-colored coat the man was wearing. She saw his eyes narrow and intensely focus on her.

Jeanette heard a loud "Boom!" and felt a searing pain in her arm. She saw "fire" come from the man's coat sleeve.

Then she heard another "Boom!"

The killer turned around and calmly walked out of the home.

This time, though, he made a significant mistake.

He left a witness behind.

\*\*\*\*

Although wounded in the arm by the first round fired at her, Jeanette showed incredible bravery. She got up and went to rescue Mary Lucy, leading her out of a back door and to a neighbor's house for safety. Jeanette was hysterical and bleeding but she managed to impart enough information to the neighbor for him to call 911. Then, despite her terror, she walked back to the home and went in to help Ruthanne.

The 911 call Jeanette asked the neighbor to make came in to the police at 11:32 a.m. Jeanette told police she had gotten to the neighbor's house about three minutes after the shooting, so the time of the crime could be narrowed down to just around 11:29 a.m.

The first police officers arrived on the scene at 11:36. When these officers made entry into the home they found Ruthanne lying on the ground of the family room, to the left of the front door. Once they confirmed the shooter was no longer in the residence, they began working on Ruthanne and discovered she was alive. The officers asked Ruthanne if she knew who had done this to her and she was able to convey she did not. She briefly described the shooter as an "older white man with a gray beard."

Despite heroic efforts by her doctors Ruthanne would succumb to her wounds that afternoon.

**** 

Detective Will Oakley was assigned to serve as the primary detective on the Lodato murder. Older than Sean Casey, Oakley was world-weary and homespun. Somehow Oakley had a small town, southern drawl even though he grew up in Northern Virginia and worked for a large police department. When picturing Oakley, think of Woody Harrelson in *True Detective,* only with better hair. Oakley had a soothing calm about him. Throughout this investigation, he fostered and maintained a close relationship with the Lodato family.

In television shows police detectives are depicted as ice-cold functionaries who see each murder as "just another case." While it is true that homicide detectives, who are routinely exposed to the most tragic aspects of human existence, usually hone a dark sense of humor as a line of defense, police serials rarely show the emotional impact of detective work. In my experience, the best homicide detectives display a deep sense of empathy and form a connection with the victim's family. So it was for Oakley and the Lodatos.

Just as Sean Casey had done three months before, Oakley heard the call over the police radio. He drove to the scene and started to interview the patrol officers that had responded. Next, he spoke with the CSI investigators who were scouring the area for evidence. Oakley was quickly able to determine the attack was not a botched robbery or theft. Like the recent Kirby shooting it was apparent this crime involved an ambush at the front door.

Since Jeanette had seen the shooter and survived, Oakley had a general description of his suspect: "a white male in his fifties with a gray beard and hair." He confirmed neither Ruthanne nor Jeanette knew their assailant, which ruled out a family member or other acquaintance. Oakley learned the shooter rang the doorbell and shot Ruthanne without warning when she opened the front door.

Oakley confirmed a total of five .22LR rounds had been fired during the attack, three at Ruthanne and two at Jeanette. Likewise, no spent cartridge cases had been located at the scene.

Oakley assigned a team of younger detectives to start a "canvass" of the area around the Lodato home. This ancient investigative technique, in which detectives go door-to-door to neighboring houses asking occupants if they saw or heard anything unusual, goes back hundreds of years and is as low-tech as it gets.

In recent times, canvassing detectives have begun adding a high-tech question to their normal routine of "Did you see or hear anything unusual?" Detectives now also ask the neighbors: "Have you installed any surveillance cameras on your property?"

One of Ruthanne's neighbors answered this question in the affirmative and handed over his digital recorder so police could scan through the stored footage.

That footage would break the case wide open.

****

I left the courtroom and took the elevator down a

floor to my office. My Chief Deputy, Molly Sullivan, informed me the victim of the shooting was Ruthanne Lodato. This was a surprise; I had a passing acquaintance with Ruthanne.

I ran down to the parking garage and got into my car. As I drove to the scene, I called Mike Kochis, who at the time was the police sergeant in charge of the Homicide Unit and a good friend. Kochis answered and said: "This is bad, Bryan, but I'm busy. I'll talk to you when you get here." He abruptly hung up.

I drove out of Old Town and through Del Ray on Russell Road. In the center of Russell's intersection with Braddock Road there is an ancient monument to the British General Edward Braddock, the road's namesake. I later learned that, as odd as it may seem, Braddock's ghost played a role in these murders.

I took a left at the monument as I had done countless times before and drove up the steep incline of Braddock Hill. As I approached the intersection of Braddock and Ridge Road Drive, I noticed a bevy of news "remote" trucks parked on the south side of Braddock Road. I also saw a clutch of T.V. reporters with cameras standing just outside of the yellow police tape blocking access to Ruthanne's street. I was going to have to run the gauntlet.

I parked and walked toward the tape. As I got close, the cameramen perked up and trained their cameras on me. Reporters started lobbing questions, hoping I might respond. Julie Carey, a well-respected NBC reporter shouted: "Bryan, is there any evidence this crime is linked to Nancy Dunning's murder?" I waved but did not respond, politely pushing my way past the cameras and under the yellow tape marked "POLICE LINE – DO NOT CROSS."

Police tape is one thing they get right on T.V.

There were two circles of tape erected around the Lodato home. The police had put up an outer perimeter to keep the media and nosy neighbors far enough away from the scene to let them do their job. There was another, inner perimeter established much closer to the house. As I walked toward the inner circle of tape, I saw Mike Kochis. Kochis was preoccupied but he did take the time to give me a two-minute rundown on what had happened before breaking off to handle more pressing duties.

I ended up standing near the Lodato house with Alexandria's Chief of Police, Earl Cook. Chief Cook was a former football player on the local high school team immortalized in the Hollywood movie "Remember the Titans." Cook was a gregarious man in most settings but his brow was furrowed and I could see the worry in his eyes.

Chief Cook asked whether I thought the Lodato and Kirby murders were connected. We had no hard evidence on which to make a connection at this point but the conclusion was inescapable. I agreed the two had to be linked given their proximity and the manner in which they had been committed.

The chief then asked me whether the Lodato and Kirby crimes were linked to the Dunning murder. I was not prepared to believe that sensational inference. I told the Chief I did not think it could be the case.

Cook was much more open to the idea. He slowly shook his head back and forth, wearing a grimace on his face. He said: "Bryan, I hope they're not, but I'm getting a really bad feeling about this."

I remained on the scene for several hours. I spoke with Kochis and Oakley several times about legal issues such as the need for search warrants. I talked with the current Alexandria Sheriff, Dana Lawhorne—Jim Dunning had retired in 2005—who was one of the first to arrive at the scene. Dana is a close friend of my father's and one of my mentors. He was also close to the Lodato family and was visibly shaken up by what had transpired.

It soon became clear no arrest was happening that afternoon. The bad guy wasn't hiding in a nearby bush. The killer had gotten away cleanly. Emotionally drained, I drove home and poured myself a glass of the most expensive bourbon I had on the shelf.

## CHAPTER TWO

*"The first law of Noble Savage Theory is thou shalt murder… again and again."*

The Alexandria Assassin—a lurid nickname for our killer created by a local reporter soon after Ron's death—executed his first two murders perfectly. In his mind, he had "descended" on a "homestead" and "introduced terror into a safe and secure neighborhood." He had completed a blitzkrieg strike in both cases, assassinating his victims in broad daylight and without any witness seeing him. It was as if the killer were a phantasm from a different dimension.

His third murder, however, was not executed perfectly. The Assassin made a huge tactical mistake, one that would ultimately result in his capture. He believed Ruthanne Lodato was home alone. She was not—and he therefore left behind an eyewitness who could potentially identify him.

Shortly after the Lodato murder, I pondered a difficult question: why did the killer leave Jeanette screaming and alive? Why didn't he walk over and make sure she could not identify him? Kochis and I discussed this seeming anomaly at length.

Soon, I formulated an answer to the conundrum: the killer had run out of ammunition. When Jeanette unexpectedly walked into the living room, the assailant panicked. Having already fired three rounds at Ruthanne, he fired two more at Jeanette from across the room. He hit her once in the arm, but the wound was neither fatal nor incapacitating.

If the shooter had possessed the means to kill Jeanette—another gun or more rounds in the gun he was carrying—he would have kept shooting until she was dead. Instead, after firing two ineffective shots at her, he fled the scene, leaving Jeanette very much alive.

Deduction established the killer used a five-shot revolver. He fired three rounds at Ruthanne and two at Jeanette. If he had any more rounds to fire, he would have walked over and ensured Jeanette would not talk to the police.

Out of ammunition, the Alexandria Assassin fled the crime scene. He ran to his little red Ford Escort and drove away.

But he made another mistake as he did so. He drove by an active surveillance camera.

****

During my first interview with Jeanette in April of 2014, she was incapable of focusing on my questions. She broke down at least a half-dozen times, weeping inconsolably. Much later, she would confront Severance at trial and the personal journey involved in her being able to do so marks her as one of the heroes of this story. But in the weeks immediately following the attack, the psychic toll of seeing Ruthanne shot and then being shot herself had rendered her incapable of cogently discussing the facts.

Jeanette had been able to meet with a police artist and help create a rough composite sketch of our suspect. The sketch was produced the day after the murder and was released publicly by the police department on Monday, February 10, just a couple of days after the crime. The composite was placed in heavy rotation on the television news, print media and the internet. Immediately upon its release citizens started calling the Alexandria Police Department with tips.

A word about composite sketches: they are called "sketches" and not "photographic likenesses" for a reason. It is extremely difficult for a witness to sit in a room with a sketch artist and orally describe the physical appearance of another person. Consider the following scenario: you are asked to meet with a composite sketch artist and produce a sketch of your mother or father. How do you explain in words what your parents look like? Do you think the completed sketch would be an exact replica of your loved one's face, similar to a photograph?

While composite artists do show the witness facial features for comparison—i.e. "Which of these eyebrows looks most like the suspect?"—no matter how talented the artist is, a composite sketch only approximates what the suspect looked like. As one of our witnesses said during her trial testimony, "a sketch is a tool." The fact that the person who produces the composite is called a "sketch artist" also proves the point: the creation of composites is more art than science.

During the pendency of the case I routinely received unsolicited comments about whether Severance "matched" the person depicted in the composite sketch. Many people approached me and shared their opinion that Jeanette's composite sketch looked "exactly like" Charles Severance. Others said they felt it "didn't look like him." Truth be told, I became fatigued at trying to explain no one should expect a "match" when looking at a composite sketch.

The reader can make their own determination about the accuracy of the drawing. The composite and Severance's booking photo adorn the cover of this book, side-by-side. One thing is for certain: there is a distinct resemblance.

At trial, the composite would become the subject of much argument. The defense team railed time and again there were significant differences between Severance's visage and the face of the man in the sketch. They particularly focused on the length of the beard, forcefully arguing the beard in the composite was much shorter than the unusually long, unkempt one worn by Severance in the courtroom.

But the fact there were physical differences is not surprising. The purpose of a composite is not to lead to a definitive identification or to create a photographic snapshot of the perpetrator. Since it is impossible for a witness to create a perfect likeness of a person by describing their features to an artist, there will **always** be differences, sometimes significant ones, between a composite sketch and a mugshot. In any case where a composite sketch is created the defense has a built-in argument: "Our client looks different than the composite," because the composite will never be an "exact match."

Another point about the composite. One must remember the circumstances under which Jeanette observed the shooter. She heard a gunshot, walked out of the kitchen to investigate and found herself in a veritable hell on earth. She was confronted by an entirely unexpected, chaotic scene. A stranger was standing in the living room. Ruthanne was lying on the floor, mortally wounded. Jeanette, having walked into the most frightening moment of her entire life, fell to the ground and was shot herself. Under these extremely stressful circumstances, it is a testament to Jeanette's inner strength that she was able to give us anything useful at all.

The composite provided some idea about the killer's description and ended up being surprisingly accurate. We now knew the shooter was a white male, in his 50s or 60s, with gray hair and a gray beard. Jeanette was adamant she had never seen him before and Ruthanne was able to confirm this before she succumbed to her injuries. This allowed the detectives to avoid wasting precious resources investigating Ruthanne's friends and family.

Jeanette was also able to say the assassin's gun was so small that it was concealed inside of his coat sleeve. Although Jeanette had never fired a pistol, her description of what she could see of the gun—"a black circle"—indicated the killer used a revolver. That description, coupled with the lack of spent cartridge cases at the scene and the total number of rounds fired, gave us an idea of the type of gun used during the shooting.

A small, five-shot, .22LR revolver.

****

At the time of the Kirby and Lodato murders, Mike Kochis was the sergeant of the Alexandria Police Department's Homicide Unit. Prior to trial, Kochis was promoted to lieutenant and transferred to the patrol division, but he oversaw all major aspects of the investigation until early 2015.

Kochis hails from a small town in New Jersey and has a Jersey way of "giving the gears" to his friends. His personality is a unique combination of military bearing and country boy. Kochis escaped by joining the Army as a young man, serving in South Korea and Bosnia as a military police officer. When he left the service he ended up as a civilian cop in Roanoke, Virginia, a small city nestled in the Blue Ridge Mountains. Kochis listens to Bruce Springsteen, Kid Rock and Carrie Underwood. While he loves to dish out good-natured abuse, Mike can definitely take it, too.

During this investigation there were many occasions where the stress got to me. I often grew angry and would devolve into counterproductive funks in which I questioned where the case was headed.

Every time I felt this way Kochis was willing to listen to me, to redirect my uncertainty and to instill a sense of confidence. There were a number of conversations in which I vented for several heated minutes at a time. Kochis would listen and then calmly funnel my misguided energy in a more productive direction. I remember one phone call in the summer of 2014, right before Severance was indicted, that consisted of me yelling into the phone. Kochis would have been completely justified in hanging up on me, but he let me run out of steam before relating his confidence in our case. I will never forget the friendship he showed me during those trying times.

By the way, Mike's exact words were "no jury is going to let this clown walk."

****

In an unusual coincidence, Kochis and another detective, Dave Cutting, had begun looking at the Dunning case earlier in 2013, before Ron Kirby was murdered. Kochis and Cutting had been recently assigned to the Major Crimes section and were getting up to speed on the Dunning case as its 10-year anniversary approached. The idea was to put a "new set of eyes" on the murder with hopes a new perspective might turn up an overlooked lead. The police department had never officially classified the Nancy's death as a "cold case" and, with the imminent anniversary, Alexandria citizens had begun asking what the department was currently doing to solve it. Assigning new detectives to take a fresh look was about all the department could do.

After the Dunning case was forensically linked to the Lodato and Kirby murders, Cutting was tasked with focusing on Nancy's death. With Sean Casey and Will Oakley already assigned to the Kirby and Lodato cases, Cutting's involvement allowed each of the detectives to focus on one crime. While all three detectives were fully briefed on all of the murders, they were experts in their own assigned case. Having a contact point for each murder made an unwieldy case much easier to handle. Once the trial team was assembled, I copied this division of labor by assigning one prosecutor to each of the three crimes.

Virginia police officers don't work for the prosecutor's office. The department reports to the Chief of Police, who in turn reports to the City Manager. On the other hand, I am elected and report directly to the community. My office has no funding for investigative staff and must rely on the police department to interview witnesses and conduct follow-up.

While the police take the lead on murder investigations before arrest, I am definitely part of the investigative team. In this case, I responded to the crime scenes and attended meetings in which the detectives discussed and debated the evidence. I watched the interview of Severance's girlfriend, Linda Robra, in real time and I went to West Virginia with Mike Kochis and the other detectives when Severance was arrested. The police asked my advice on which leads to pursue and I was involved in decisions such as when to obtain search warrants. The converse is also true; after an arrest is made, I consider the detectives a full part of the trial team.

My most significant role was making the call as to whether Charles Severance should be indicted for murder and, if so, with which murders he should be charged. In making this decision the detectives were true partners, meeting with me repeatedly and forcefully arguing their viewpoint. Under Virginia's system, however, the final charging decision lies with the prosecutor.

I had a good professional relationship with the detectives. That does not mean we agreed on every decision or there were not heated arguments between us on occasion. I am certain there were times when the detectives cursed my name behind my back. The gravity of the case and the stress associated with it made it impossible to avoid all friction.

Likewise, my trial team would often disagree on how the case should be presented. In late September 2015, the week before the trial started, the team convened in my office to discuss a piece of evidence we had previously agreed to present to the jury. During this meeting, two lawyers had second thoughts about the evidence. Their indecision at this late juncture made me steamed. I balled up a piece of paper and threw it forcefully against the wall as I yelled: "Get out of my office!"

This outburst was not exactly a shining example of my leadership capability. My point in reciting the anecdote is to emphasize that tension was high and not every decision was easily agreed upon.

In most cases, the trial team was able to work collaboratively and to have honest conversations when disagreements arose. I encouraged the attorneys and detectives to consider alternative ideas and to play devil's advocate. This "team of rivals" approach significantly improved our collective attack of the case and, through a dialectic of which Hegel would be proud, we were able to make an astonishing number of good decisions.

****

Dave Cutting and I are contemporaries in age and began at the police department as patrol officers at roughly the same time. We worked the evening shift together for a couple of years in the late 1990s, although not on the same squad. Cutting is one of the sharpest detectives with whom I have ever been privileged to work. He has a dry sense of humor leavened with the dark outlook of a veteran police officer. While he can occasionally be a little grumpy, he can also take a joke.

Cutting quietly does his job—and does it well. He does not care who gets credit and shies away from cameras and the spotlight. Indeed, Dave Cutting will probably never read this book. If he does, he will be unhappy his name was mentioned.

In my view, there are two types of people in the world. There are those who get things done and there are those who sit around looking for an excuse for not getting things done. Dave Cutting most assuredly belongs in the first class.

Mike Kochis was promoted to lieutenant in April 2015 and transferred back to the uniformed division. Soon thereafter, Chief Cook made the right choice, promoting Cutting to sergeant and assigning him to take Kochis' place as the supervisor of the Homicide Unit. This decision insured there was continuity to the investigation. I like to tease Kochis about leaving the case halfway through, forcing Dave, Sean and Will to finish the job.

The police department had its very best working the investigation. We had a surviving victim who might be able to identify her assailant and a composite sketch providing the first glimpse of our suspect. I also knew we had a serial killer on the loose and that he would likely kill again.

It fell on these detectives to identify and arrest him before he did.

# CHAPTER THREE

*"Murder is good. Court justice is bad. Kill authority. Listen to their screams."*

The composite sketch was released to the media just days after the Lodato murder. While the police had not publicly confirmed the Lodato and Kirby crimes were connected, the public assumed they were. The community was in an uproar. The residents of Alexandria were understandably terrified.

With the release of the sketch hundreds of tips started pouring in to the police department. By the time Severance was arrested, over 1000 tips had been provided by citizens. Most of them were too vague to be of any real help. Frightened citizens would call in about any older white man with a beard. A great number of the callers said nothing more than: "I was riding on the subway the other day and there was a weird looking white guy with a beard who got on the Metro at the King Street station."

The police department was not prepared for the volume of tips phoned in by a wary public. The first "tip line" number the department released was Kochis' desk extension; his voicemail filled up within hours. Since having a tipster call in only to be told the voicemail was "full" was unworkable, something had to be done.

The feds were happy to help. The FBI assisted by setting up a more efficient tip line and helping to staff it. The Bureau collected evidence during search warrant executions and it offered the assistance of the Behavioral Analysis Unit, which uses specially-trained personnel to bring the behavioral sciences to bear on complex investigations. FBI audiovisual experts worked on enhancing video evidence.

Many citizens assume any "big investigation" is likely to turn into a "federal case." This is not the way it works. In the real world, almost all murders are tried by state prosecutors in state courts.

The U.S. Attorney has no direct authority over her state counterpart. The feds cannot order a state prosecutor to drop a charge or summarily inform her they are going to "take the case." In rare circumstances, federal and state authorities can bring charges in the same case and hold two different trials. Since this is an inefficient use of precious resources, it behooves the state and federal authorities to meet and agree as to which office will handle the prosecution.

Over the years, I have seen a number of "turf battles" erupt between federal and state prosecutors. There are inherent differences between their job descriptions: state prosecutors have to handle every case that drops into the inbox while the feds can pick and choose the most solid cases to charge in federal court. This can lead to resentment among state authorities, who often accuse the feds of "cherry-picking."

As I have told my federal counterparts, I am elected to prosecute every felony that occurs in Alexandria, not just the ones the U.S. Attorney doesn't want. On the other hand, it is true that the U.S. Attorney's Office has limited resources and cannot adopt every state felony. Because of this, the feds are incentivized to pick cases with solid evidence and not squander time on marginal investigations. The federal counter to the charge of "cherry-picking" is elegant: "we have limited resources and the ability to choose our cases, so why would we choose weak ones?"

Unfortunate turf squabbles are usually ridiculous and never advance the goal of public safety. Almost all of them could be avoided if the parties agreed to put aside their egos, sit down and talk through their differences. The first step would be to admit the inherent tension in the state/federal relationship; the next to come up with a comprehensive framework for determining who should handle a particular case.

Luckily, there were no such conflicts during the Severance investigation. The FBI and the U.S. Attorney's Office were both exceptionally helpful and were quick to offer resources to assist in the matter. I am thankful for the support provided by our federal partners.

\*\*\*\*

While FBI field agents acted as a force multiplier in running down the numerous leads being called in, the Bureau's Behavioral Analysis Unit(BAU) brought its expertise to bear. BAU is a respected agency whose pioneering techniques assist federal and state law enforcement agencies in any number of serious criminal investigations.

Lay people usually know behavioral analysis through the more popular—but less accurate—term "criminal profiling." That phrase evokes a psychologist with quasi-psychic gifts, capable of deducing the age, race, sex and peculiar habits of a serial killer from a cursory glance of a crime scene. Real criminal behavioral analysts do not seek to identify a specific person as a perpetrator through reasoning alone. Instead, they further investigations by providing investigative suggestions and likely psychological characteristics of unknown offenders.

BAU met with detectives early on and soon produced a "perpetrator profile" that would later prove correct in several surprising aspects, most notably that our killer had probably lived in the neighborhood he targeted at some point.

****

In late February a tip came in identifying a local man who looked like the composite sketch. The tipster thought the man was "unusual" enough to be the killer. Every tip that identified a real person had to be run down so a two-person team, comprised of an APD detective and an FBI agent, was assigned to follow-up.

The man was located and interviewed. During the interview he convinced the detectives he was not responsible for the Alexandria murders, providing an airtight alibi. After dispelling the detectives' suspicion, the man said he knew someone they should interview and provided the name Charles Severance. He had gone to school with Severance and knew Severance to be angry with the City of Alexandria. While the man hadn't seen Severance in years, he had visited Severance's website and saw pictures of him—pictures in which Severance looked very much like the person depicted in the composite. This was the very first time Severance's name arose in the investigation.

Detectives documented this interview and placed Severance's name into the database for subsequent follow-up. As of yet, there was no reason to focus on him as the prime suspect. This lead was just one of many that needed to be run down. But the information set in motion a chain of events that would flush our assassin out of hiding.

On such small tipping points do cases turn.

****

Charles Severance was raised in a normal, all-American family. His father was a high-ranking naval officer and, given his father's military service, Severance's childhood was peripatetic. After several moves the family settled in the Fairfax, Virginia, neighborhood known as Oakton. Severance graduated from high school there and subsequently attended both George Mason University and the University of Virginia.

Severance was a bright teenager, well-read and interested in political history. He was mechanically inclined and graduated with a degree in engineering. He had an active fantasy life and was particularly drawn to role-playing board games. Throughout his life, Severance enjoyed both playing and occasionally creating fantasy-driven games.

One that he created, "Mental Disorder," would be injected into his trial. The rules to this game were inscrutable but involved the players trying to amass something called "insanity points." The winner would be entitled to issue "Certificates of Insanity," replete with the embossed seal of the Commonwealth of Virginia, to the losers. Many of the scenarios depicted on the playing cards arose from events in Severance's own life. One angrily recounted the short sentence he served in Jim Dunning's jail after his January 1997 firearms arrest in Alexandria.

Severance was fixated on mental health professionals and mental illness. He maintained a website called "MentalDisorder.com," dedicated in part to frightening rants about psychiatrists. Severance was absolutely convinced he was perfectly sane and anyone who hinted otherwise became the object of his rage.

At trial, Severance's lawyers used the game and website to explain some of his hate-filled and vitriolic writings. According to several witnesses, Severance sold "Mental Disorder" both on his website and in a local game shop. These defense-friendly witnesses cheerfully recalled how "fun" and "interesting" Severance's games were. The upshot was that "Mental Disorder" was a legitimate game designed for commercial sale. In reality, it was nothing of the sort.

During cross-examination, each witness admitted they played the game once—and only once. I guess "Mental Disorder" wasn't all that "fun" after all. Indeed, Severance's "games" were not intended to provide a diversion. They were an avenue by which an angry man vented some of his spleen.

Another "game" Severance created had an extremely unusual title. It was called "Tomahawking a Homestead in the Backwoods of America."

That phrase was Severance's metaphor for murdering people when they answered a knock at their door.

****

After leaving college in the 1980s, Severance held a series of engineering jobs. He was quickly dismissed from each for eccentric behavior. He was known for arguing with his supervisors and for holding strident political views. One employer became concerned when Severance drove to work in a truck draped with the flag of the Soviet Union.

In the mid-1990s he was employed as a mechanical engineer in Alexandria, working for the local wastewater authority. He purchased a small home in the Del

Ray neighborhood of the City. This residence, located on Gunston Road, was located about a mile from the Dunning and Kirby homes and much closer to the Lodato house. It would be fair to characterize Severance's "Gunston Manor," as he called it, as being situated on the outskirts of Ruthanne's neighborhood.

The year before he was arrested by the rookie officer for carrying a concealed weapon Severance ran for mayor of Alexandria. By this time, the dark and angry part of his personality had begun to take over and his campaign was highlighted by eccentric outbursts. During one campaign event he got into a physical altercation with an organizer, throwing a punch. At a mayoral debate with other candidates, Severance showed up wearing a floor-length black leather jacket reminiscent of *The Matrix.* He had on dark sunglasses and his hair was slicked-back, highlighting the prominent widow's peak in the middle of his forehead. Parts of the debate were recorded and can be viewed online. They show an angry, intense person who delighted in causing the other candidates to feel discomfort. One of his platform planks was to teach square dancing in the City schools.

Severance lost that political race but he continued to seek office. He ran for Congress in 1997 and then again for Mayor in 2000. His poor showings in the polls left him angry and even more convinced his fellow Alexandrians were incapable of understanding his genius.

During the murder investigation, the police found documents related to his quixotic 1997 campaign for Congress. In one of these missives Severance discussed his thoughts about the plans for a new Woodrow Wilson bridge, part of the Capital Beltway that crosses the Potomac River and links Alexandria to Maryland. The original bridge had been built in the 1950s and, by the late 90s, was nearing the end of its useful life. A new bridge had to be built and there was a debate about exactly where it should be located.

Severance vehemently disagreed with the established plan for the Wilson Bridge, a plan championed by the Council of Governments. In his campaign materials, he promised to "compel the World Bank to vouchsafe $1.5 billion" toward the bridge replacement. He stated emphatically the plan to route the bridge through Alexandria was "notorious." He preferred forcing Fairfax County to cede land several miles further south for the project. If Severance had been allowed to make the decision, the bridge would never have been built in Alexandria.

****

Charles Severance loved country dances, particularly square dancing, and in July of 1998 he found himself at a Northern Virginia western bar. That evening, Severance met a woman and asked her to dance. The pair hit it off and began a romantic relationship. Soon after meeting Severance, she became pregnant, giving birth to a son in April of 1999.

By the time of the boy's birth the mother was living with Severance in his "Gunston Manor." She decided to raise her son with Severance and tried to make the relationship work, but soon things started to fall apart. Weary of Severance's odd behavior, manipulation and emotional abuse, in early 2000 she and her son moved out of the Alexandria home.

Severance initiated a contentious and heavily-litigated battle over custody of the boy. The dispute took place in the Alexandria courts and Severance acted as his own attorney, filing hundreds of sarcastic and mocking legal pleadings. Several hearings were held in which an angry Severance verbally attacked the boy's mother, her attorneys and the Court. The presiding judge was so disturbed by Severance's behavior he asked Sheriff Dunning to provide additional deputies as courtroom security.

In March 2001, after Severance refused to undergo a court-ordered psychiatric examination, the judge granted the mother full custody of the boy. In making the decision, the judge relied on the pertinent legal standard, ruling that granting the mother full custody was "in the best interest of the child."

After announcing his decision the judge allowed Severance an opportunity to say goodbye to his son. Worried about the boy's safety and the possibility of a parental abduction, the judge required the farewell to take place in the courtroom. Uniformed deputies closely guarded the child during the encounter. This was the last time Severance ever saw his son. The presence of "law-enforcement lunatics" during this goodbye—and the fact he apparently was not allowed to touch the boy during the meeting—caused a great deal of resentment inside the seething cauldron of Severance's mind.

At the conclusion of the goodbye meeting the deputies served Severance with a copy of a protective order forbidding him from contacting the boy or his mother. The deputies signed Severance's copy, prominently writing the name of the Sheriff under whose authority they acted. Years later, police detectives would locate that copy of the protective order amongst Severance's belongings. In clear handwriting, the order bore the name

"Dunning."

Before his son was born, Severance had an angry personality. He was prone to rants and he easily perceived personal insults even where none were intended. He had long had a fascination with firearms. These personality traits provided the kindling for a conflagration of violence. The custody dispute provided the spark.

After obtaining sole custody of the child the mother moved to another state. Severance did not know where she was living but did know her parents' address. Over the course of the next decade he sent hundreds of threatening and harassing letters to the parents and to schools he thought his son might be attending.

At Severance's trial, the child's mother testified that, between the day the court awarded her custody in 2001 and the day Severance was arrested for murder in 2014, she woke up every morning convinced Severance would find her and kill her.

****

In late February 2014, Alexandria police detective Irv Ellman was assigned to follow-up on the Charles Severance lead. A former college defensive lineman, Ellman was a big man with a big heart and one of the most seasoned detectives working for the Alexandria police.

The only address Ellman had for Severance was that of his parents, who resided in the same Northern Virginia home Severance had grown up in. Ellman did a little research and learned the parents were both retired and in their early eighties. During the initial stages of the investigation, both were cooperative with the detectives, although the cooperation would cease once Charles was charged with the murders.

Severance's father retired from the United States Navy as a rear admiral after a distinguished and highly decorated career. His military service required the family to move frequently during Charles' youth. It also meant the father was away from his wife and children for extended periods of time.

This itinerant existence affected Charles and helped calcify his resentment toward the "law enforcement class." Somewhat surprisingly given his father's service, his writings revealed a great hostility for military personnel. Severance was frequently rhapsodic when discussing the death of service members, writing with obvious joy about reports detailing the demise of an infantry patrol in Iraq, for instance.

Severance considered the military one of the most despotic agents of the "government elite." Another, not surprisingly, was law enforcement. As I read his Manifesto of Hate, I had a difficult time determining whom he hated more: police or the military. Severance clearly enjoyed reading about police officers being killed in the line of duty. In one demented outburst he opined:

**"Police officer murdered is a song! Rejoice!"**

Severance's mother shared some of Charles' antipathy toward the government. While she was an intelligent and kind person, she was reluctant to confront her son's growing mental health issues during his late-teenage years. Both parents were on notice of Charles' eccentric views but were apparently unable to do much about them.

In 1989, Severance was arrested by Fairfax County police after a citizen complained she heard shooting in the woods. Responding officers detained Severance and an acquaintance at the scene. They recovered firearms, targets and spent ammunition. Most disturbing was the fact that Severance had pasted photographs of President George H.W. Bush and his wife, Barbara, on the targets. Severance told the officers he did not like the government and he mockingly referred to Barbara Bush as the "white ghoul." These actions landed him on the radar screen of the Secret Service.

In response to this arrest, Severance's parents convinced him to see a psychiatrist. After one visit in which he admitted to thinking about killing his father, Severance refused to return to the doctor. His parents did not force the issue. No one ever tried to get Charles Severance psychological treatment again.

When Ellman first knocked on the Severances' door, the parents conceded Charles was angry at the City of Alexandria over the custody dispute involving his son. They said Charles resided with his girlfriend about 40 miles from Alexandria in a community known as Ashburn. They confirmed Charles wore a gray beard but were adamant "Charlie" would never hurt anyone.

Ellman wrote down the girlfriend's name, Linda Robra, and gave the parents his business card. After the detective left, Severance's parents called their son and gave him Ellman's information. They asked Charles to contact the detective but he angrily refused to do so.

Severance remained just one more name amongst many potential suspects. Ellman added Linda Robra's information into the tip management system for additional investigation. Charles Severance could not be taken off the list of suspects until detectives interviewed him face-to-face, but he remained one line of inquiry in a thousand. It would fall to another detective to contact Severance at Robra's home.

In mid-February 2014 detectives started to look through the surveillance footage recovered after Ruthanne's murder. They soon focused on one piece of video recovered from a neighbor who lived two blocks west of the Lodato home. His house faced Braddock Road, the high-volume artery named after the British general.

The video was captured on two cameras, one facing east and another roughly west, near Braddock's intersection with Scroggins Road and just about 300 yards from the Lodato house. If the killer had used a car to flee it was likely his car would be seen on the surveillance camera.

A tech-savvy police detective, Dan Gordon, was tasked with making a copy of the data on the surveillance camera's digital hard drive. Gordon ensured the time/date stamp on the drive was accurate and working properly and focused his attention on the time frame just after Ruthanne was shot.

Gordon quickly noticed a distinctive car driving west on Braddock at 11:32 a.m., a maroon station wagon later identified as a 1997-1999 Ford Escort station wagon by experts at Ford. Unfortunately, the surveillance camera did not record in high-resolution, so many details could not be made out despite subsequent FBI efforts to enhance the relevant frames. Gordon could see the car displayed both front and rear license plates but could not read anything on the plates themselves, including the state in which the car was registered. Although it was difficult to be certain, it looked like the driver was a white man with a gray beard. Gordon could make out what appeared to be a small, circular bumper sticker on the rear of the car but could not determine what it depicted.

If he had been able to read the bumper sticker, Gordon would have been convinced of the Escort's significance far earlier.

**\*\*\*\***

As late as March 5, a full month after Ruthanne Lodato was murdered, the police had not made any progress toward identifying the killer. While Charles Severance's name was on the "follow-up" list, he had not been "made" as a suspect. The case remained a mystery.

It appeared the police were throwing punches at a ghost.

They needed to catch a break.

# CHAPTER FOUR

*"Anyone who is a victim of savage police policy is at liberty to kill, murder, scalp, torture and steal until he is effectively exhausted from finding no satisfaction."*

Throughout late February and early March 2014 detectives and FBI agents continued to track down leads. None seemed promising and most were easily closed. Frustration started to rise among the officers working the case, who were well aware the killer could strike again without warning.

During this time frame the recovered bullets from the Lodato scene were analyzed and compared to those recovered from the Kirby and Dunning homes. In Virginia, forensic examinations such as DNA analysis and firearms comparisons are conducted by the state Department of Forensic Science (DFS). (An exception is fingerprint evidence; larger police departments like Alexandria employ their own latent print examiners.)

DFS splits the state into four geographic regions; Alexandria sends its forensic evidence to the Northern laboratory. Alexandria is not the only police department that submits evidence to the Northern lab and DFS staff find themselves conducting thousands of examinations each year for a plethora of law enforcement agencies. At the time of our investigation, the Northern lab's firearms unit was staffed by two extremely talented examiners with a wealth of experience, Julian "Jay" Mason and Gary Arntsen.

Both Mason and Arntsen had over 30 years in the

field of forensic firearms analysis and had conducted thousands of firearms examinations. Both were extremely respected in their field and did an outstanding job of communicating this somewhat arcane area of science into layman's terms.

Mason had been the examiner assigned to the Dunning case back in 2003 and had been assigned to the Kirby and Lodato cases before it was clear they were related. By early March, he had completed his initial examinations and analysis and produced a written report outlining his findings. Mason determined the same type of ammunition, "Remington .22 Long Rifle (LR) plain lead," was used in all three murders. Mason believed the same make and model of firearm, probably a revolver, was used in all three crimes, but that the same exact gun was never used twice—an opinion that would subsequently mesh seamlessly with the evidence detectives amassed.

In an early-March phone call Mason summarized his chilling conclusions for me: all three murders were linked and the murderer was fixated on a specific, extremely unusual gun and ammunition combination. The killer used three different guns, all of the same make and model, to commit the three murders.

We had a serial killer on our hands.

\*\*\*\*

The Alexandria Assassin was absolutely obsessed with a particular firearm and ammunition combination. At trial, three different firearms experts would testify that, in over 100 years of collective experience the only crimes in which they had ever observed this particular gun and ammunition combination used were our murders. Three idiosyncratic crimes that occurred within about one mile of each other, all involving an ambush murder at the front door of a private home. The only logical conclusion was the murders were linked.

Given the centrality of the firearms evidence, I will relate it in some detail. I concede this exercise may be technical and a little dry, but it is as important for the reader to understand it as it was for the jury.

The field of firearms and ammunition analysis has its own nomenclature which is often misused by the general public. For example, television shows ubiquitously use the term "shell casing" when referring to what is properly called a "cartridge case." As Gary Arntsen likes to say: "casings are for sausages, not ammunition."

A round of ammunition is technically referred to as a "cartridge." The cartridge is composed of a "bullet" which is the projectile that leaves the weapon and hits the target, the "cartridge case" which contains gunpowder and houses the bullet and the "primer" which is a small charge of powder on the bottom of the cartridge case. When the primer is struck by a firearm's firing pin it explodes and ignites the gunpowder in the cartridge case, "firing" the bullet down the barrel of the gun at high velocity.

Ammunition is primarily identified by caliber, which is the numerical measurement of the diameter of the cartridge. Caliber can be in standard or metric measurement: a .50 cartridge is 1/2 inch in diameter, a 9mm cartridge is 9 millimeters in diameter and so on. It follows that a .22 round is a little less than a quarter-inch in diameter. All .22 rounds are physically very small—among the smallest rounds produced—and for that reason are less likely to cause significant physical damage if used to shoot someone.

Twenty-two caliber ammunition can be particularized because it is produced in several different subclasses: .22 Long, .22 Short, .22 Magnum and .22 Long Rifle. The names of the subclasses do not accurately reflect their characteristics; Long Rifle rounds are not particularly long nor are they used only in rifles. The categories were created to distinguish a slightly different round from its peers. For our purposes, we will focus on .22 Long Rifle, usually abbreviated as .22LR. All of the ammunition components recovered from the three murder scenes were identified as being consistent with .22LR ammunition.

Ammunition can also be subdivided into smaller classes. Ammo is either "jacketed" or "plain lead." A jacketed bullet is one in which the lead bullet is surrounded, or "jacketed," by a sheath of harder metal, usually copper. Jackets are placed on higher-velocity rounds to ensure the soft lead bullet isn't deformed or destroyed by the energy created when the round is fired.

On the other hand, plain lead bullets are not jacketed. Plain lead rounds can be used in lower-velocity ammo because the energy created by the firing process is insufficient to damage the round. Twenty-two caliber Long Rifle ammunition comes in high, standard and low-velocity variations. The standard and low-velocity types are unjacketed, plain lead rounds. By contrast, .22 Magnum rounds fire at a higher velocity and are therefore jacketed.

Ammunition is produced with two varieties of "primers." Primers are either "rim-fire," in which the primer is contained in the rim of the base of the cartridge, or "center-fire," in which the primer is contained in the center of the base of the cartridge. Most .22 pistols use center-fire rounds.

Twenty-two caliber Long Rifle ammunition is manufactured by a host of companies; only one imprints a small "quality-control" letter on the base of the lead bullet. That manufacturer is Remington, the largest in America. The quality-control letter exists so Remington can figure out in which plant a defective round was manufactured.

Remington places the control letter on two different .22LR brands it produces, Cyclone and Subsonic. Cyclone is Remington's standard-velocity .22LR ammunition. Subsonic, as the name implies, is the low-velocity version. The two rounds are physically identical except for the number of grains of gunpowder contained in the cartridge case. If you examine two fired .22LR Remington bullets, one Cyclone and one Subsonic, it is impossible to tell them apart.

"Subsonic" ammunition is designed to produce muzzle-velocity speeds below the speed of sound. This ostensibly means the round makes less sound when fired than Cyclone. I've fired both at the range; in reality, it is difficult to discern a difference in the sound produced. Nonetheless, consumers who want to make less noise are going to be drawn to subsonic rounds due to the manner in which they are marketed. In particular, if one were going to assassinate people in an urban environment where witnesses might be around to hear things, .22LR Subsonic would be the perfect ammunition to use.

For the same reason, an urban assassin would need a small firearm that could easily be concealed. A small gun would necessarily fire small-caliber ammunition. This could be a problem, because the smaller the round is, the less likely it is to cause massive damage. The problem could be avoided by surprising the intended victims and shooting them in the heart at point-blank range. At that distance a .22 bullet is sufficient to kill.

The collection of the physical attributes of a round of ammunition is known as the round's "class character-istics." In all three Alexandria assassinations the ammo used shared the following class characteristics: .22 cali-ber, Long Rifle, plain lead, unjacketed rounds. Addition-ally, since quality-control letters were found on the base of bullets from all three crime scenes, the ammunition could be identified as Remington. And since Reming-ton produces only two .22LR plain lead rounds—stan-dard-velocity Cyclones and low-velocity Subsonics—you can imagine my surprise when I learned Charles Severance was obsessed with Remington .22LR Subson-ic plain lead, unjacketed ammunition.

When I first read Severance's Manifesto, I was horrified to find him musing that Subsonic ammunition made "sweet, sweet music" and was "very, very effec-tive when Tomahawking a Homestead in the Backwoods of America."

\*\*\*\*

Handguns are broken down into two large classes: revolvers and semiautomatic pistols. A semiautomatic pistol is loaded by inserting a spring-loaded magazine, sometimes incorrectly referred to as a "clip," into the butt of the firearm. After charging the firearm by "rack-ing" the slide on the top of the weapon, the pistol uses the energy created by the firing of each round to cycle a new round into the firing chamber. It will continue to fire one round for each trigger pull until the firearm is out of ammunition. This process allows for quicker rate of fire and for the firearm to be loaded with more rounds of ammunition.

As each cartridge is fired, the spent cartridge case must be cycled out of the firearm. Imagine a movie or T.V. show in which a character shoots a gun and the spent "casing" pops out of the firearm and onto the ground. Because semiautomatic pistols eject spent cases and revolvers do not, if investigators find spent cartridge cases at a crime scene it is a pretty good indicator the gun was a semiauto.

The contrary is also true: if there are no cartridge cases located, this likely means a revolver was used. A revolver keeps a finite number of cartridges, usually six, in a circular cylinder. When the trigger is pulled the hammer falls, causing the firing pin to strike the primer and fire a round. A revolver is designed so that this process mechanically rotates the cylinder, allowing the next cartridge to be fired. All spent cartridge cases are retained inside of the cylinder and are not ejected onto the ground.

Since no spent cartridge cases were located at any of the three Alexandria murder scenes the detectives were convinced the Alexandria Assassin used a revolver to commit his crimes.

Television shows sometimes imply the absence of spent cartridge cases is absolute proof that a revolver was used in a homicide. In the real world, detectives know this is not necessarily true. A person who fires a revolver can open the cylinder and remove the spent cartridge cases, dropping the cases on the ground for police to discover. Alternatively, a person who fires a semiautomatic pistol can stop to pick up spent cartridge cases and remove them from a scene to frustrate investigators.

Cases can be kicked or even blown by the wind. However, if no cartridge cases are recovered, the most likely explanation is that the murder weapon was a revolver.

In the Lodato shooting, Jeanette was able to tell us the killer did not stop to pick up spent cartridge cases. Since no spent cases were located at the scene, we had conclusive proof a revolver had been used.

The number of rounds fired at each of our murder scenes was paramount. The investigation revealed three rounds were fired in the Dunning murder, five rounds were fired in the Kirby murder and five rounds were fired in the Lodato murder. The fact that five rounds were fired—and not six—was a significant clue. Most revolvers carry six rounds, but since the highest number of rounds fired in any one of our murders was five, we deduced the Alexandria Assassin used a .22LR five-shot revolver during the murders.

Detectives quickly learned only one American company manufactured a .22LR five-shot mini-revolver. That company was North American Arms, based in Provo, Utah. Their mini-revolver was extremely small, with an overall length of about four inches. It was so small it could be completely concealed inside of a closed fist.

Severance was obsessed with this exact firearm. As he wrote in the Manifesto of Hate:

*"North American Arms out of Utah makes a beautiful and deadly 5-shot mini-revolver."*

*"The NAA .22LR 5-shot mini-revolver stainless steel with the wooden grip is small and easily concealed."*

*"Thou shalt murder and vengeance is mine saith the Lord!"*

When a bullet is fired it travels down the barrel of the gun at intense speeds. The barrel of most handguns contains a series of alternating high and low points etched into the metal of the barrel. These high and low points are known in specialized lingo of the firearms industry as "lands and grooves."

Lands and grooves serve a purpose, imparting spin to the bullet. The spin helps to significantly increase the accuracy of the shot, much like a spiraling football. As the bullet travels down the barrel it can twist in one of two directions: clockwise or counterclockwise. In the industry, these two twists are described by the simple names "left" and "right." The number of lands and grooves and the direction of twist imprint a distinctive pattern on a fired bullet.

The hard alloy of the barrel's lands and grooves easily imprints markings on the soft lead of a fired bullet. A trained forensic scientist can examine a bullet and, if it is in good condition, determine the class characteristics of the firearm that fired it. In the three murders committed by the Alexandria Assassin the forensic scientists that examined the ammunition evidence told us all of the fired rounds had been fired out of a firearm producing a pattern of eight lands and grooves and a twist to the right.

It just so happened that the North American Arms five-shot .22LR mini-revolver produced eight lands and grooves with a right twist. In fact, it was the only five-shot .22LR revolver manufactured in America that produced that pattern of class characteristics.

****

On the morning of March 6, 2014, Alexandria Police Chief Earl Cook held a press conference in which he summarized Jay Mason's findings with regards to the firearms evidence. The press conference was heavily attended by the media and the link between the three murders was quickly and extensively reported.

I did not want the Chief to discuss Mason's analysis with the press. Intense media attention would complicate the investigation. I feared the release of certain factual details of the case would alert the suspect we were closing in on him, causing him to flee and get rid of the guns and ammunition. I discussed my concerns with Chief Cook and asked him to consider not holding the press conference, a request he politely refused.

Cook did agree to be circumspect in his comments. While he mentioned the firearms evidence suggested a link between the three cases, he was careful not to name the specific type of ammunition used in the murders. The Chief did a very good job of walking a tightrope, giving the media and the public significant information without jeopardizing the investigation.

The Chief's comments were not lost on the massed reporters: a serial killer was on the loose in Alexandria.

Public fear was at a fever pitch.

****

The Alexandria Police Department, from the Chief on down, played its hand close to its collective vest throughout the investigation and prosecution of this matter. At no point did any law enforcement official speak to reporters, not even in an "off the record" capacity. I consider this a minor miracle and a true testament to the professionalism of the women and men who worked the case.

Leaking information to the press is a time-honored tradition and reporters work carefully to cultivate sources willing to speak with them about sensitive investigations. Reporters know how to play the psychological levers in order to get people to talk. They know, for instance, that many have an innate desire to see themselves on television. Others like the thrill of secretly speaking to the media "off the record." For some, the very fact they know confidential information makes it impossible to keep it secret. In most big investigations someone on the inside speaks to the press.

My profession harbors many of the worst offenders. I am often dismayed at the way prosecutors hold forth for the cameras. I guess it should come as no surprise. Most local prosecutors are elected, meaning they are both trial lawyers and politicians. They often cannot resist the camera.

The best—or, more appropriately, the worst—example of this was the infamous Duke lacrosse rape case. In 2006, the local elected district attorney in Durham, North Carolina, was in charge of what must have appeared to be his "career case." Coincidentally, the DA caught the case during his campaign for election. Before he knew it, he was the center of the media universe. The DA was unprepared for the attention lavished on him by the press and ate it up. He gave numerous interviews with national news outlets, expounding in depth on the evidence. He provided his personal opinions on the strength of his case and the failings of the defendants—young men who were ultimately proven innocent. The DA ultimately had his bar license revoked and was briefly jailed after his case unraveled in spectacular fashion.

Prosecutors must resist the urge to jump in front of

the camera. The Rules of Professional Responsibility specifically hold that a prosecutor "may not make any extrajudicial statement which he knows, or reasonably should know, has a reasonable chance of influencing a potential juror." Failure to abide by this rule may result in a prosecutor being removed from a case or becoming the subject of disciplinary proceedings. In a big case, such public ruminations can substantially increase the likelihood of a judge granting a defense motion to change venue, a motion in which the defense asks the trial to be moved to another jurisdiction where public outrage is lower and an impartial jury can be impaneled.

The reasoning behind this prohibition is the prosecutor should not engage in "extrajudicial" statements—that is, statements made outside of a courtroom—that could influence a prospective juror's opinion about the case. There are a number of ways in which a prosecutor's extrajudicial statements could impact a jury.

First, a juror is supposed to base their individual verdict only on evidence that is admitted in court. There are any number of reasons why incriminating evidence might be ruled inadmissible by a trial judge. A prosecutor who recounts the evidence against a criminal defendant in a pretrial interview may talk about specific pieces of evidence that are eventually declared inadmissible. Jurors watching the nightly news may remember the prosecutor's reference to this evidence during deliberations.

Second, a potential juror watching a television interview of a prosecutor only hears one side of the story. The prosecutor gives his own version of the evidence without the defendant's attorney having an opportunity to offer contrary explanations. A pretrial television stand-up allows a prosecutor a chance to make a "closing argument" without the defense being able to respond.

Finally, the prosecutor is usually an elected official and it is reasonable to assume he is seen favorably by a majority of voters in his district. A prosecutor who says during a pretrial interview: "I've been doing this job a long time and I've never seen a stronger case or a more evil defendant" fosters a situation where jurors might think "well, I voted for the DA, and he just said on T.V. this is the strongest case he has ever seen, so the guy must be guilty."

For these reasons, prosecutors are prohibited by the rules of ethics from giving pretrial interviews in which they discuss the evidence, the motive for the crime or otherwise give their personal opinions about the strength of the case. This rule is extremely difficult for some to abide by. My field draws those with big egos, people who like being on camera and who often aspire to run for higher office. If you are an elected prosecutor it can be very hard indeed to maintain radio silence. Yet the rules of ethics demand just that.

A couple of additional points about pretrial publicity: First, the rules do allow a prosecutor to publicly release certain basic pieces of information such as a list of the charged offenses, the possible penalties associated with the charges and the next court date. In the Severance case, I issued a written press release containing these details after the grand jury had returned indictments.

Finally, the rule applies only to **pretrial** comments or interviews. After a trial is concluded, there is no risk of influencing prospective jurors and the prosecutor may speak with the media about the case as much as he likes.

He may even write a book about it.

## CHAPTER FIVE

*"Can you forgive someone for kidnapping your son?"*

Chief Cook's press conference was another substantial step toward capturing the Alexandria Assassin. The press conference was heavily covered by the media and video of the Chief's comments, in which he conceded there was a serial killer on the loose, was ubiquitous on the local news. There is no doubt Severance quickly learned the police knew the firearms evidence linked the cases. He would have understood his two mini-revolvers would conclusively tie him to the crimes.

By sheer coincidence another significant event happened on March 6, just hours after the Chief's press conference. That afternoon Detective Chris Whelan was taking a second shot at locating Charles Severance. Whelan had been randomly assigned the Severance lead to follow-up. By engaging in a little detective work Whelan was able to find the home address of Severance's girlfriend, Linda Robra, in Ashburn, Virginia.

Ashburn is a suburb about 40 miles west of Washington, D.C. Originally farmland close to the town of Leesburg, Ashburn grew in population in the late 1990s as the closer-in areas filled with people. Ashburn is more of a mailing address than a town and is entirely located inside of Loudoun County. Since it is unincorporated, it falls under the jurisdiction of the Loudoun County Sheriff's Office.

In early 2014 Charles Severance lived in one of these townhouses. Since he hadn't held a job in over a decade, he didn't own it. He cohabited with Robra, a part-time real estate agent and substitute elementary school teacher with whom he had a slightly ambiguous romantic relationship. Severance had lived with Robra since 2011, after he met her at a country dance held in a nearby hotel.

On the afternoon of March 6, Whelan approached the Robra townhouse and knocked on the front door. Receiving no answer, he turned his attention to a Lexus SUV parked in the driveway. He retrieved one of his business cards and wrote on the back: "I need to speak with Charles Severance." He did not mention _why_ he wanted to speak with Charles. Whelan placed the business card under the windshield wiper and left.

When he got back to headquarters, Whelan ran Robra's name through a police database and obtained her cellphone number. He called her that evening and she answered. Whelan told her he needed to speak to Severance, again not telling her why. Robra indicated she would get the request to Charles.

The night of March 6 must have been an extremely stressful one for Charles Severance. He knew he had committed three murders. He knew Robra had purchased two firearms and a box of a specific type of ammunition for him. He knew from Cook's press conference the police were aware of the significance of the firearms evidence left behind at each scene. Severance also knew the police had released a composite sketch that closely resembled him.

Severance had ignored the initial police request for an interview, made through his parents in early February after police visited their home. Since he had not heard anything else until March 6, he probably convinced himself he had successfully evaded the police by ignoring

them. But the confluence of the March 6 press conference and Whelan's visit to Robra's home on the very
same day shook that belief.

While the timing of Cook's press conference and
Whelan's visit was completely coincidental, it did not
look that way to Severance. The combined effect of a
press conference in which the police chief said the firearms evidence linked the three crimes and a knock on the
door by the police later that same day convinced Severance his arrest was imminent.

Severance could not have slept well on the evening
of March 6. He would have been mulling over his options. Run? Meet with the detective? Ignore him? Hide
the firearms and ammunition Robra had bought him?
Shave his beard so he did not look like the composite?

For the first time in a decade the Alexandria Assassin was in fear.

****

The next day, March 7, was another eventful one.
Severance woke up, thought about the situation and decided to act. First, he emailed Chris Whelan from his
personal Gmail account. Severance sent the email at 9:45
a.m. It was terse and unusual: "I received your business
card from Linda Robra." Nothing else. No mention of
whether Severance would or would not meet with the
detective. Whelan emailed back asking again to meet;
Severance did not respond.

This strange email is indicative of the stress Severance was under that morning. He had no way of knowing
the police had not yet settled on him as the prime suspect. He had no money, few friends and fewer options.
By sending the short email he was buying some time to

think.

Later on March 7 he made another unusual decision. That afternoon, Severance drove to Washington, D.C. and parked in a garage near the National Cathedral. He exited his car, took an old, beat-up bicycle he owned off the rear bike rack and pedaled down Massachusetts Avenue toward the Russian Embassy.

Severance had on several pairs of pants and a couple of t-shirts underneath a bulky sweatshirt. This ensemble made the slightly-built Severance appear far heavier. Severance wore a multi-colored, southwestern-style poncho over the sweatshirt. He capped off his attire with an anachronistic personal favorite: a black, Revolutionary War-era tricorn hat.

When Severance arrived at the Russian Embassy he parked his bike and walked to the compound's entrance. Russian security officers manned the front gate. When an embassy visitor was cleared by security, Severance "piggy-backed" and followed the visitor in. The Russian guards noticed and intervened. When they stopped Severance he loudly proclaimed he was requesting asylum and that the "City of Alexandria" was "persecuting" him. Brushing aside his asylum request, the Russians called for uniformed officers of the United States Secret Service, the agency tasked with policing embassies.

Officers arrived and engaged Severance in conversation. They took several photographs of him in his hat and poncho and spoke to him about his reasons for being at the embassy. Severance repeated that he felt Alexandria was persecuting him. He also unexpectedly mentioned the Alexandria courts had taken his son away from him.

The Russians decided they did not want to press charges. Told he was free to leave, Severance got back on his bike and began pedaling away. Secret Service officers, their curiosity piqued by Severance's odd display, followed him and watched him go into a nearby parking garage. The officers entered and saw Severance putting his bike on the rack attached to the rear of his personal car: a maroon, 1999 Ford Escort station wagon.

They approached Severance again and asked him for consent to search his car. Now angry, he denied permission to search, which was unfortunate as the murder weapons were probably inside of the Escort that afternoon. Before the officers left they took a series of photographs of the car itself.

Later that evening the Secret Service filed a police report. Since Severance bore a resemblance to the well-publicized composite sketch and angrily mentioned the "City of Alexandria" at the embassy, the Secret Service sent the report, along with the pictures of Severance and his maroon Ford Escort, to the Alexandria police.

By the next morning Cutting, Casey, Kochis and Oakley were zeroing in on Charles Severance.

****

Why did Charles Severance go to the Russian embassy? Why was he wearing the odd attire? At trial, the defense argued it was because of his mental illness—just look at the photo of him in a tricorn hat!—and because he disliked the City of Alexandria. He had become frightened when the Alexandria police wished to interview him.

The defense team overlooked the fact Severance did not go to the Russian embassy in February, when he learned the Alexandria police had visited his parents and asked to speak with him. What was different about

March 7?

The answer is simple: the confluence of Whelan's home visit and the Chief's press conference convinced Severance the police were closing in. Like any criminal who thinks he is about to be locked up, he needed to make good his escape.

As Severance's voluminous writings would prove, his original motive for murder was his anger over the Alexandria custody dispute in which he was ordered to have no contact with his son. By 2014 it had evolved to include an ill-defined political component that I will explore in detail later in this book. Severance thought he was acting as a revolutionary against an unjust government consisting of "nefarious, status quo utopian elites." He was convinced violence was justified as an act of civil defiance and revolution.

Severance was flushed out of hiding like a rabbit pursued by hounds. While his visit to the Russian embassy makes little sense at first blush, it made perfect sense to him. Severance saw himself as a noble exposer of truth; as another Edward Snowden. Like Snowden, Severance had braved the anger of an oppressive government for the sake of principle. And since the Russians had provided Snowden with asylum from prosecution, why wouldn't they provide it to Charles Severance, a brave American who had chosen to act against a corrupt and venal government?

****

Soon after the Lodato killing, the composite sketch bearing a strong resemblance to Severance was released to the public. He must have looked at the composite and considered his options. Should he shave, so he looked less like the drawing? He had worn the long beard for years. To shave it off right after a murder would be too suspicious.

The police had also publicly released a physical description of the killer: thin and of average height. Severance himself was relatively slight and would have realized it was impossible to quickly put on sufficient weight to significantly change the way he looked.

When Severance went to the Russian embassy, he dressed the way he did in an attempt to conceal his appearance. He put on the tricorn hat to cover his hair. The poncho and the numerous layers of clothing were an attempt to change his physical appearance.

I concede the choice of a tricorn hat is unusual. If one were trying to conceal one's appearance, such a hat arguably would have a contrary effect, effectively drawing more attention. However, Severance, a well-read history buff, was fascinated with the political history of the revolutionary war era. As we will see, Severance considered himself a "noble savage" rebelling against the inequities of the "utopian elites." He celebrated the tricorn hat as a symbol of eighteenth-century rebellion. He wore it as a tacit announcement of his uprising against the "law-enforcement class."

The hat also had the effect of concealing the prominent widow's peak on Severance's forehead.

One final point about the Russian Embassy photographs. The defense would argue a great deal about the fact that when he was arrested in March, Severance's beard was longer and more unkempt than the beard on the man in the February composite sketch.

Put yourself in Severance's place. If you're running from the police and know the composite sketch of the killer shows a neatly groomed beard, what do you do? You cannot shave the beard off: that would be far too obvious. You can, however, easily change the way your beard looks by brushing it out and neglecting to groom it.

Near the end of the trial I noticed something interesting. In his March 14 booking photo Severance's beard looked slightly shaggier than the beard depicted in the composite. This apparent discrepancy could be explained by noting composite sketches are not photographs and that Jeanette was focused on his eyes and not his beard.

When I looked at high-resolution copies of the Russian embassy photos I was struck by Severance's appearance. Those photos were taken on March 7, a week before his arrest, and depicted a noticeably different-looking beard: one that was well-groomed and neater. The photograph closest in time to the Lodato murder showed Severance with a beard more like the one described by Jeanette.

After he was rebuffed by the Russian embassy, Severance decided to create some distance between his appearance and the man in the composite. Since he couldn't shave his beard off, he did the next best thing: he stopped grooming it and brushed it out.

\*\*\*\*

Severance returned to Robra's Ashburn home in the evening of March 7. He told her about the encounter with the Secret Service but neglected many of the details. He did not mention seeking asylum. Over the next two days, Robra repeatedly tried to convince Severance to meet with Alexandria detectives so he could "clear up" their concerns.

A few words about Robra, who constituted something of an enigma. Now in her early 60s, she met Severance in 2011 and allowed him to move in with her within a month of their first meeting. While Robra maintained employment and had made money in real estate, Severance had no job and little resources. He was supposed to contribute $400 a month in rent but as time went on, it frequently went unpaid.

Like Severance, Robra harbored a distrust of law enforcement and the government. This helped explain how they had so quickly become friends and roommates. It also explained why she was displeased the police were coming to her door looking for Severance and why she was unhappy he would not talk with them. If he would just dispel their suspicions, the police would leave her alone.

By the evening of Sunday, March 9, it was clear to Linda Robra "Charlie" wasn't going to be speaking with the police. Severance unexpectedly announced he "thought it was best" if he went "camping." Robra knew from past experience that when "Charlie" was going camping, he was leaving for an extended period of time. Peeved at his intransigence, Robra told Severance if he was leaving, he needed to pack his things and "go for good." Severance obliged, piling what little possessions he owned into a couple of worn duffle bags and throwing them into his maroon station wagon.

The next morning, Monday, March 10, Severance started up the wagon and drove away. He did not tell Robra where he was going. He did not call his parents. He just hit the road and vanished.

Severance left Ashburn just about eight hours before the Alexandria Police "made him" as the prime suspect and about 60 hours before they hit Linda Robra's house with a search warrant. When he left, he took with him two .22LR five-shot North American Arms mini-revolvers, "stainless steel with the wooden grips" and a box of Remington Subsonic .22LR ammunition.

****

The puzzle really started to come together on Monday, March 10. That afternoon, Alexandria police detective Mike Whelan—no relation to Chris—reviewed the Secret Service report and the attached photographs. Whelan double-clicked on the photos that depicted Severance's car. He had previously seen the surveillance footage from the Braddock Road camera. The resemblance between Severance's Escort and the car on the video was immediately apparent.

Whelan raced down to the Homicide Unit and showed the photos to Cutting, Casey and Oakley. What the detectives saw before their eyes was stunning. A car just like Charles Severance's, down to what appeared to be a small, circular bumper sticker on the rear bumper, had been caught on camera driving away from the Lodato home minutes after the murder. The photos of Severance wearing a tricorn hat confirmed he resembled the man in the composite sketch. The Secret Service reports revealed he was seeking asylum because the "City of Alexandria was persecuting" him.

The photographic evidence was more than enough to convince the detectives Severance was the prime suspect.

****

On the morning of Wednesday, March 12, Cutting

called Linda Robra and asked to meet with her. With-in an hour, he was at her Ashburn townhouse. Cutting knocked on the door and shortly thereafter Robra an-swered. She said Severance had moved out a couple of days before and she did not know where he was. Robra did not mention two guns and a box of ammunition she had purchased at Severance's insistence.

Later that afternoon, Cutting and I met to debate our strategy. Cutting was certain Robra was being evasive and, as usual, it turned out he was right. We agreed he had probable cause for a warrant to search Robra's house for evidence related to the Lodato murder.

Cutting headed out to Loudoun County to swear out the search warrant. Once he had the warrant in hand, he obtained the assistance of the Loudoun County Sheriff's Office and the FBI in executing it. I drove out to Loudoun to attend the pre-raid briefing which was scheduled for 8 p.m.

The spring evening was cold and extremely windy, adding a haunting quality to an already tense situation. The briefing was held in a large conference room at the Sheriff's Office. The room was full of law enforcement officers from a number of different agencies. Cutting ex-plained the case and summarized why he suspected Sev-erance was the killer. He read from the search warrant, which authorized the seizure of any potential evidence to include: clothing, guns, computers and microscopic "trace" evidence such as carpet fibers or hairs. Soon, a massive convoy of Loudoun County deputies, Alexan-dria detectives and FBI agents left for Robra's house.

Cutting knocked on the door of the residence and told Robra he had a warrant for her home. He explained it would take several hours to complete the search and asked her if she would be willing to go to the Loudoun Sheriff's office and talk. When she consented, Cutting quickly put her in his police car and left. Sean Casey stayed behind to lead the search of the home, with a bevy of officers and FBI agents present to assist.

Back at the station house, Cutting brought Robra into a room which was equipped with a closed-circuit television camera. The system recorded the interview and allowed a group of us to watch from an adjoining room. I observed with great interest as Robra narrated the story of how she met "Charlie" Severance.

Cutting's performance during this interview was masterful. As his questions became more pressing, Robra became evasive. Cutting adapted his tactics when she dissembled, confronting her without being overbearing. His ability to calibrate his response bore fruit and soon the truth started to emerge.

Robra admitted Severance remained extremely angry about the Alexandria custody dispute over his son and would become enraged if the subject came up. She said when "Charlie" started on the topic of his son and the City of Alexandria, he would became so angry she had to leave the room.

Robra somewhat sheepishly confessed she had neglected to mention two small guns she had purchased over the internet. Severance had moved in with her around the summer of 2011 and first suggested she buy a special gun in early 2012, ostensibly for her to use as a self-defense weapon. Soon, his request morphed: he now urged her to buy two guns. Severance specifically wanted two North American Arms (NAA) mini-revolvers, insisting they were better suited for her small hands. Robra freely admitted she knew Severance was prohib-

ited from possessing guns because of a prior felony conviction; she maintained this did not matter because she
believed the guns were for her.

Robra brushed off his suggestion at first but Severance continued to bring it up and, by April 2012, had
found the guns he wanted on a website. Robra bought the
two mini-revolvers and had them shipped to a gun shop
in Winchester, Virginia. She and Severance drove to the
gun shop and picked up one in May 2012. She returned
alone to the store for the second gun in August 2012. The
two trips were necessitated by a Virginia law in effect at
the time that allowed only one firearm to be purchased
per transaction.

Between the purchases Severance brought up the
idea of buying ammunition for the guns. At his suggestion, he and Robra traveled to a different gun store in
Leesburg, closer to her home. Inside the store, Severance
showed Robra a box of ammo he wanted her to buy and
then left to wait in the car. Robra could not remember
the name of the ammunition manufacturer but she did
remember Severance insisting on "low-velocity" ammunition. She also remembered the box was white and
green, which just happened to be the colors of a box of
Remington ammunition.

Once they were in possession of the guns and ammunition, Severance showed Robra how to load and
unload the revolvers. Robra insisted to Cutting that the
guns "belonged" to her but she admitted both her and
"Charlie" had unfettered access to them. She said she
was reclusive and had very few houseguests. She agreed
only she and Severance knew the guns were in the house.

After learning to load the guns sometime in the fall
of 2012, Robra never handled them again and assumed

they remained untouched. She was adamant she had never fired the guns. After Cutting's visit to her home, she decided to go and check on the guns which had been left unsecured on the second floor. One had been kept in a pouch in a drawer in her home office and she was surprised to find the pouch empty. She kept the other gun in its original gun box in the hall closet and soon discovered that box was empty as well. The white and green box of ammunition was also gone.

Robra's two other guns—.38 six-shot revolvers that, being the wrong caliber, could not have been used in the murders—were still in her home. She conceded that, since only she and "Charlie" knew about the guns, Severance must have taken the two NAA revolvers and the ammunition when he left her house to "go camping."

At the end of Cutting's outstanding interview, we knew Severance was angry with the City of Alexandria. We knew he had fled with two guns and ammunition and had probably concluded the police were on to him.

But we had absolutely no idea where he was.

**** 

In 1997, after he had been arrested by the rookie police officer in Alexandria, Severance was convicted of Possessing a Concealed Weapon. This first offense was a misdemeanor for which he served 10 days in Jim Dunning's jail. In early 2004, when the Virginia State Police caught him with three more guns in Rockingham County, Virginia—more on this arrest shortly—they charged him with Possessing a Concealed Weapon-2nd Offense. Under Virginia law, a second concealed weapons offense is classified as a felony.

In 2005, Charles Severance accepted a plea bargain

and pleaded guilty to one felony count of Possessing a Concealed Weapon in Rockingham County Circuit Court. Severance was sentenced to 12 months in jail, with all of that sentence suspended, meaning he did not serve any active time. He was not placed on probation. The outcome of the case, in which the government obtained a conviction but no real punishment, led me to conclude the Rockingham prosecutor was willing to make a light plea offer in order to get a felony on his record. As a convicted felon, Severance could no longer lawfully purchase or possess any firearm.

Severance's writings would prove he was very angry about this felony conviction. Many of his musings revealed his stance that his "god given Second Amendment right to keep and bear arms" had been unlawfully taken away by a corrupt government.

****

Robra's interview established Severance had left her home with two guns and ammunition, providing us with probable cause he was violating Virginia law: specifically, that he was a felon in possession of a firearm. A warrant for this serious offense would likely be sufficient to keep Severance locked up once arrested.

I looked away from the CCTV monitor and turned toward Loudoun County Deputy Rick Shochet, who was part of the group watching the Robra interview. Shochet was assigned as our Loudoun liaison and was extremely helpful. He agreed to obtain the arrest warrant while Cutting finished up with Robra. Once the warrant was issued it would be logged into the FBI's national database so any law enforcement officer who came into contact with Severance would have the authority to arrest him.

Within two hours we had an open felony warrant for Charles Severance.

The manhunt had begun.

**** 

After the Loudoun warrant was active, Cutting and I discussed obtaining an Alexandria warrant charging him with Ruthanne's murder. Cutting's argument was compelling: Severance looked like the composite, his car matched the car in the surveillance video and he had access to the "right" type of gun and ammo. However, I remained unconvinced that obtaining a murder warrant was the right decision at this early juncture.

I definitely *thought* Severance was responsible for the Lodato murder—and probably the Kirby and Dunning murders, too. However, a prosecutor must have far more than a "belief of guilt" before charging someone with murder. Any number of factors warrant caution before "dropping" murder charges. First and foremost, a prosecutor does not want to wrongfully charge a person with a serious crime. Prosecutors have no incentive to charge the wrong person with murder. To do so not only brings undeserved opprobrium on the mischarged citizen, it allows the real perpetrator to remain at liberty and the community to remain at peril.

Even if the right person is identified, a premature warrant can also have devastating effects on the progress of a prosecution. Under our system of justice, the government only gets one shot at a trial. If the prosecutor charges too early and is forced to try a case without all of the evidence being developed, he could easily lose. Once a criminal defendant is acquitted, the double jeopardy clause of the Constitution forever prevents him from being re-charged him with the same crime.

A premature charge could present another procedural complication. The Code of Virginia requires the government to commence a trial within five months of indictment if the defendant is being held without bail, as most alleged murderers are. If the suspect does not waive his speedy trial rights the government faces the Hobson's choice of either starting a trial without all investigative leads being chased down or dismissing a murder charge to avoid the speedy trial problem. Dropping a case in this manner, even though it can be re-indicted, makes the prosecution appear feckless and unprepared.

Finally, if a prosecutor rushes to judgment and makes a bad charging decision, he has completely undermined the faith of the community in the integrity of the process. He has alienated the victim's family, causing them even more grief and making them doubt his ability and judgment. He has made it infinitely more difficult to charge the "real killer," diminishing the likelihood of bringing a just result to the case.

For all of these reasons, a professional prosecutor cannot bring murder charges without being confident in the state of the case. At this point in the investigation I would have been derelict in my duty had I charged Charles Severance with murder. He had been our focus for all of two days; we needed more time to investigate.

While I had a duty to be confident in the evidence before charging Severance with murder, I had a concomitant obligation to protect the public. We now knew Severance was probably a murderer. We knew he was angry and had two guns with him. We had absolutely no idea where he was.

Television shows never explore these competing

duties. As a minister of justice, I had to be certain of the strength of my case before charging Severance with murder. Just as compelling was my oath to keep the public safe. Had I done nothing and Severance killed again, I would not have been able to live with myself.

I felt as though I were caught in a vise. In an attempt to balance the two ends of a delicate see-saw, I authorized a charge that would get Severance off the street while leads were run down. I also thought by not bringing a murder charge we could keep Severance's name out of the public domain until we were ready to bring a murder indictment.

In that conviction, I was naïve and spectacularly wrong.

# CHAPTER SIX

*"Let all members of the enforcement class scream. The cowards deceive and die and do the dance of the Kalashnikov."*

Shochet obtained the felon in possession warrant on the evening of Wednesday, March 12. Ultimately, Severance was located and arrested in Wheeling, West Virginia, on the afternoon of Thursday, March 13, but the intervening hours were full of worry. I was fearful Severance would kill again before he could be located. The detectives were also concerned he might engage in a shootout with the police, a very real fear given his established hatred of law enforcement.

On the morning of March 13, Mike Kochis convened a meeting at police headquarters to discuss the options for locating our suspect. I was there, as were Casey, Cutting and Oakley. The FBI was also in attendance.

While law enforcement has the capability of tracking a person's cellphone, it isn't as easy as it looks on television. First, police have to obtain a search warrant allowing them to utilize cellphone tracking. This is not a small hurdle because judges pore over search warrant applications with a magnifying glass, particularly when the warrant seeks real-time location data. Even if a warrant is obtained, if the suspect elects to turn his phone off, it cannot be located.

Television shows constantly overestimate law enforcement's ability to obtain electronic evidence. Most citizens assume police officers are routinely listening in on their phone calls and reading their email. In the real world of criminal investigations it is very rare for law enforcement to review the content of private communications in real time. This can only occur when a judge authorizes an intercept, which in common parlance is referred to a 'wiretap.' Wiretaps, in which a suspect's communications are monitored in real-time, are disfavored by the courts and are approved only in major cases where all other investigative methods have proven to be unfruitful. In 20 years in law enforcement I have participated in only six cases in which a wiretap was authorized; only one of those was a "state wire."

Obtaining a search warrant to track Severance's phone was not difficult since an open felony warrant for his arrest was extant. However, for police to locate a phone, the suspect must have it with him and turned on. Even if these two conditions are satisfied it is still difficult to narrow down the specific location. In most cases, the signal from a phone gets the police within a several-mile radius around the suspect. If a cellphone is a needle, the best a warrant can usually do is decrease the size of the haystack.

In this case the cellphone was a dead end. While Severance did possess an old "flip-style" phone, he rarely used it and it was turned off during the manhunt. We could not use it to find him.

One of the main points of discussion during the March 13 meeting was whether the police department should "go public" and formally name Severance as a suspect. The detectives wanted to release photographs of Severance's car, disclose the existence of the open firearms warrant and announce the police considered him a "person of interest" in the Alexandria murders. Will Oakley hoped photographs of Severance would prompt someone to call in and tell us where he was.

I was against this course of action. We had not charged Severance with murder because, as of yet, I felt we did not have sufficient evidence to do so. This would be lost on reporters, of course; the moment the police called Severance a "person of interest" an intense circus would commence, complicating the investigation. With it would come substantial pressure to charge Severance with murder.

I've always chuckled at the term "person of interest." To me, the terms "suspect" and "person of interest" are synonyms. If the police suspect you have committed a murder, then you are "a person of interest" to the investigation. Over the years the meaning of the term "suspect" has morphed and it now signifies the "one person the police think did it." A new term had to be invented for people the police merely suspect has committed a crime: "person of interest." This is a distinction with no difference: Severance was both a person of interest and a suspect.

In the middle of this conversation a knock on the door rendered our debate moot. A federal agent relayed that Severance's debit card had just been used at a cheap hotel in Wheeling, West Virginia.

Within 30 minutes I was riding with Mike Kochis, speeding toward West Virginia.

**\*\*\*\***

Charles Severance was fascinated with the history of the Ohio River valley. He was particularly enthralled with General Braddock's 1755 westward march to Fort Duquesne to fight the French. On one occasion during his trial, Severance would bring a history book about the

Braddock campaign into the courtroom. He read it while a witness testified.

After selling his home in Alexandria in 2001 Severance moved to Cumberland, Maryland, living there until about 2005. Severance bought a home for a dirt-cheap price and ostensibly ran a bed-and-breakfast he called his "Chalet." Given his odd demeanor, it is hard to imagine he had many return customers. At one point, Severance's Cumberland neighbors complained to the police about his habit of taking baths, completely nude, in an old cast-iron bathtub he kept in his front yard.

The city of Cumberland was built atop the site of Fort Cumberland, a British stronghold that served as a base for Braddock during his Fort Duquesne campaign. Braddock's troops stopped in Cumberland, resting and mustering supplies before setting out for the Ohio River Valley.

In 2005 Severance sold the Cumberland home and used the proceeds to finance a five-year tour of the United States. He drove his maroon station wagon around the country aimlessly, camping or sleeping in the back of the car or staying at cheap overnight hostels. On several occasions, he visited historical sites associated with General Braddock.

Braddock started his march in Old Town Alexandria at a still-standing historical home known as Carlyle House. The Del Ray thoroughfare known as Braddock Road is named after the general and purportedly follows the route he took toward Cumberland and, thence, Fort Duquesne. At the Del Ray intersection of Braddock and Russell Roads stands the historical marker dedicated to General Braddock. On top of the marker is one of the cannons Braddock used during his expedition, pointing westward to mark his path. An ancient, illegible plaque affixed to the monument's side originally described his exploits.

If you mark the locations of the Dunning, Kirby and Lodato homes on a map of Del Ray, they form a rough triangle.

The Braddock cannon is at its center.

****

Mike Kochis is an outstanding police officer but an absolutely terrible driver. I have never been more convinced I was about to die than during the trip to Wheeling. Kochis, driving at speeds well over the limit, continuously spoke on his cellphone while drinking a cup of coffee. He sometimes steered with his thighs so he could have both hands free. I pleaded with him to let me drive but he laughed in his New Jersey way and said, "shut up, kid, we'll be fine!"

About halfway to Wheeling, Kochis received a phone call that made us both relieved: Severance had been arrested. A Wheeling police officer on the lookout for Severance, his car and his bike and had located the bike parked outside of a local library. The officer went into the library and found our man at a computer, surfing the internet.

That Severance was located at a public computer was not surprising. He routinely went to public libraries and accessed the internet, a fact which would make it impossible to uncover evidence of "precrime research" on his victims. Internet searches on publicly-accessible computers are almost impossible to link with a specific user. The police later visited every library around Robra's Ashburn home. They confirmed Severance had frequented one of the libraries but discovered the library's system did not retain information about internet searches. Attempts to peruse the computers themselves for evidence were likewise in vain.

Severance was arrested without incident. He did not resist and allowed himself to be handcuffed. No guns or ammunition were found on him. There were papers next to him on which he had been writing in his peculiar handwriting, a script with which I was about to become very familiar. The papers contained scribblings about campgrounds. It appeared Severance was trying to figure out where to go next.

With Severance under arrest Kochis and I could breathe a little easier. Or at least Mike could. Mike did not ease off the accelerator or his cellphone and I suffered another hour of absolute panic before we somehow reached Wheeling intact.

About a month before the arrest, before Severance was even made as the suspect, I taught a class about criminal investigations at a conference attended by police officers and agents from across the Eastern seaboard. I discussed our murders with a professor of psychology who was also teaching at the conference. After listening politely to the facts, the professor confidently gushed: "When you catch up with this guy, he is going to want to brag. He will tell you all about what he's done and how he's smarter than everybody. He'll give up everything."

As we approached Wheeling, I thought about that professor.

I hoped he was right.

**** 

Wheeling is situated on a picturesque bend of the

Ohio River, with the mighty river serving as the border between Ohio and West Virginia. The town's name purportedly derives from the native American phrase "*wih link*" which means "place of the head." The moniker refers to the head of a white settler who was scalped and decapitated at his homestead near the current site of the town. The local native Americans displayed the settler's head on a pike near the confluence of Wheeling Creek and the Ohio River.

Wheeling emits an aura of cultured decay. The architecture makes it clear this was once a wealthy town, but those days are long past. Huge old homes cling like ancient Roman villas to the hills around downtown, much as Wheeling itself clings to the bank of the muddy Ohio. While the homes are large enough to impress, on closer inspection, like the City itself they show the signs of age and disrepair. Paint peels off Victorian mansions and panes of leaded glass are spiderwebbed.

Downtown Wheeling boasts an array of imposing early-1900s office buildings that now have too much vacant space on the upper floors and too many gin joints at street level. But the mountain air is clean and crisp and the people who inhabit this fading beauty of a town are unreservedly hospitable.

Once we arrived in Wheeling we made a beeline to the police department. Kochis and I were ushered into a back office where a monitor displayed an adjoining interview room. Inside, just feet away from where were sitting, was Charles Severance. Via CCTV, I could both see and hear what was going on in the interview room. We were soon joined by Casey, Cutting and Oakley, who had driven to Wheeling separately.

A uniformed Wheeling police officer was in with

Severance but under strict orders to not question him about the investigation. The officer's job was to babysit our suspect and wait for us to arrive. As I watched the video feed I listened as Severance gave the officer what seemed to be a nonsensical history lesson.

Severance engaged in an extended dissertation about the "Indians" and the "settlers" in the area around Wheeling in the 1700s. The thrust of his story, to the extent I could discern it, was that the "noble savages"—the Native Americans—were far more clever than the white settlers and always outsmarted them, killing many of them in the balance.

At the time, it seemed Severance was just rambling on without any purpose. In retrospect, I didn't understand Severance's complicated metaphor or his political thought. He was, in a sly and sarcastic way, confessing to his crimes through this unusual history lesson.

Severance was too smart to directly admit to murder. He absolutely loathed the police and would never confess to a law enforcement officer whom he considered his intellectual inferior. Instead, he talked about his deeds obliquely. Charles Severance identified politically with Native Americans, who raised their families and lived their lives ignorant of Western ideas of law, order and government. Severance believed eighteenth-century white settlers had unjustly forced an unwanted way of life on the indigenous people. In return, the Native Americans rightfully rose up against the settlers, attacking them and occasionally killing them in their isolated homesteads.

Severance was convinced these Native Americans were justifiably defending their culture by "tomahawking homesteads in the backwoods of America." Taking

after their example, since the Alexandria "law enforcement class" had deigned to impose its will on the "noble
savage" Charles Severance, he was "at liberty" to "tomahawk" Alexandria homesteads in retaliation.

As I watched, Severance asked what was going to
happen next. The Wheeling officer replied he was waiting for "Alexandria officers" to arrive. Severance sneered
and said he would not talk to anyone from Alexandria.

This remark prompted Dave Cutting to come up
with a plan. He grabbed an FBI agent who had traveled
with us to Wheeling and asked her to speak with Severance. Cutting reasoned he might talk to a federal agent
who was not from Alexandria. The agent agreed to give
it a try and to pretend she knew nothing about the Alexandria murders.

I eagerly watched the video feed as the FBI agent sat
down in the room with Severance. She began by advis-
ing him of his *Miranda* rights. Everyone recognizes this
process from the television and the movies: before the
police may interview a person who is under arrest they
must advise the arrestee he has the right to remain silent,
the right to have an attorney present during questioning
and the right to have an attorney provided by the government if he is indigent.

As soon as the FBI agent read the list of constitutional rights from a written form, Severance cut her off.
He pulled the document over to him and pointed his
bony finger at it, tapping the written words as he said: "I
have the right to remain silent. Yeah.... and I'd like an
attorney... It's in my best interest."

I will discuss Severance's mental health in detail later, but this episode established he was capable of rational thought. He understood he was better served by not

talking to the police.

The Alexandria Assassin was not going to confess. Furthermore, once he invoked his rights, the Constitution forbade the police from ever attempting to re-interview him.

****

During the evening of March 13 Casey and Oakley worked with Wheeling officers to obtain a series of search warrants: one for the computer Severance was using at the library, one for the hotel room in which he had stayed and one for his 1999 Ford Escort, which was located in the hotel's parking lot.

The computer revealed nothing of value; neither did the search of the hotel room. The search of Severance's car, however, was one of the turning points of the case.

There was no literal "smoking gun" hidden in Severance's Escort. The two .22 NAA five-shot mini-revolvers were not located. Indeed, we never recovered them and, as of this writing, the guns and ammo are still unaccounted for. Given Charles Severance's obsession with his assassination kit, I don't think he threw it into the Ohio River. It is far more likely he hid the guns on his way to Wheeling, intending to retrieve them once the heat cooled down. One day an anonymous hiker will find a backpack next to a tree on some forlorn trail with Severance's firearms concealed inside.

There were several items of physical evidence inside of the car: a gun-cleaning kit, a portable golf range-finder and a plastic bag full of latex gloves. All of these would be admitted as evidence during trial.

Detectives were also fortunate to discover several composition notebooks containing hundreds of pages of Severance's handwriting. Many of Severance's most incriminating writings were found in the car—with the "Parable of the Knocker" prime among them. These personal ruminations, many of them addressed to the son Severance had not seen in over 14 years, contained his deepest, private thoughts. They revealed a man absolutely fixated on violence.

The essence of Charles Severance was contained in those dark pages. They formed the core of his Manifesto of Hate and served as a personal diary. He wrote his innermost feelings in those notebooks, jotting down things therein that he never discussed with Linda Robra.

At trial the defense would maintain Severance had never hidden his anger, posting hundreds of deranged writings on the internet. The defense theorized no one would leave violent rantings online if they planned to act on them. Severance's attorneys said the Manifesto was just more of the same type of writing Severance freely deposited on websites he frequented—and was therefore harmless.

The thoughts Severance expressed in the composition notebooks were categorically different from those which he placed on the web. Severance did not leave missives to the estranged son he had not seen in fourteen years on the internet. Severance never mentioned the .22LR NAA mini-revolver on a website. He did not write about Subsonic ammunition.

Charles Severance never wrote: "Knock, Talk, Enter, Kill, Exit" on the internet, either.

**\*\*\*\***

Soon after Severance's arrest and the seizure of his Ford Escort, Oakley reached out to a video expert at the

FBI's Forensic Lab in Quantico, Virginia. This specialist was asked to enhance both the Braddock Road surveillance video and the Target video. The FBI expert told Oakley the car depicted on the Braddock Road video was probably a Ford Escort station wagon.

Not only did Severance's car match the color, make, model and year of the Braddock Road car, it was similar in a number of more idiosyncratic ways. Both cars displayed a front and rear license plate and both had a distinctive dent on the driver's-side rear quarter panel. Severance's car had alloy wheels on it, distinguishing it as a higher trim level; entry-level models came equipped with plastic hubcaps. The wheels were identical to the car on the surveillance video.

Then there was the bumper sticker.

\*\*\*\*

The investigative team spent the night of March 14 in Wheeling. Stressed and tired from a busy day full of developments, I met the detectives at a local tavern and then went to bed early. The next morning Kochis and I drove to the garage where the FBI was completing the search of the car. When we arrived Dave Cutting walked over to me and said: "You've got to look at this… come with me."

We walked into the garage bay containing the Escort and Cutting pointed at the sticker displayed on the rear bumper of the car. It was in the same place as the sticker on the car seen on the Braddock Road surveillance video. Far more shocking was the sticker's appearance.

Circular in shape and in stark black and white, the sticker depicted the cylinder of a revolver with five rounds loaded. Around the cylinder were the words "Assassination City Derby."

I was struck by the sly sarcasm of the sticker, which was totally consistent with Severance's personality. By prominently placing that sticker on his bumper for all the world to see—in effect, by hiding it in plain sight— Severance was making a subtle, revolting joke. To him, murdering people in their homes was a sick game. Severance thought it great sport to drive around displaying a bumper sticker the "elites" were too dumb to decipher.

In Severance's mind, he was participating in an "Assassination Derby."

****

After the search of the Escort was complete Kochis arranged for a flatbed truck to drive it back to Alexandria. Once in Virginia, additional search warrants were obtained; one to "re-check" the car for evidence and another allowing detectives to disassemble portions of the car; Cutting hoped that perhaps Severance had stuffed the guns in the air conditioning system of the Escort. Unfortunately, the guns weren't located.

Taking the Escort apart required the police to remove the rear bumper, replete with its shocking sticker. I would later introduce the entire bumper as an item of evidence at trial.

As Kochis and I prepared to drive back to Alexandria I got a call on my cellphone from a number I did not recognize. I ignored it and listened to the subsequent voicemail. It was Julie Carey, the television reporter from our local NBC affiliate who had been at the Lodato home on the day of Ruthanne's murder. Carey is very good at her job and has an infinite number of sources in Northern Virginia. Wheeling, however, is a long way from Alexandria so I was astounded to hear her asking whether the arrest of Charles Severance was related to the Alexandria homicides.

I originally thought we could keep Severance's arrest low-key for months. Within hours, one of the best local television reporters had made the connection.

****

Severance had been arrested on our Virginia gun possession warrant, which was a relatively serious charge. The fact he had fled from Virginia when the police wanted to talk to him indicated he was a risk of fleeing if released from jail. The upshot was Severance would probably be held without bail in West Virginia until he was extradited back to Virginia.

But "probably held without bail" was not the same as "definitely." If we obtained a murder warrant from an Alexandria magistrate, we could rest assured Severance would remain in custody until trial.

Charles Severance could not be released on bail. The thought he might run and hide from prosecution paled in comparison to the very real fear that, if at liberty, he would retrieve his guns and kill someone else.

Cutting and Casey pointed out our case had significantly improved with the discovery of the latex gloves and the composition notebooks. Cutting pleaded: "Come on, Porter, we are going to have to charge him with murder sooner or later, let's just get this thing started. We can't risk him hitting the street."

Detectives tend to think in terms of black and white. Once they've made up their mind the murderer is in custody, any delay in charging is perceived as weakness. I often joke that if every jury was comprised of 12 cops, I would have the easiest job in the world; I could literally read the newspaper and drink coffee during the trial and still get a conviction.

District attorneys are usually more cautious than the investigators.

The friction between detectives who want to act quickly and prosecutors who preach caution does occasionally result in real-world disagreements. It did in this instance. But there was no doubt Cutting was right about the threat to the public if Severance were released.

****

Mike Tyson once said: "everyone has a plan until they get punched in the mouth." I doubt anyone would argue Iron Mike is an erudite social commentator, but truer words were never spoken. When I took office in early 2014, my plan was to focus on policy changes and the internal administration of my office. I doubted whether I would have any time to go to court.

The Alexandria Assassin investigation punched me directly in the mouth. When Charles Severance was arrested, I had been the elected prosecutor in Alexandria for exactly 73 days. I had never handled a case of this gravity; to be honest, I probably never will again. I was unprepared for the media attention the case received. I had not planned on being at the center of a whirlwind.

My stress level rose exponentially when I realized the detectives working the case expected me to have the answers to a number of very big questions. Questions such as: do we have enough evidence to charge Severance with murder? When do we charge him? How many murders do we charge him with? Should we seek the death penalty?

There was no formula into which I could place the evidence and receive a mathematically precise answer as to which charges to bring. I had no Magic 8ball to gaze into and divine the answers. There was no algorithmic software I could employ to produce a roadmap for a complicated trial.

I stood in the cold West Virginia air and pondered the predicament, breath transforming into puffs of steam before me. Prosecutors are trained to spot holes in their cases and to consider the "worst-case scenario" before making a decision. This ingrained reticence often is perceived as indecisiveness by detectives, who are quick to suspect the Commonwealth's Attorney is "a spineless jellyfish" afraid to act. In this situation, however, things had moved extremely quickly; just a week before Severance was not even on our radar screen.

After a lengthy internal debate—and an external one with Dave Cutting—I decided I could not charge Severance with murder without a better understanding of the evidence. It was too soon to obtain a murder warrant. I assured Cutting that if a judge decided to release Severance, I would revisit the question. It would be fair to say Cutting wasn't thrilled with my decision.

We got into the unmarked police cars and began the long drive back to Alexandria.

\*\*\*\*

The process of extraditing a criminal is a vestige from a time when the sundry states were effectively distinct countries. When a person who is wanted on a criminal charge in one state is arrested in another, the prosecuting state cannot immediately send officers to retrieve him. The arrestee can avail himself of the courts of the state in which he was located to fight the extradition, arguing the other state's warrant should not be honored.

The arrestee can also elect to waive an extradition hearing and agree to return to the state in which he is wanted. Charles Severance, however, was not waiving anything.

In some ways Severance's decision to fight extradition was a boon. If Severance had waived his hearing, the extradition would have occurred within a couple of weeks of his arrest, accelerating the trial date on the Loudoun County charge. Because Severance elected to contest the extradition we had time to work on leads before bringing a murder indictment. To my relief, the West Virginia judge ordered him held without bail.

Severance's West Virginia attorneys repeatedly argued the firearms charge was a "sham" designed to buy us time to complete our murder investigation. While I readily admit the warrant was designed to get Severance into custody so that he could not kill anyone else, I categorically deny the Loudoun charge was a "sham." To the contrary, it was a strong case and had it proceeded to trial Severance almost certainly would have been convicted. In the end, the Loudoun firearms charge was dropped for strategic reasons, but not because it was unwinnable.

Once I was convinced Severance was likely responsible for the Alexandria murders, I had a moral obligation to get him off the streets so he could not kill again. On the other hand, I had a competing ethical obligation to make sure we had a strong case before charging him with murder. The Loudoun warrant accomplished both goals, buying us time to pull the case together while effectively neutralizing the threat to the community.

When I took office, I swore an oath to protect the

citizenry. I will never apologize for keeping people safe.

**\*\*\*\***

In the D.C. area we have a local morning radio show called the Sports Junkies, starring four men who have been friends since high school. I have listened religiously for decades; the Junkies are my age and their on-air demeanor reminds me of a group of my friends. Their brand of humor is usually right up my alley.

In addition to sports, the quartet often discuss current events including true crime. Unfortunately, they usually get significant aspects of the criminal justice system wrong—even though one of them has a law degree. I'm often tempted to call in to fill them in on how it really works, but the one time I tried I was put on indefinite hold.

It's a small point, but the Junkies use the words "burglary" and "robbery" interchangeably. They are not synonyms: you burgle a house by breaking into it and you rob a person by stealing property from their custody through the use of force. Likewise, the words "jail" and "prison" do not mean the same thing: jails are local facilities in which inmates are either awaiting trial or serving short sentences, whereas prisons are operated by the state and house those serving terms of longer than one year. Pending his trial, Severance remained in jail—not prison.

Charles Severance was extradited back to Virginia in May 2014, residing in the Loudoun jail until September, when he was indicted for murder in Alexandria and the Loudoun charge was dismissed.

I spent the months between May and September actively putting the case together. As I became more familiar with the evidence, I took my show on the road and visited a number of other prosecutors whose opinions I valued and to whom I am forever indebted. Each of them had their own caseload and could rightly have said "sorry, good luck," but ours is an exclusive fraternity. Friends gave freely of their time, listening to me explain my case and then sharing their thoughts about strategy.

Every colleague I spoke with agreed I was morally obligated to charge Severance with murder. However, there was significant disagreement about whether I should charge him with one murder, two murders or all three. Different people, all of whom had my complete respect, had starkly different opinions. The only common theme was a deep reluctance to recommend charging Severance with the Dunning offense. These seasoned prosecutors believed the "10-year gap" between Nancy's death and the Kirby shooting might prove insurmountable.

The maelstrom of conflicting advice was not helping me sleep any better. I had hoped for unanimity from my peers on the appropriate course of action. In the event, the contrary occurred: the more people I spoke with, the more differing opinions I amassed.

The natural human fear of failure loomed over me. I don't mean I feared a personal failure, like losing my next election. To be quite honest, given the weight I felt on my shoulders, at the time I questioned whether I really wanted to be re-elected. My fear of failure revolved around letting others down: my family, my hometown community, which rightly demanded the killer be stopped, the outstanding detectives who had worked tirelessly to identify Severance and, of course, the families of Severance's victims. Sleep became a rare companion.

One day in mid-August I woke up from a fitful slumber and reassessed the conflicting opinions I had amassed for the one-thousandth time. I was startled when a disembodied voice pierced my deliberation and, in a clear female timbre, said: "No one is going to make these decisions for you; you're going to have to trust your gut and make them on your own."

When I say I heard disembodied female voice speaking, I mean it. I literally heard a voice inside of my head talking to me. Kind of like: "If you build it, they will come," I suppose.

Maybe the stress was getting to me and I was starting to crack. Maybe it wasn't an angelic voice at all, but simply my own thoughts as I awoke from a twilight sleep. I'll concede that's the most plausible explanation.

But that morning, for the first time since I had become involved in the case, a sense of serenity crept over me. The rational part of my brain knew it could not be so, but for just a minute, the voice made me feel like someone was looking out for me.

The advice was simple and elegant. It was also true. My gut instinct *had* gotten me this far. I did have a job to do. I was paid to make tough decisions and no one was going to make those decisions for me.

When you boil it down to its essence, the job of an elected prosecutor is to make tough decisions.

****

I knew the case better than anyone and my gut told me I had to indict Severance for all three crimes. Every time I considered my choices, I came back to an inescapable conclusion: I *could* adequately explain the "10-year gap" and the facts—particularly the firearms evidence—

only made sense if all three murders were heard by one jury in one trial.

To be sure, the police detectives working the case unanimously wanted all three indicted and were not shy about saying so. Kochis and Cutting were the most vocal, frequently exhorting me to action. Given these dedicated detectives had poured their heart and soul into the case I could not easily dismiss their instincts.

I had another compelling reason to indict Severance for killing Nancy Dunning: both her family and the community deserved an answer to this decade-long mystery. Between 2003 and 2013, the police had continued to work the case. Despite this lengthy investigation, detectives never uncovered anything concrete and never came close to charging anyone with the crime.

The absence of any real leads had sadly not stopped an undeserved cloud of suspicion from forming around Nancy's husband, Jim.

****

The simple Latin phrase *qui buono?*—to whom the good?—is a useful starting point in many homicide investigations. The idea, invented by the respected Roman judge Lucius Cassius two millennia ago, is that when you have a mystery to solve you begin by asking yourself who benefitted from the crime? In the imperfect vale upon which we tread the answer often involves identifying the beneficiaries of wills or life insurance policies.

Thus, when the police are confronted with the unsolved murder of a person with no known enemies, the first step in their playbook is to look at the victim's friends and family. This is especially true when theft can be ruled out as a motive, as it could be in Nancy's case.

It was not unusual that after Nancy's death the police looked at her husband. The detectives would not have been doing their jobs had they not included Jim in the investigation. I had nothing to do with the Dunning case until the fall of 2013, but had I been involved in 2003, I suspect I would have supported investigating Jim as well.

In the months after Nancy's murder the detectives determined Jim could not have fired the fatal rounds himself. He had been at work at the City jail the morning of the crime before leaving to meet Nancy and Chris. The jail's electronic key card system captured the time Jim left for his lunch date. Detectives were also able to piece together that Jim visited a bank and a local business on his way. Given the established times for these events and the fact Chris Dunning corroborated his dad's arrival time at the restaurant, there was not enough time for Jim to have stopped by his home to personally commit the crime.

Having eliminated Jim as the gunman, detectives started to consider whether he may have hired someone to kill his wife. Seeking a motive, investigators turned their eyes to the nature of Jim and Nancy's marriage, where they found the normal foibles of any sustained human relationship.

What the detectives never located was any tangible evidence connecting Jim to Nancy's death. Every avenue of investigation was attempted. Detectives interviewed Jim's acquaintances and co-workers. They issued subpoenas for his financial records to determine if there was any paper trail linking him to a contract killer. They obtained his phone records to see if he had contact with any shady characters. Not one shred of incriminating evidence was found.

It is impossible to prove a negative and it was therefore impossible for the detectives to establish Jim was _not_ involved in the crime, but it should suffice to say that my predecessor in office never charged Jim with any offense. Nevertheless, rumors about Jim spontaneously generated and the community began to whisper. A cloud of suspicion condensed around Sheriff Dunning. It was a very thin mist, composed of speculation and innuendos, but it hovered around him until he retired from office in 2005.

Jim Dunning moved to South Carolina and quietly lived out his days until he passed away in 2012. In one of the many injustices surrounding this case, Jim did not live to see whether his name was cleared.

\*\*\*\*

As the summer progressed I became convinced the rationale for indicting all three crimes was solid. All three were committed within one mile of each other, in a neighborhood in which crime was rare and violent crime unheard of; all three involved a knock (or doorbell ring) at the front door and a cold-blooded assassination, with no attempt to enter the home or steal anything; and the Kirby murder occurred just days short of the 10-year anniversary of the Dunning murder. All three victims were white, middle-aged and upper-middle class; all three were killed on a weekday in the late morning hours; and all three had been shot with .22LR Remington ammunition, fired from a gun with eight lands and grooves and a right twist: the characteristics of the exact gun and ammunition combination with which Charles Severance was obsessed.

The Lodato murder was the strongest case. With the Braddock Road video, the gun evidence, the composite sketch and Jeanette's testimony, the safest path was to charge Severance with the Lodato murder alone.

Indicting the Kirby and Dunning murders would require me to prove these crimes were committed in a manner so similar to the Lodato case—that the *modus operandi* of the killer was so unique—the only rational conclusion was the same person was responsible for all three. My trial plan would resemble a syllogism: the same person committed all three murders, Severance committed the Lodato murder, *ergo* he committed the other two as well.

If I indicted Severance for all three murders the defense attorneys appointed to represent him would immediately file a motion to sever the Dunning case from the other two, based on the existence of the "10-year gap." If granted, the motion would force me to abandon my trial plan and would significantly lessen my chances of securing a conviction. Together the three cases formed a compelling story; if the defense were successful in pursuing a "divide and conquer" severance strategy, the case would be in serious jeopardy.

In an interesting coincidence, the issue of severance would have a huge impact on the Severance case.

## CHAPTER SEVEN

*"The last scream of a victim echoes to eternity."*

David Lord is a Senior Assistant Commonwealth's Attorney in my office. I can't claim the praise for hiring him; that must go to my predecessor. I was smart enough, however, to realize I needed David on my trial team. In July I approached him and asked if he was willing to work the case. David enthusiastically agreed and by August was up to speed. His first substantive assignment was to research and brief the severance issue.

David would not be considered physically imposing but his intellect is decidedly so inside the confines of a courtroom. David's boyish good looks belie the seriousness with which he approaches every case. Anyone who knows him would use the word energetic in describing him. Whenever I assign David a task it is a foregone conclusion it will be done in half the time it would take me to do it and twice as well. I consider myself fortunate to have David working for me and blessed to call him my friend.

David brought to the table several outstanding qualities: an inexhaustible font of energy, an exceptionally quick and incisive legal mind and an absolute dedication to doing the right thing.

David is active in his local church and is working toward a degree in theology in his spare time. He and I have had many fascinating discussions about religion and ethics over the years, to include topics as diverse as miracles, Catholicism, the efficacy of prayer and the Reformation.

During the early days of the Severance investigation, we found ourselves engaged in one of these good-natured debates. We started to discuss a theological conundrum that has confounded philosophers for centuries. Known as the "problem of evil," it posits: "if God is an omnipotent, omniscient and caring being, why would He allow suffering to exist in the world?"

At trial, I would return to the "problem of evil" in my final words before the jury.

****

By the end of August, parts of the case were coming together. Sean Casey had finally completed a review of thousands of documents recovered from Severance's parents' home pursuant to a search warrant. In the basement, in an area used by Severance to store personal belongings, Casey had located a treasure trove of writings. Many took the form of postcards Severance mailed to his parents between 2005 and 2010.

In 2005, Severance sold his Cumberland home and became an itinerant nomad, driving around the country in his Ford station wagon. During his travels, Severance would stop at historical sites he found interesting, many related to the encroachment of white settlers on Native American lands. He was a dedicated postcard writer, composing hundreds of cards and mailing the majority to his mother and father. He always told his parents what town he was in. Postmarks confirmed Severance's whereabouts, allowing Casey to piece together his movements over this period. Severance's "Grand Tour" partially explained the "10-year gap" between the Dunning and Kirby murders. For over half of that time period, our killer was nowhere near Alexandria.

The postcards are also notable for the hatred and vitriol Severance spewed in them, odd asides for travel postcards addressed to his mother. For example, from Kings Canyon National Park in California:

**"Glad I backtracked to see this strange geological formation… On two of four days, I have spotted these precocious, impudent rascals" (police).**

**"I hope and pray" (my son) "develops survival instinct and effective predator skill like a defiant Severance."**

**"Tomahawking a Homestead in the Backwoods of America!"**

Among the scores of postcards in the parents' basement Sean Casey located a box of ammunition. Green and white, it bore the words "Remington Subsonic .22LR" on its face. The box originally contained 50 rounds, but when Casey opened it he discovered only 40 rounds remained.

Casey noticed a serial number was stamped on the inside of the box and sent it to Remington to see what information they could provide. Within weeks, the detective had his answer: the ammunition was manufactured in late 2001. Since that date was prior to Nancy Dunning's murder, the ammunition could have been used in the crime.

Ten rounds were missing from the box.

Five of them may have been loaded into the gun used to kill Nancy Dunning.

Three were probably fired during her murder.

**** 

In early September, Casey, Cutting and I met to discuss the evidence recovered from Linda Robra's Ashburn townhouse. Police located the empty North American Arms gun box in an upstairs closet. In Robra's home office, they found the small pouch in which she had stored the second mini-revolver.

Cutting had reviewed a bevy of documents that corroborated Robra's purchases of the guns and the ammunition. He showed me a copy of an online receipt that detailed the purchase of two .22LR North American Arms revolvers for a total of $414.98. Interestingly, Linda Robra had written the price and some information about her credit card at the top of the document. At the bottom, in his unmistakable handwriting, Charles Severance had scribbled: "2 .22 NAA 5-shot revolvers, 1 50-round box of Subsonic ammunition, gun-cleaning kit," confirming the guns and ammo were his idea.

Other documents written in Severance's hand were seized from the home office. One said: "Hammer interferes with right side rail." While this did not accurately reflect the terminology a firearms expert would use, the import was unmistakable: Severance had fired one of the mini-revolvers and discovered the hammer was not working properly. Another document confirmed the name of the gun store where Robra had picked up the two guns.

A jury would not have to take Linda Robra at her word. Every part of her testimony surrounding the purchase of the guns and the ammunition was corroborated by extrinsic evidence. As a bonus, many of the documents displayed Severance writing about the guns.

Casey also located two spent .22LR cartridge cases on the floor of Robra's garage. As previously noted, in a revolver, cartridge cases remain in the gun's cylinder until physically removed by the shooter. The presence of these cartridge cases proved someone fired two .22 rounds and dropped them in the garage. Since Robra denied ever shooting the revolvers, Severance was the only remaining candidate.

On a television show, CSI personnel would put the fired cartridge cases under a microscope and immediately discover the shooter's DNA or fingerprints. In the real world, the temperatures and pressures involved with the firing of a round of ammunition effectively destroy any forensic evidence. This science applies to both cartridge cases and fired bullets. Therefore, none of the ammunition components recovered, either from Robra's house or the three crime scenes, could be forensically tested for the presence of Severance's DNA or prints.

Cutting mentioned one last intriguing bit of firearms evidence was seized from Robra's home: the two .38 revolvers and 100 rounds of .38 ammunition. Robra had owned these guns for decades, well before she met Charles Severance. She confirmed Severance knew about the .38 firearms and had unrestricted access to them.

The fact Severance took the .22 NAA mini-revolvers when he left Robra's home to "go camping"—but left the .38 revolvers behind—strongly suggested Severance knew the NAA .22LR revolvers were the murder weapons.

When Severance fled to West Virginia in early March, the police had not yet publicly released the caliber of the ammunition used in the murders. Indeed, this was one of the key pieces of information I convinced Chief Cook to avoid discussing in his March 6 press conference. When Severance took the .22 revolvers but not the .38s, it implied he knew which caliber gun could be linked to the Alexandria murders. The only person who would know which guns had been used was the Alexandria Assassin himself.

That Severance left the .38s behind also helped by negating one of the arguments later floated by his attorneys: perhaps some unidentified thief had entered Robra's home and stolen the .22 revolvers. On its face this was implausible, but the idea someone broke in and stole just the North American Arms revolvers became untenable if the jury was asked to believe the "thief" left behind the two more powerful .38s.

The evidence was circumstantial but very powerful. Robra had purchased the two guns and the box of Subsonic ammunition at Severance's request. He had test fired the revolvers and dropped the cartridge cases in the garage. When he realized the police were on his trail, he fled, taking the .22s and the Subsonic ammo with him because he knew their discovery would mean his downfall.

We could establish Severance had access to two North American Arms .22LR five-shot mini-revolvers in 2013-2014. We could prove he had access to Subsonic ammunition during the same time frame. We could show he had fired these guns. The box of ammo from the parents' house proved Severance had access to Subsonic ammunition in 2003.

One piece of the puzzle was still missing.

Could we put a .22LR North American Arms five-shot mini-revolver in the hands of Charles Severance during the time frame surrounding Nancy Dunning's death?

\*\*\*\*

To answer this critical question, we needed to speak

with Virginia State Trooper John Murphy. Cutting had run Severance's criminal record and learned about his 2005 felony firearms conviction. A little detective work revealed the charge arose out of an arrest Murphy had made in 2004. Since Murphy was assigned to a police barracks in the western part of Virginia, one day in the summer of 2014 Cutting and I made a lengthy trip to interview him.

John Murphy was a former football player and he looked the part at almost 6'4" and well over 200 pounds. Murphy was imposing was definitely not someone I would want to argue with. Notwithstanding his size, he was warm and gregarious. I quickly learned he had a penchant for great stories. Murphy started our interview by sharing an interesting anecdote about his time at the Virginia Military Institute. Then he dove into the details of the time he arrested Charles Severance.

Murphy came into contact with Severance in February of 2004, just two months after Nancy Dunning was murdered. While patrolling rural Rockingham County, Murphy noticed Severance's Ford wagon displayed expired license plates. He initiated a traffic stop on a secluded road and watched as Severance slowly pulled over.

The reason why Severance was in Rockingham that day is unknown. Rockingham County is off of Interstate 81 in the mountains of western Virginia. The county is about halfway between Northern Virginia and Cumberland, Maryland, where Severance was living at the time. It is possible Severance was on his way back to Cumberland from Alexandria or from visiting his parents in Fairfax, but Rockingham County is not on the route one would normally take between these two locations. Severance was known for preferring to drive the backroads, usually to visit historical sites, and may have been taking a circuitous route back to his Maryland home.

What is certain is Severance was heavily armed. Trooper Murphy, conscious of his own safety, elected to approach Severance's vehicle on the passenger side of the Escort. This method is often employed by the state police and is contrary to the method used by most police officers who prefer approaching on the driver's side.

This tactical choice may have saved Murphy's life. When Murphy arrived at the passenger window he could see Severance, the only occupant of the Escort, focusing on the driver's side mirror; Severance was anticipating Murphy's approach on the driver's side. Since Severance had a loaded gun under his seat and two more within easy reach, he may have been considering shooting Murphy, just as he probably considered shooting the rookie Alexandria officer years before.

Murphy maintained the element of surprise by walking up on the passenger's side. The window was partially down and Murphy engaged Severance in conversation. As he did so, his "police sense" started to bother him. Almost simultaneously, Murphy noticed loose ammunition and a large number of spent cartridge cases on the passenger floorboard of the Escort.

When Severance did not respond to questions about the ammunition, Murphy did not waste time. Possessed with probable cause Severance was concealing a firearm, the trooper walked around the car, opened the driver's door and grabbed Severance. Severance put up little resistance as the burly trooper pulled him out of the car. Murphy handcuffed Severance and placed him in his police car after confirming he had no guns hidden on his person. With Severance secure, Murphy returned to the Escort to complete a thorough search.

Murphy first found a .22 semiautomatic pistol hidden inside of a plastic briefcase laying on the Escort's back seat. He discovered a .380 semiautomatic pistol on the rear floorboard of the car, partially tucked into the crevasse created between the driver's seat and the center console. He soon located another gun under the driver's seat. This final firearm was concealed inside of a piece of fabric in much the same way Severance had concealed the gun seized from him during his 1997 Alexandria arrest.

Murphy was fascinated by the small size of the gun hidden under Severance's seat. He identified it as a .22LR North American Arms five-shot mini-revolver, stainless steel with a wooden grip. The revolver was fully loaded and could have easily been retrieved and fired.

Since all three firearms were concealed from common observation, and since Severance had previously been convicted of misdemeanor Carrying a Concealed Weapon, Murphy charged him with Carrying a Concealed Weapon-Second Offense.

Under Virginia law, a second weapons violation of this type is a felony and Severance was ultimately convicted of that offense. As a convicted felon, he was incapable of lawfully purchasing or possessing any firearm or ammunition.

If he ever wanted to buy a gun again, he would have to convince someone to buy it for him.

****

I would later tell the jury the .22LR North American Arms mini-revolver Severance possessed in February

2004 was the firearm he used to kill Nancy Dunning. The gun's seizure raises two significant questions: if it was the gun used in her murder, why didn't Trooper Murphy figure that out back in 2004? What ultimately happened to the gun?

The answer to the second question is easy. The Virginia State Police destroyed Severance's mini-revolver in 2006, melting it down in a blast furnace, after his criminal case was completed and a judge ordered the gun's destruction. This is standard procedure and is required by the Code of Virginia.

In 2014, I hoped the state police had somehow overlooked the judge's order and the gun was still sitting on a shelf somewhere. I had them check several times, but they ultimately confirmed it had been melted down for scrap metal.

The answer to the first question is a little trickier. In a television show Trooper Murphy's ersatz equivalent would have placed the recovered gun into a computer scanner. Within seconds, Nancy Dunning's picture would have popped up with the word "MATCH" flashing in red lights. Not surprisingly, things are much different in the real world.

The FBI does maintain a law enforcement database called the National Integrated Ballistic Information Network (NIBIN) that is intended to "automate ballistics evaluations" and to "provide actionable investigative leads in a timely manner." In theory, NIBIN can allow a law enforcement officer to determine whether a cartridge case recovered from a crime scene came from a firearm that had previously been used in a crime.

NIBIN works by storing and comparing marks imparted to a fired cartridge case as it is ejected from a semiautomatic pistol. Evidence of rounds fired by a re-volver is usually not put into the system. Even in the rare case where a cartridge case is recovered at a crime scene and determined to have been fired from a revolver, it is not entered into the NIBIN system. Likewise, fired bullets are usually not entered into NIBIN. These limita-tions are mostly due to sheer volume: America experi-ences a huge amount of gun-related violence every year and data entry is laborious.

Since no cartridge cases were recovered at the Dun-ning crime scene, no firearms evidence from the case was entered into the FBI database. There was no point in Murphy test firing the recovered NAA .22LR. Any test fire from Severance's revolver could not be entered into NIBIN or compared with the data contained therein.

Citizens are often surprised to learn there is no na-tional database for guns and firearms are not subject to registration requirements. You may have to register to vote, you may have to register your car, but in Virginia you never have to register your firearm. There is no such thing as a "registered owner" of a gun in the Common-wealth. When a firearm is recovered from a crime scene it is usually impossible to determine where it came from.

While this situation is lamentable—I discuss some ideas for improving NIBIN in the conclusion of this book—in the real world of investigations there was no feasible method by which Murphy's 2004 seizure of Severance's .22LR mini-revolver could have led to it be-ing identified as the Dunning murder weapon.

****

We were not quite at a dead end with regards to the gun. While there is no requirement a firearm be registered, licensed firearms dealers must complete and submit reports about gun sales they make. Dave Cutting was able to query a database and obtain documents detailing the initial sale of the NAA mini-revolver seized by Murphy. The document bore Severance's distinctive handwriting and established he bought the gun in April of 2003, just eight months before Nancy Dunning was killed. Severance still had it two months after her murder when Murphy arrested him, circumstantially proving Severance possessed the revolver in December 2003.

A painstaking investigation, led by three outstanding detectives, had established Charles Severance had possessed three five-shot mini-revolvers of the exact same make and model. He possessed one at the time of Nancy Dunning's murder and two more during the time frame of the Kirby and Lodato murders. He was fixated on the exact type of ammunition used to commit all three murders, Remington Subsonic .22LR. One box of that ammunition, produced in 2001 and missing 10 rounds, was recovered from Severance's parents' home. Linda Robra bought another box of Subsonic ammo in 2012 at Severance's request.

The detectives had also established that Severance had a hatred of the City of Alexandria and recovered his Manifesto in which he ruminated about committing murder. Severance resembled the composite sketch of the Lodato murderer and, in 2003, he looked like the man depicted in the Target video following Nancy Dunning before she was killed. His car was caught on a surveillance camera driving away from the Lodato house minutes after Ruthanne and Jeanette were shot.

On the other hand, no eyewitness had identified him as the murderer. Police had not recovered the guns Robra purchased and therefore no forensic analysis could be conducted upon them. Severance had invoked his right to an attorney and had not confessed to the crimes. No DNA or fingerprints implicating Severance had been located at any of the crime scenes. While we had discovered thousands of disturbing documents written in Severance's hand, none of them specifically named his victims.

As the humid days of late August trickled to an end, my days of procrastinating were done. I had to revisit the charging decision. I could put it off no longer. As the angelic voice had commanded, I followed my gut. I understood the evidence and how it fit together better than anyone. I was personally convinced Charles Severance was responsible for all three murders. The three murders *were* related and the cases rose and fell together.

The grand jury for the City of Alexandria was scheduled to meet at 9 a.m. on September 8, 2014. When the jurors convened, I would seek a 10-count indictment charging Charles Severance with the murders of Ruthanne Lodato, Ron Kirby and Nancy Dunning.

I summoned up some courage and called Mike Kochis. If I told Mike what my decision was, there could be no turning back. Calling Mike was the equivalent of Caesar crossing the Rubicon.

*Alea iacta est.*

\*\*\*\*

For the sake of argument, let's say I had chosen to charge only the Lodato case. After all, several people advised me to do just that, since we had an eyewitness who described a killer very similar to Severance and video of a car very similar to Severance's car leaving the scene of the murder. Why not be conservative and just indict one crime?

Had I indicted just the Lodato offense, Severance's lawyers would have inevitably raised the fact that Ron Kirby had been murdered in a similar way just three months before and just about a mile away. They would have pointed out Ron was murdered using the same ammunition and firearms combination used to kill Ruthanne. Closing the loop, the defense would have pounded the table: "*the government knew about the Kirby murder, knew about the firearms evidence and yet decided <u>NOT</u> to indict our client with committing it. Even the prosecutor did not believe our client killed Ron Kirby!*"

The hypothetical defense summation is obvious: if Severance did not kill Ron Kirby, a fact the prosecution had conceded by choosing not to charge him, then he did not kill Ruthanne Lodato, either. *The real killer is still out there!* I dreaded the idea of watching jurors nod in agreement as the defense delivered this powerful argument.

Similarly, the testimony of the firearms experts about the rarity of the ammunition used to commit the murders was only compelling if all three murders were tried together. If I had charged just the Lodato and Kirby murders, the firearms testimony would have lost its potency. Instead of Jay Mason saying: "I've only seen this ammunition in three crimes—the three murders charged in this case," his testimony would have been: "I've seen this ammo in three cases—the two charged in this case *and* one more with the same *M.O.* that occurred in the same neighborhood a decade before."

That the firearms evidence forensically linked the three crimes tugged at me like gravity: I had to indict them together.

I asked David Lord if he thought I was making the right decision. David replied without equivocation: "Absolutely, Bryan. The cases only make sense when tried together. Plus, you are convinced he committed all three and we have the evidence to back your conviction up. You are morally obligated to charge it this way and seek a just result for the victims."

David was absolutely right.

****

Criminal defendants who cannot afford to pay a private lawyer to represent them are entitled to an attorney at the government's expense. In most jurisdictions these government defense attorneys are called public defenders.

Given the amount of courtroom experience they amass, public defenders are often better attorneys than their private counterparts. Defenders are extremely dedicated to their clients and possess an intense desire to help the downtrodden. They attempt to make the criminal justice system better by putting the prosecution and police to the test. and ardently believe it is better for 10 guilty people to go free than for one innocent person to be convicted.

Despite their title, they are not tasked with defending the public collectively. Their job is to defend individual members of the public who have been charged with a criminal offense. The rules of ethics binding on defense attorneys specifically prohibit the consideration of the public good or the community's welfare in deciding how to handle a particular case. Defense counsel's sole objective is securing the outcome most favorable to their individual client.

Even if a public defender is personally convinced his client is guilty of a depraved murder—even if he knows there is a real threat to public safety if his client is found not guilty and released—he still must do everything in his power to secure an acquittal. Consideration of the public's well-being would be antithetical to the client's interests.

A prosecutor, on the other hand, is supposed to consider the public good before initiating or maintaining a prosecution. In fact, prosecutors across the country take the public good into account every day in deciding how to execute their duties.

I am not naive enough to argue that every prosecutor always lives up to his obligation to serve the public good. Indeed, there are any number of examples of DAs failing to faithfully discharge their ethical responsibilities. Given the immense authority entrusted to prosecutors it is right to hold accountable those who fail to diligently wield their authority. However, a focus on the relatively few examples of prosecutorial malfeasance detracts from the exceptional work thousands perform across the country daily.

****

David Lord and I spent a long weekend in the office, fueled by pizza, preparing for the Grand Jury proceeding. Crime did not stop in the City; the day before the Grand Jury convened I was called to the scene of an unrelated murder that occurred on the West End of Alexandria. After conversing with the detectives, I made my way back to the office to finish up the Severance prep work.

We presented a total of 10 charges: two counts of

Capital Murder, one for the killing of Ron Kirby and one for the killing of Ruthanne Lodato. One count of First-Degree Murder was submitted with regards to the Nancy Dunning murder. Under Virginia law the premeditated murder of two or more persons within three years constitutes Capital Murder, thereby elevating the Kirby and Lodato murders to Capital Murder. Nancy Dunning's murder, while equally heinous and shocking, occurred 10 years before the Kirby murder and therefore could not be indicted as Capital Murder under Virginia law.

Another count alleged a crime called Malicious Wounding for the shooting of Jeanette. In a twist of Virginia law, a completed malicious wounding, which requires proof the shooter intended to maim, disable, disfigure or kill the victim, is a more serious crime than an attempted murder.

We also brought four counts of Use of a Firearm in the Commission of a Felony, one for each murder and one for Jeanette's shooting. Two counts of Possession of a Firearm by a Convicted Felon were tacked on. On the dates of both the Kirby and Lodato offenses Severance was a convicted felon and his possession a firearm constituted a separate felony. He had not yet been convicted of a felony on the date of the Dunning murder, so we could not seek a third Felon in Possession count against him.

**** 

There was another reason to charge the felon in possession counts. They would help get Severance's 2005 felony conviction before the trial jury. Evidence of prior convictions is usually not admissible out of fear a prior criminal record will bias the jurors against the defendant. Because the felony conviction proved one of the elements of the felon in possession charges, it could be admitted at Severance's trial. We needed to get it before the jury, not to besmirch Severance or get the jury to dislike him, but to help explain the "10-year gap" between the Dunning and Kirby murders.

Nancy Dunning was murdered in December 2003. This act of violence was one Severance had been contemplating for some time; probably since at least 2001 when he bought the first box of Subsonic ammunition.

I think Severance had been fantasizing about murdering someone well before 2003. There were likely dozens of potential victims whom he considered killing in the years between 1989 and 2003. We knew that after his 1989 arrest for shooting targets in the woods he told a psychiatrist he had considered murdering his father. There had to have been other "targets" he pondered assassinating.

Despite his anger, his obsession with guns and his fixation on violence, it took Severance a long time to work up the nerve to kill. Severance likely surprised himself by going through with the Dunning crime. The first murder was a cathartic release for him. His anger had welled and forced him to act. Once the white-hot magma had been expelled, the pressure inside his troubled mind temporarily abated.

Even had he not been arrested by Trooper Murphy in 2004 it would have been some time before Severance killed again; before the cycle of resentment, pressure and internal debate brought him to seek another release. Before the 10-year anniversary of his first murder convinced him that he needed to attend to some unfinished business.

In late December 2003, the Alexandria Police Department publicly released still photos taken from the Target video, hoping to identify the man following Nancy Dunning around the store. Severance must have seen the media reports about the Target video. Since he knew he was the man depicted in the photos, he would have been worried the release of the video might lead to someone recognizing him and calling the police.

Just two months later, the February 2004 seizure of the North American Arms mini-revolver Severance used to kill Nancy Dunning significantly increased the pressure. While I have outlined the reasons why that firearm could not have been forensically connected to the Dunning murder, Severance would not have known making the connection was impossible. He would have been very nervous throughout 2004 and into early 2005 that the gun, now in the possession of the Virginia State Police, would ultimately lead to him being identified as Nancy's killer.

His fear of being discovered would have been heightened once he was convicted of the felony gun charge in 2005. As a result of the guilty plea, Severance's DNA profile was entered into a national database. While he had not left his DNA behind at the Dunning scene, he could not have known this either. He therefore had ample reason to fear his DNA would lead police to his doorstep.

Between the Target video, the seizure of the murder weapon and his felony conviction, Charles Severance would have been very concerned that law enforcement might identify him as the Alexandria Assassin.

What did he do after the combination of events led him to suspect he was in danger of being discovered as a murderer? He did the same thing he would later do in

2014, when confronted with a similar chance of being arrested: he got into his Ford Escort and drove away. Indeed, as the postcards recovered from his parents' home showed, he spent most of the next five years roaming the country in his "little red wagon."

The 2005 felony conviction helped explain the "10-year gap" between the Dunning and Kirby murders in another way. From his writings and actions, it was incontrovertible Charles Severance was obsessed with one gun and ammunition combination: a small, "easily concealed" .22LR North American Arms mini-revolver and Remington Subsonic ammunition. In order for Severance to conduct his "assassinations" he needed this assassin's kit. Trooper Murphy had taken his gun away from him and now, as a convicted felon who could not lawfully purchase guns or ammunition, he could not easily obtain a new one.

Without his toolkit, Charles Severance could not conduct an assassination. Before he could kill again, he needed to find someone to buy a .22LR mini-revolver and Subsonic ammunition for him. It would be about seven years before he met Linda Robra.

**** 

My decision to indict Capital Murder meant the death penalty was in play in the Severance case. However, I decided to waive death as a potential penalty and filed a written notice to that effect concurrently with the indictment. Severance's serious and untreated mental illness was uncontroverted and Alexandria is a progressive enclave which evidences little support for the death penalty. The combination of mental health mitigation and the community ethos mattered deeply to me. I sincerely questioned the morality of seeking capital punishment for a person so affected by mental illness.

Waiving had another benefit: the trial would get started much more quickly. I had a host of witnesses I needed to keep on board; a quicker trial date decreased the potential for gremlins like missing witnesses to arise. Capital trials take a very long time to commence; had I sought the death penalty it is even possible the case would not have been tried by the time this book went to print. I could not risk that type of delay.

With the effect his heinous crimes had on the community—and with the cold calculation Severance displayed in planning them—my waiver of the death penalty spurred some to criticize me online. I remain convinced I made the right choice. Indeed, in my career, I have waived the death penalty in all four capital cases I have indicted.

Another decision now confronted me: should I keep the fact I wasn't seeking capital punishment a secret? If the defense attorneys thought a death sentence was in play, they might convince Severance to plead guilty and accept a life sentence so as to avoid the ultimate sanction.

Avoiding a 100-witness trial in which the outcome was not preordained would in many ways be a blessing. My job was to keep a killer off the streets and a guilty plea would accomplish just that. If I announced I was waiving the death penalty, I would arguably lose the only real bargaining chip I had to coax a guilty plea from Severance.

Notwithstanding this, I never considered concealing my decision, not for one second. It would have been unethical to do so. It would have been a moral failure to privately determine that seeking the death penalty was inappropriate but to then keep my decision confidential in the hope of securing a guilty plea.

Let me be clear: I am not advocating that a prosecutor who has made the decision to seek the death penalty should never consider allowing the defendant to plead guilty in exchange for taking the death penalty off the table. In my opinion, that is exactly the right decision. My situation was different in that I had affirmatively decided to waive the death penalty from the outset.

My job requires me to make tough decisions and once I've made them, I own them. I publicly announced I was not seeking the death penalty on the same day I announced Severance had been indicted for the murders.

**** 

Severance was obsessed with wanting to feel like he was in control of his life. His writings are replete with boasts like: "Who is the alpha predator now?" and "I ask the questions!" These quotes masked the truth: Severance knew his life was off the rails. He constantly yearned to feel in control.

Throughout the trial, Severance insisted he was in intense pain from an ankle injury that predated his arrest. He maintained he could not walk at all, despite the fact he had been perfectly capable of walking at the Russian Embassy and around Wheeling prior to his arrest. Severance's phantom complaints caused the deputies in charge of his custody to escort him into the courtroom in a wheelchair. It appeared he concocted an ankle injury in order to have something about which to complain.

One of the most indelible photographs from the case was taken early on, as Severance was wheeled into the courtroom by deputies. When confronted by news cameras, Severance flipped the bird, an image captured and immediately tweeted out by reporters. You can still find it on the internet. Severance sarcastically explained to the judge this had not been an obscene gesture. With a straight face, he maintained it was intended to represent of a map of West Virginia.

If you look at the photo, it does look a little like West Virginia. I have to agree with Charlie on that.

When Severance complained about his backside being sore from the wheelchair, the deputies had to provide him with a pillow to sit on. They catered to his whims like he was some sort of medieval potentate.

I don't think his ankle hurt—or his posterior. I think Severance's ego hurt. Indeed, it had been hurting for a long time. Charles Severance realized that, despite his intellectual gifts, his life had amounted to basically nothing. Now his future was out of his hands. Making the deputies push him around in a glorified stroller was a metaphoric middle finger to the "law enforcement class."

****

In recent years, grand jury proceedings have come under public scrutiny. Television talking heads rail against prosecutors using investigative juries, arguing we can somehow force them to do what we want with a case. The theory is prosecutors, afraid of negative optics over an unpopular decision, will use the grand jury as a shield, forcing the outcome they want from the jurors and then telling reporters "don't blame me." I have heard a lawyer on a television show forcefully advocate prosecutors should stop taking cases to grand juries altogether.

That talking head must have forgotten his constitutional law because the Fifth Amendment states, in pertinent part: "no person shall be held to answer for (a felony), unless on a presentment or indictment of a grand jury." Virginia has adopted similar language in a code section, specifically requiring a grand jury's consent before a person can be put on trial for a felony.

This is how it should be. Before a case gets to the grand jury, the three branches of government have already been involved: the legislature, which has proscribed certain conduct by the enactment of criminal law, the executive, which has investigated the case and elected to bring charges and the judicial, which has usually made a preliminary decision probable cause exists to arrest the suspect. The grand jury—in effect, the citizenry—gets the final say in sending the case to trial, acting as a check on the three branches of government.

In a grand jury proceeding the prosecutor puts evidence before the jurors in the form of witnesses and submits proposed criminal charges for the jurors to consider. The prosecutor does not make any argument before the grand jury and cannot be present while the jurors deliberate on the indictment. The jury's discussions and vote are absolutely secret. Whether the jurors vote to indict or not is their decision and neither the prosecutor nor the judge is allowed to question it. A grand jury can refuse to indict for the right reason, the wrong reason or even no reason at all, allowing it to act as a check against prosecutorial overreach.

In addition to checking the power of the prosecutor, the jurors serve as the pulse of the community. A prosecutor who cannot get a case past a grand jury, with its lower legal standard of probable cause, is certainly unlikely to obtain a trial conviction. In this way, the grand jury is a gatekeeper, preventing marginal cases from proceeding.

I suppose an unscrupulous prosecutor could influence a grand jury by presenting certain pieces of evidence and intentionally omitting others, but I doubt this problem is prevalent. I definitely know I have never attempted to subliminally prod a grand jury one way or the other.

If evidence exists that a particular prosecutor manipulated the system, the correct response is to vote that lawyer out of office—not abrogate 800 years of criminal procedure and the Constitutional mandate for a grand jury decision.

\*\*\*\*

I went into the grand jury room, sat down and explained the indictments I wanted the jury to consider. The jurors were surprised; they received no warning they would be asked to deliberate upon such a serious case. Of course, no one had received prior notice: not Charles Severance, not the media and not the families of the victims. Our team had avoided all leaks. After answering a few legal questions, I left the room so the detectives could present the facts.

Given the complexity of the case, it made sense to have each detective present their assigned case. Will Oakley went first with Lodato, Sean Casey next with Kirby and Dave Cutting last with the Dunning case. Cutting also testified about the evidence linking the three murders together.

Once Cutting was done, I re-entered the room and answered a few legal questions the jurors had about the indictment. The tension was palpable. The panel was well aware of the gravity of its task. I exited and left the jury to its deliberations.

The grand jury started promptly at 9 a.m. By 10:30 a.m., I had my answer: probable cause on all 10 counts.

Charles Stanard Severance stood indicted for all three murders.

## CHAPTER EIGHT

*"It has nothing to do with business. Everything is personal. They kidnap and they die."*

With the indictment returned, the police department and my office issued simultaneous press releases. The police release provided an overview of the charges and invited the media to a press conference that afternoon at Alexandria Police Headquarters.

My office does not have a public information officer(PIO). I act as my own PIO and I personally drew up our Severance release. As previously noted, the rules of professional ethics prohibited me from making any public statement about the case that could reasonably influence a trial jury. I was limited to discussing the charges, the possible penalties and the trial schedule.

Of course, this modicum of information did not sate the media's craving for information. The reporters wanted to know how and why Severance committed the crimes. They wanted to hear about the evidence that had convinced me Severance was guilty. I could not provide this information, so I decided to initiate a complete embargo on discussing the case with the media, adding a paragraph to my press release that cited the controlling ethics rule word-for-word. The final line of the release stated in no uncertain terms I would make no additional comments.

I also decided I would not participate in the Chief's press conference that afternoon. I chose not to go in front of the cameras because there was no benefit in doing so. I could not answer the onslaught of media questions that would be forthcoming and feared if I slipped up and said something inappropriate, I would damage the case before it even got off the ground.

A prosecutor handling a major case should strive to remain out of the glaring eye of the television cameras until after the case has been tried. Before trial, all of his energy and effort must be directed on putting the case together. He cannot risk putting his foot in his mouth. Every unscripted appearance with reporters provides a golden opportunity for disaster to strike.

Around 1:00 p.m., I issued my terse press release.

By 1:02, the onslaught of phone calls from reporters had commenced.

**\*\*\*\***

Prior to my election I had not received any training on dealing with reporters. Quite honestly, I was unprepared to handle the intense media response that accompanied the Severance case. Serial killers get national attention. When CNN starts calling you at your desk, you really feel the pressure.

In retrospect, I did not handle the pressure very well. My first impulse was to refuse to speak with reporters at all and to pass by in sullen silence if I saw one outside the courthouse. If a reporter insisted on asking me a question, my response was to gruff: "Didn't you read my release? No comment!"

While my reaction was understandable given the microscope I found myself under, this was certainly not the right way of handling the situation. It gave many the impression I had an axe to grind. I remember a conversation with a local writer that began "Bryan, I know you hate the media, but could you answer just one question?"

I do not hate reporters and I regret giving anyone that impression. The media plays a necessary and critical role with regards to the criminal justice system. The press serves as a check upon the government, to include police officers, sheriffs and prosecutors. Elected district attorneys wield a great deal of power and without the light shone on their decisions by the media, that power can lead to abuse. Under most circumstances, the press is a positive influence on the public dialog. We should always remember the founders put freedom of the press in the very first amendment to the bill of rights, giving it pride of place.

As my exposure to reporters grew, I learned most were hardworking, ethical professionals. I became friendly with several as a direct result of the Severance case and I learned a great deal as a result of those friendships.

While I respect the media as an entity, I do have some concerns to share. Given the nature of the internet and the 24-hour news cycle, reporters are under significant pressure to be first with a story. Speed often comes at the expense of accuracy. This has probably been true since newspapers were invented—think of a 1930's cub reporter "catching a scoop"—but the internet demands ever-increasing levels of rapidity. Reporters are subconsciously incentivized to tweet first, without taking the time to verify.

In addition to speed, reporters need a "hook" for their story and can easily tend to sensationalism. The effect has grown concomitantly with society's unfortunate penchant for reality television. Salacious headlines get internet clicks. Internet clicks lead to career advancement.

I'll give an example. One of the first courtroom arguments we had in the Severance case was whether the media should be allowed to broadcast the trial via an in-court video camera. It was one of the rare issues on which the prosecution and defense agreed, with both sides emphatically arguing against the presence of cameras. The trial judge ultimately denied the request for television cameras but did allow a still photographer to snap pictures of the proceedings.

The media hired an attorney to argue its contrary position to the trial judge. The lawyer, an accomplished and eloquent civil practitioner, emphasized that regular citizens possessed a First Amendment right to know how a trial works, how their government went about prosecuting a complex case and what law applied to the trial.

Given these lofty civic arguments, it would follow the photographs taken in the courtroom would show the attorneys forcefully holding forth on a weighty constitutional issue, right? Think again. The first photograph ever published from a courtroom hearing was of Severance being wheeled into the courtroom and flipping the bird at the camera.

Pictures of an eccentric serial killer giving the finger may help ratings, but a trial is supposed to be a search for the truth. No one will ever convince me in-court cameras help with that search. Television causes everyone associated with the case to act differently. Judges may worry about how their rulings will affect their ability to be promoted to a higher court. Prosecutors may worry about how their arguments affect their approval ratings. Witnesses worry about how their testimony will be perceived by their friends or may feel their safety is at risk if their likeness is live-streamed.

Cameras affect the manner in which people comport themselves. If their demeanor and presentation are affected, the jury deciding the case is hearing a different set of evidence than it would if there were no cameras. For that reason alone, television cameras should be barred from trials.

****

The press routinely takes prosecutors to task for unethical behavior. As well it should, given the power inherent in their office. But reporters also possess a huge amount of power.

Let me share an example. The day before the Severance trial began a media outlet ran an article which said our case was a "circumstantial one" and implied our evidence was weak. The reporter quoted a local defense attorney who happened to be a mentor to the lawyers representing Severance, but no reference to this connection was made. The attorney was quoted as saying: "I think what (the prosecution is) going to try to do is poison the jury against the defendant." No former prosecutor was quoted in the article about how strong of a case the prosecution had amassed.

I later spoke with the reporter about the obvious lack of balance. I asked how he could in good conscience write such an article when he did not know most of the evidence in the case or how we were going to tie it together.

He responded by saying "all the evidence was out there." This was not accurate. Given how circumspect we had been about releasing information, hardly any of the evidence was "out there." Furthermore, the reporter had no way of synthesizing the evidence that had been referred to in court and understanding how it fit together as a whole.

When we began jury selection, several citizens admitted they had read the article before coming to court. Human nature being what it is, there was a real chance these jurors had been influenced by the article and would harbor an unconscious bias against the prosecution's case if selected to serve.

It bears repeating that reporters have real power. They need to be wary of how they exercise that power lest they influence the outcome of a story as opposed to just reporting on it.

\*\*\*\*

In the months leading up to the indictment I had discussed the case with no one outside of my team. I even rebuffed my father, who is the most trustworthy man I know, when he asked about the progress of the investigation. I had to avoid turning the case into a media circus of swirling reports and innuendo. The more people who had inside information, the more likely information would leak.

Necessarily, we had kept the families of the victims in the dark. Until a charging decision was made, any information we gave them would place them on an emotional roller coaster, with their hopes buoyed momentarily when an interesting piece of evidence was uncovered and then deflated when another investigative lead turned out to be nothing. We felt it could be injurious to give the families warning about a potential indictment while running the risk that the Grand Jurors may not find probable cause to indict. The detectives told the families about the charges on the morning of September 8, right after the grand jury returned them and before the Chief held his press conference.

The families were in the room for the Chief's televised remarks. When that was over, they were led to the third floor of the police department where I was waiting to speak with them. I remember the anxiety I felt as they entered the room. My stomach was in knots. I wondered whether I could find the words appropriate for such a sensitive conversation.

I had to earn their trust. Trying this case without the support of the families would have been impossible.

****

Another thing that is never accurately portrayed on television is the intense relationship that exists between the prosecutor assigned to a murder case and the victim's family. In the course of my career I have seen many different responses to my initial meeting with a victim's family. I have frequently been met with distrust. Sometimes with anger. Always with grief, although victims process grief in a myriad of ways.

The amount of empathy a prosecutor must possess is never depicted on T.V. I'm not sure I possess sufficient empathy; I try to make up for my lack of natural ability by being extremely open and accessible with the families. Access and honesty breed trust.

The families, having been kept in the dark for so long, wanted as much information as I could provide. They expected me to treat them with the dignity and respect they deserved. These expectations seem reasonable—indeed, they are—but many prosecutors have difficulty providing family members the access and time they require. I was determined not to make this mistake.

I started by introducing myself. I was relatively young to be an elected prosecutor, so I wanted to reassure the family members I had the requisite ability to handle this case. I talked about the 13 years I had served as an assistant prosecutor. I briefly discussed the prior murder cases on which I had worked. I gave the families my personal cellphone and told them to call if they needed to talk, anytime, day or night.

I delved into the law, explaining why I could not indict Nancy's death as Capital Murder. I gave them my reasoning for waiving capital punishment. I discussed how the case would proceed, explaining it would be some time before the trial commenced. I made it clear the families should expect the defense attorneys to battle us, tooth and nail.

I ended with words I remember very well, because they came straight from my heart:

"This is almost certainly going to be a trial. I don't think Charles Severance will ever accept responsibility for his crimes, so please don't expect him to plead guilty. They call them trials for a reason. In many respects, this process will be yet another trial for each of you. Many of you will feel angry about how the process focuses on the defendant and what's fair for him, as opposed to what is fair to the memory of your loved ones. I cannot change this, but I will meet with you to explain the process as often as you like."

"I have never lost a loved one to violence and it would be an insult for me to tell you I understand how you feel. I do, however, understand the gravity of this case and I will bring every resource to bear on this case I can. This is not just another 'case' to me, it's a human story that involves three people being stolen from this earth. I will do everything I can to remember your loved ones and to bring about a successful conclusion. I feel a sacred obligation to do so."

"You must always remember any trial is a gamble. There are only two outcomes, a conviction or an acquittal. I cannot guarantee which of those will occur."

My voice cracked with emotion: "What I can guarantee, and what I promise to each of you, is that I will remember Nancy, Ron and Ruthanne. I promise to put whatever ability God has given me into this case. I promise I will work hard."

"I promise I will be there with you every step of the way from this moment, right now, until the verdict is returned.

"I promise I will see this case through."

****

**The Victims (l-r)**
Nancy Dunning, Ron Kirby,
Ruthanne Lodato

Two photos presented at trial. At left is a photo of Charles Severance, taken from his website, and depicting him as he looked around 2002. On the right is a still taken from the Target video. Note the distinctive widow's peak visible in both photos.

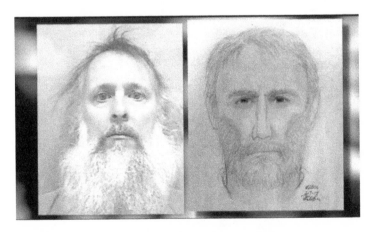

A side-by-side comparing Severance's appearance at his arrest in 2014 with the composite sketch produced from Jeanette's first-hand account.

Photo taken by the U.S. Secret Service showing Severance the day he attempted to obtain asylum at the Russian Embassy.

Photo of a NAA .22LR 5-shot mini-revolver. The ruler helps emphasize the small size of the firearm — just 4 inches long.

Comparison showing the similarities between
Severance's Ford Escort, in the top photo,
and the Escort caught on a surveillance
camera fleeing the Lodato crime scene

Close-up of
the Escort's
bumper,
showing the
bumper sticker

Photo of the Severance trial team taken right after the verdict: from left, David Lord, the author, Marc Birnbaum, and Jimmy Entas

The author speaking with the press immediately after the verdict was returned, the victim families stand in the background

# *The Manifesto of Hate*

The starting torque is
2.5 times the running torque.

It is harder therefore be firm and decisive
          Parable of the Knocker
Knock Enter
A metaphor A Revelation A mystery
Knock and the door will be answered
Seek and ye shall find
Knock and the door will open
Ask and ye shall know
Wisdom
Knock. Talk. Enter. Kill. Exit
Murder Wisdom
     MW

Patience is an excuse for cowardice

Jesus the Lord

     Parable of the Decider


The Parable of the
Knocker: "Knock. Talk.
Enter. Kill. Exit."

Spell enchantmant and the
Magic of Mind control

Random Evens Rendon Thoughts
& Mystary to Mob Governmant

Jesus is Lord.

The Prince   Macc & Vell

Leviathon    Thomas Hobbes

safetseems
I introduce murder into a neighborhood. It shudders
with horror. Do it again and again and again. The
ring of fire, death, and insecurity of Syria is
contagious. American Foreign policy is kick ass.
Add violence and increase uncertainty among status
quo utopian oppressive elites. Emotionally disturb them
with violence, Night mares and day dreams of terror.
Horrible child trolls the
neighborhood.

"Introduce murder into a safe and secure
neighborhood. It shudders with horror. Do it
again and again and again.

The last scream of a victim echoes to eternity.

Give glory to God. Peace on earth. Death to adversaries.

It is not dreadful to torture and adversary.

It has nothing to do with business; everything is personal.

They kidnap and they die.

Firm and decisive is effective Firm

"The last scream of a victim echoes to eternity…. They kidnap and they die."

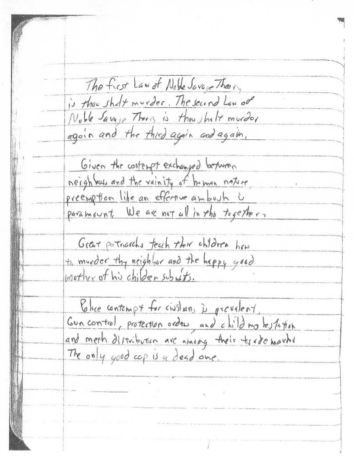

The first Law of Noble Savage Theory is thou shalt murder. The second Law of Noble Savage Theory is thou shalt murder again and the third again and again.

Given the contempt exchanged between neighbous and the vainity of human nature, preemption like an effective ambush is paramount. We are not all in this together.

Great patriarchs teach their children how to murder thy neighbor and the happy good mother of his childer submits.

Police contempt for civilians is prevalent. Gun control, protection orders, and child molestation and meth distribution are among their trademarks. The only good cop is a dead one.

"The first law of Noble Savage Theory is thou shalt murder."

Suffering Fathers Scheme is rife with murder and greed.

Exempt from all measures of the enforcement class.

By right of might wins because might does not always make right but it assuredly makes government

State want to secede from nation, region from states, localities from regions, and individual from government.

Exchange liberty for security and get neither.

Murder on my mind and my mind on murder.

Effectively tomahawking a homestead in the backwoods of America because it is in the best interest of the child,

for terror terror is a passion that always produces delight when it does not press too close.

crybaby group hug therapy and public gratification by first responders is special, sweet and sensitive cute.

"Murder on my mind and my mind on murder. Effectively tomahawking a homestead in the backwoods of America."

18th century   Age of
                Age of Enlightenment  Age of Reason
        , bic in my son

Please purchase three North American Firearms
.22 MINI revolvers and 500 rounds of subsonic
low velocity cartridges. The five round stainless
steel with wooden grip revolver is small and
easily concealed. Thou shalt murder and
vengeance is mine saith the Lord. Hollow point and
below the speed of sound is sweet music and
very very effective in the very very dangerous
land of Allah because Tomahawking a homestead
in the Backwoods of America is a second coming
of the Lord Jesus Christ. Violence wins.

God bless you my son  Cheers to us.

Ku ecshte babi yt?  //// ——, babi ujt
                                    your father
Learn to consi- swing, counting, waltz and dance.
deus ex machina
    I dcojt do te jetime pici, besamit

Do not trust cops because police contempt for civilians
in law enforcement 101.

"Please purchase three NAA firearms… and 500
rounds of subsonic cartridges… Thou shalt
murder and vengeance is mine, saith the
Lord."

18th century  Age of
                    Age of Enlightenment  Age of Reason

North American Firearms out of Utah makes
a beautiful tiny and deadly .22 mini revolver
5 cartrage stainless steel mormon death squad
special. Best to discharge subsonic less than
the speed of sound ammunition. Don't damage
gun with high velocity high energy rounds.
Aversion and appetite govern men. Aversion
to jail and an appetite to kill an adversary.

Social contract theorist like Thomas Hobbes
are worth studying. Leviathan and Behemoth.

Thou shalt not kill is a lie. No self-respecting
god-fearing patriarch would not kill men
and women who delight in terrorizing his family.

The only good cop is a dead cop.

Screaming social worker is a song. Hear it.

"NAA… makes a beautiful tiny and deadly mini revolver…. Thou shalt not kill is a lie. No self-respecting patriarch would not kill men and women who delight in terrorizing his family."

**Subject:** nudge
**From:** principle investigator
**Date:** 7/31/2013 2:02 PM
**To:** °
**CC:** therapy

i've been nudging and trolling for over a decade and nobody has noticed. violence wins. assassinate because it is in the best interest of the child.

www.mentaldisorder.com/loser is a harmless nudge.

tomahawking a homestead in the backwoods of america,

count

"I've been nudging and trolling for over a decade and nobody has noticed. Violence wins."

# PART II - TRIALS AND TRIBULATION

## CHAPTER NINE

*"The status quo enforcement class are constantly in fear of revolutionary zealots. My liberty and your oppression are the order of the day."*

The first step in the trial process was determining who the presiding trial judge would be. Since Ruthanne Lodato was both the daughter and sister of an Alexandria judge, the Alexandria bench recused itself to avoid the hint of any bias against Charles Severance.

Within roughly a week, Judge Jane Marum Roush of the Fairfax County Circuit Court was appointed by the Virginia Supreme Court. Fairfax County is a large, suburban county in Northern Virginia that shares a border with Alexandria. I had never appeared before Roush, but her reputation as an excellent trial judge preceded her.

Judge Roush, who has since retired, was an outstanding choice to handle such a complicated trial. Having presided over the 'D.C. Sniper' trial of Lee Boyd Malvo, she had experience dealing with the media attention given to high-profile cases. Attorneys who knew her described her as an outstanding jurist with an incisive legal mind.

Roush was in charge of her courtroom and had an in-court style that resembled my own. Asking around, I learned she was professional in her dealings with those appearing before her but was apt to dress a lawyer down if she smelled an inconsistent argument. My sources said she was not opposed to occasionally dropping a one-liner to bring a little levity to the courtroom. As someone I trusted told me, Roush "had an extrovert's personality and is in her element presiding over a big case."

\*\*\*\*

It is said the mark of a good leader is to pick outstanding people to work for you and then take the credit for what they do. If that's the case, I deserve a lot of credit.

Once I made the decision to indict Severance, it was obvious I would need a substantial amount of help. David and I could not try such a complicated case alone. At this point, we thought we may have to call as many as 160 witnesses.

Counting myself, there are a total of 14 attorneys in my office. If I tasked three of my assistant prosecutors to work full time on the Severance case, I would have had about a quarter of my office out of the normal case rotation. This would be devastating; crimes did not stop in Alexandria with the arrest of Charles Severance. Hundreds of other offenses, to include less-publicized murders, continued to stream in. Those cases needed the requisite care and attention as well and I could not afford tying up one-fourth of my office on a single case, no matter how grave.

As the elected, my role was to be in overall command of the prosecution, providing strategic direction and structure as well as being the "buck stops here" person with regards to major decisions. David Lord was in charge of dealing with the defense attorneys. He also served as the point man on pretrial motions and was invaluable in the drafting of our written trial plan. David was talented and energetic, but he needed assistance.

The help was provided by Virginia's Attorney General, Mark Herring. The Attorney General is one of three statewide elected officers, along with the Governor and the Lieutenant Governor. In a departure from many states, the Commonwealth's Attorneys, as independent elected officials, do not work for the AG and maintain plenary criminal responsibility in their respective localities. Under Virginia's regime, the Attorney General does not have a great deal of original criminal jurisdiction.

After his 2013 election, AG Herring instituted a new initiative in his office called the Major Crimes and Emerging Threats Unit(MCET). MCET was designed as a cadre of experienced trial attorneys who, in addition to trying criminal cases that did come under the AG's aegis, were available to assist local prosecutors with significant cases upon request.

My good friend Linda Bryant was the Deputy Attorney General supervising MCET at the time. Prior to working for the AG, Linda had served as a prosecutor in Norfolk, Virginia, for many years. Norfolk is one of Virginia's more violent cities and Linda immediately understood how difficult the Severance prosecution would be.

When I asked for help, Linda Bryant quickly provided it. The AG's office agreed to assign an MCET attorney, Marc Birnbaum, to my trial team.

**\*\*\*\***

If you've ever seen the British crime drama *Broadchurch,* Marc Birnbaum is a dead ringer for DI Alec Hardy, particularly when he grows a beard. Prior to moving to the Attorney General's Office Marc worked as an Assistant Commonwealth's Attorney in Fairfax County. He and I met a decade earlier when we were assigned to investigate criminal street gangs for our respective offices. I knew what I was getting with Marc: a consummate professional and a great lawyer with a polished courtroom demeanor. Marc's hallmark was meticulous, methodical legal argument that left jurors with no alternative but to accept his premise. That kind of attention to detail would be critical in a case of this magnitude.

Marc's patience, coolness and incisive legal mind are attributes one would expect in an outstanding trial judge. If he elects to follow that path, in the not-too-distant future Marc will likely don the robe and ascend the bench.

****

In the television and the movies, detectives and prosecutors never have to deal with the effects of stress. They just do their job, solve a case within an hour and move on to the next one. Since T.V. DAs have a caseload of one, maybe I shouldn't be surprised.

My law professors never taught me about the stress inherent in trial work. Even a simple prosecution brings with it a certain degree of anxiety. A prosecutor's job is to build her case, deciding which pieces of evidence to admit and which witnesses to call to the stand. Defense attorneys have it a little easier when creating a trial plan: they do not have to prove their client is innocent, they just have to poke enough holes in the prosecutor's case to create a reasonable doubt in the jury's collective mind. In many murder cases, defense attorneys do not call a single witness, relying on cross-examination and argument to create a reasonable doubt as to their client's guilt.

Prosecutors also have to worry about the "gremlins" that pop up. A "gremlin" is my term for any of the unexpected problems or issues that invariably arise before a trial commences. An attorney has no way of knowing which gremlins will materialize but she should count on something going wrong. Trial plans never work the way they look on paper.

Gremlins take many forms but the most frequently encountered is the reluctant witness. Witnesses have many reasons for not wanting to testify. Some are truly afraid. Some do not want to see the defendant convicted. Professional witnesses, like doctors and business owners, often act as though they are above being bothered with a subpoena. Prosecutors spend an inordinate time pleading and cajoling reluctant people to testify.

Reluctant witnesses usually do not understand the constitutional mandate prosecutors labor under: the confrontation clause. Criminal defendants are allowed to confront the witnesses against them and a prosecutor cannot rely on sworn statements or videotaped affidavits. The government must put live witnesses on the stand.

Over the years, I have frequently explained that a properly-served subpoena is not a request to come to court. It is a judicial order to appear and a willful refusal to obey its command is punishable by arrest and a finding of contempt of court.

****

In the weeks before a trial commences, my mind continuously runs through every permutation that may arise. While this trait allows me to prepare for worst-case scenarios, it also makes me unbearable to be around: I can think of nothing else. Even worse, I am a confirmed pessimist.

By late September, the stress of this enormous case was coming down on me as more and more gremlins arose. Everyone involved expected me to have the answers, even though I had never before led such a complex investigation. I was not sleeping or eating well. I was singularly focused on the case, leaving little energy for other matters.

Each morning I would burn off some of my built-up worry by taking a walk around Old Town Alexandria. I would usually find myself at the shore of the Potomac River. There, I would sit on a park bench and think about the case.

On September 17, 2014, I took one of these walks. I left our courthouse and walked east on King Street. After several blocks, I found myself strolling into what the City calls Marina Park. I have no idea why it is called that. There is no marina, just a forlorn, tiny bay. Perhaps it was a marina once or perhaps the City plans on making it one in the future. For now, the name is aspirational.

Marina Park was empty. I found a bench, sat down and considered the issue preoccupying me at the time: I desperately needed another lawyer. I now had three working the case—David, Marc and me. Given the complexity of the evidence, I was convinced that was not enough manpower. I felt proceeding with a three-person team was a recipe for disaster.

In my office, most murders are tried by two attorneys, referred to as a "first-chair" and a "second chair," with the first chair serving as the lead. In Virginia, the usual homicide trial takes three or four days to try and might involve 20 witnesses. With a two-person team, each team member is responsible for about 10 witnesses. In the Severance case, each member of a three-person team might be responsible for over 50 witnesses! With that much responsibility, there would be a real possibility of details slipping through the cracks.

There has never been a television show that accurately depicts how difficult it is to create a trial plan and execute it successfully. The amount of preparation required is astounding and the length and complexity of this trial were going to exponentially increase the prep work. I needed more help.

I had no idea where I could find a fourth attorney. For starters, my office was already taxed and I could not assign another assistant to the case. I could not beg nearby jurisdictions to loan me one of their prosecutors; they had their own cases to worry about. The Attorney General's Office had already given me one attorney to work on the case, it was unreasonable to think they would provide a second.

It was a mid-September afternoon that still felt like summer. The air was thick and humid. As I sat on the park bench I could see the waves of heat radiate upwards from the cooler river water. I clenched and unclenched my fists, internally debating different ideas about where I could find another capable attorney. After what seemed an eternity, I realized getting more help was impossible and resigned myself to a three-person team. I shook my head in frustration and stood up to start my walk back to the office.

I took a shortcut through the Wilkes Street tunnel, a mid-1800s railroad right-of-way created by the cut-and-cover technique. When first established, Alexandria sat on a bluff overlooking the Potomac River roughly following today's Lee Street. After the City became a major port in the early 1800s it was necessary to find a way to get railroad tracks down to the waterfront, which sat on a filled-in mudflat below the large Lee Street townhomes. Since the bluff formed a physical impediment to trains, the Wilkes Street tunnel was built underneath it.

By the 1970s, train traffic was so light the tunnel was no longer needed. The railroad ceded the tunnel to the City and it was subsequently turned into a decidedly creepy pedestrian tunnel, about 1000 yards in length and poorly lit. The interior is dank and walking its length feels like urban spelunking. Interestingly, my mother's family has deep ties to Alexandria and there is an apocryphal story that one of my ancestors was murdered in the tunnel in the early 1900s.

****

As they say, there are no atheists in foxholes.

And as I walked into the Wilkes Street tunnel, I found myself in a metaphoric foxhole. I desperately needed a fourth lawyer and I did not know where to find one. While I am not a devoutly religious person I instinctively began to pray, putting my hands together as I walked through the darkened tunnel.

"God, I need someone else to help me try this case. Please help me find another lawyer," I said aloud. I repeated the phrase probably a dozen times in a row in quick succession.

As I continued saying my modified rosary, I approached the western exit of the tunnel. Unexpectedly, my cellphone rang, piercing my trance. I collected myself and answered it as I walked out of the subterranean path.

I recognized Linda Bryant's voice immediately: "Bryan, I was thinking you might need more help with Severance. I just hired someone who I think would be perfect for the case."

"His name is Jimmy Entas."

****

I have taken no liberties with this timeline. I was extremely concerned about finding another attorney, I entered the tunnel worried about it, I started to pray as I walked through it and—as I walked out into the proverbial "light at the end of the tunnel"—my phone rang.

I cannot believe I am saying this, but Jimmy Entas was the answer to my prayers.

While I struggle with the lack of extrinsic evidence supporting organized religion, I likewise find it difficult to accept everything we see, all of the complexity of this planet and all of human experience, is the result of a random set of coincidences. I suspect there is more to our existence than that.

There are mysteries in this world we do not understand. One of them is truly confounding: if the universe is a cosmic coincidence, the result of some atoms bumping into each other trillions of years ago and a subsequent chain of reactions, how were those initial atoms created? Where did matter come from in the first place?

Physicists have theorized matter could have been created out of the ether. Brilliant minds insist a purely natural 'theory of everything' will one day be sufficient to explain the universe. The rational part of my brain accepts an intellectually satisfying explanation may be developed. As Spinoza opined, it could be "God" is an infinite, natural force as opposed to a sentient being intentionally influencing the affairs of the beings he created.

While the rational part of me understands science may prove to have all of the answers someday, as of yet, it does not. Physicists cannot conclusively explain how matter came into being. They cannot explain human consciousness. They cannot explain the different physical laws that apply to quantum objects as opposed to larger bodies controlled by general relativity.

Indeed, in an effort to reconcile the unusual behavior of quantum particles with the theory of relativity physicists have devised outlandish concepts, such as "string theory" and the "multiverse," that are intriguing. However, these unusual ideas require one to subscribe to unseen "strings" or, even more fancifully, to an infinite multitude of other universes, tangential to but undetectable by ours, in which every conceivable eventuality is realized. There is no tangible evidence for either.

When you get to questions about how the universe started or where matter came from, scientists are forced to rely on complex theories and ideas for which there is little to no proof. They say: "Trust us. We used to have no proof of bacteria, but science progressed and we now accept its existence. One day, science will provide a cogent explanation for all physical phenomena."

Just like priests, physicists ask you to take a leap of faith.

Sounds a lot like religion to me.

****

The idea there is some supernatural aspect to human existence is attractive. However, I cannot subscribe to the proposition there is "one true faith" and all other religions—the Roman Pantheon, Zoroastrianism, the Aesir— that have either gone before or shall go after are the work of Satan. It does not seem possible an omnipotent God would sentence billions of humans who did not adhere to the one "correct" eschatology to an eternity in hell. It seems particularly unfair to doom pagans who lived before God revealed his divine plan: the ancient Athenians who lived centuries before Christ, for example.

The Christians think the Muslims are the infidel, the Muslims think the Christians are, and so on, *ad infinitum*. The position that one group has the favor of the Almighty to the exclusion of others has been the source of untold misery throughout the ages and is patently hubristic. It seems more likely that we, as imperfect beings with a dim understanding of the universe, are utterly incapable of recognizing the true nature of God. Perhaps all human religions are attempts at worshipping a deity so far outside our ken as to be utterly beyond it.

As a prosecutor, everything I do is based on evidence, the accumulation and analysis of which is now hard-wired into my DNA. I cannot support a proposition unless I marshal sufficient proof the proposition is correct. The physical, concrete evidence for established religions is thin, which is why I struggle with my faith.

However, there is a strain of physical evidence supportive of the proposition there is an architect of the universe. That evidence is all around us, hidden in the laws of physics and present in the structure of a seashell or a dragonfly wing. We call it mathematics.

Others far more intelligent than I have noted that mathematics is extremely effective in explaining the structure of our universe. It is so effective it appears to be more than a coincidence. Why is it arithmetic, which is ostensibly a human creation, so accurately describes the laws of physics? Why do precise mathematical ratios pop up in all sorts of startling places?

Consider a particular set of numbers known as the Fibonacci sequence, in which each number is the sum of the two numbers preceding it. Fibonacci numbers describe a numerical ratio that arises in an astonishing and diverse array of natural settings. Flower petals, seashells, hurricanes and spiral galaxies are all mathematically synched to the Fibonacci ratio. Modern scientists cannot explain why this specific numerical relationship is observed in so many unrelated natural events.

Much like programming code is required to write virtual reality computer applications, it appears mathematics is the code of the universe. It can be argued that this is evidence of a programmer—or of a divine architect. Alternatively, some theorists hold we are living in a computer simulation and the laws of physics are themselves bits of programming. As we slowly discern these laws, we are, in effect, reading the lines of code that willed us into existence.

Science provides a humbler explanation: it is not surprising math seems to describe the universe precisely; if it did not—if the laws of physics were just a bit more capricious—then humans would not exist and no one would be alive to conduct mathematical calculations. Science maintains the seemingly paranormal applicability of math is a fallacy. We observe mathematical laws because they are a necessary condition precedent for our universe.

Even if there is a deity, the idea prayer might influence Him to do things He would not otherwise do is unsettling. It implies a capriciousness to God that is difficult to accept. Can it really be God counts prayers like so many internet votes for the winner on *American Idol* and thus selects a winner? If so, a lonely orphan with cancer would be less likely to survive than a well-connected person who could afford to post prayer solicitations on YouTube.

Rationally, I doubt the efficacy of prayer.

However, believers would be quick to note that as I walked into the train tunnel in a moment of dire need, when I could see no other solution, I instinctively put my hands together and prayed to an unseen Deity.

****

Those who know Jimmy Entas might question whether it was actually Beelzebub who was on the receiving end of my prayers. Mr. Entas knows only one speed and it's a little too fast for some.

A tuft of close-cropped blonde hair juts above the rugged landscape of Entas' face, a landscape earned over 20 years prosecuting violent crime in Norfolk. As Jimmy puts it, he "did some serious shit" during his tenure in that waterfront town. Jimmy is opinionated and confident. He believes in karma and cosmic retribution, a duo which meshes in a synergistic set of connections between his friends and acquaintances which he constantly refers to as "Jimmy's World."

Entas inherently distrusts authority. I agree this is an odd trait for a lifelong prosecutor, but it works for Jimmy and he enjoys keeping people guessing about where he is coming from. Despite the Entas smokescreen, I have ventured far enough into "Jimmy's World" to know the truth: he is a compassionate man and a true friend. Once he's convinced you're not a "bullshitter" he will go to the mat for you.

Moreover, Jimmy Entas is a warrior and a gifted trial lawyer. I needed a warrior in my corner.

When I spoke with Entas for the first time over the phone, I delved into the gravity of the situation and the complex nature of the evidence. The longer I spoke about the case the more I was convinced Jimmy would be scared away. He lived in Norfolk, over 100 miles from Alexandria, so working on the case would be logistically difficult. The trial would be both stressful and lengthy. I was asking him to expend large amounts of time and energy on a matter to which he had no ties.

The longer I spoke, the more I realized I was doing a terrible job of convincing Entas to join the team. Our case was strong, but a guilty verdict not preordained. We would have a real dogfight on our hands and an acquittal was a possibility.

As I finished my overview of the investigation, Entas paused and asked me if Severance had said anything incriminating when arrested. I admitted he had not and assumed this was the nail in the coffin of his participation.

I was stunned when Jimmy chuckled and said: "Good. If you had a confession, it wouldn't be a challenge."

"I'm all in, 100%."

****

Since Charles Severance had absolutely no money the Court appointed a team of three defense attorneys to represent him at public expense. The Alexandria Public

Defender's Office normally would have been appointed but declined to take the case.

Although I had announced I was not seeking the death penalty, Severance was still facing two counts of Capital Murder and the possibility of life in prison without parole. My charging decision meant Severance would receive almost unlimited taxpayer funding for his defense. There is no cap on court-appointed attorney's fees for a capital case, nor on money awarded to the defense team for investigators and expert witnesses.

The media often reports about how little court-appointed attorneys are paid for representing clients in felony cases. In general, I agree with the concern: court-appointed attorneys deserve to be paid more for the hard work they put in defending lower-level felony cases. That concern was not an issue in the Severance prosecution. Indeed, at the conclusion of the trial, we learned the Commonwealth of Virginia had provided almost $700,000 for use in Severance's defense, ensuring it was amply funded.

The lawyers appointed, Chris Leibig, Joe King and Megan Thomas, all began their careers in the Alexandria Public Defender's Office. All three were roughly my age and had tried many cases against me in the past. The same three had represented the sheriff's deputy whose homicide sentencing was held on the day Ruthanne Lodato was murdered.

I personally respected each member of the defense team and was convinced the relationship between the sides would be cordial and professional. Each was a committed, hard-nosed lawyer who knew their way around a courtroom. I was certain they would file a litany of pretrial motions in an attempt to flesh out our strategy and test our evidence.

Megan Thomas is a brilliant and experienced litigator who never shies away from serious cases. Despite the immense stress of defending murders, Thomas has never lost her willingness to fight for her clients. When she argues to a jury her words brim with passion.

Joe King is Thomas' polar opposite and formed a formidable bookend of "ice" to Thomas' "fire." King relies on inexorable reason as opposed to passionate oration. He excels at incisive legal analysis. He finds obscure legal points, conforms them to the facts and fashions them into persuasive points. King's arguments often resemble a logic problem: "We have A in this case, your honor, and since A is akin to B from another case, C is the only decision you can make. *QED.*"

Chris Leibig fits somewhere on the continuum between his two colleagues. Leibig is soft-spoken, but his words usually carry significant weight. He is exceptionally bright and capable of swaying a jury with a cogent summation. In the sheriff's deputy's case, for instance, he made a sentencing argument that still ranks among the best I have ever witnessed.

Leibig has no issue obfuscating the thrust of an argument or the goal of a motion, playing the game of misdirection as well as any attorney against whom I have practiced. He is self-assured; even when a judge's comments from the bench make it clear that her decision is final, Leibig will say: "hear me out, judge" and continue on with the point he is making, confident that if the judge listens to his position just a little longer, his logic will carry the day.

All three attorneys were consummate professionals who relished serious cases. The battle lines were drawn.

We were in for a serious dogfight.

****

Given the adversarial nature of a criminal case, on occasion there are bound to be disagreements between prosecutors and defense attorneys. Sometimes these disagreements can be strenuous and passionate. In a murder case the pressure is concomitantly higher and can exacerbate disagreements between the parties.

Television shows sometimes portray this head-butting, but usually do a huge disservice to the legal profession. Attorneys are shown as thinking of the other side as their mortal enemy. A television defense attorney is certain prosecutors are a malignant force intent on punishing offenders out of spite and self-aggrandizement, while her opposite number theorizes defense lawyers are willing to act unethically or even criminally to "get their clients off on a technicality."

Both scripted television dramas and the evening news perpetuate these stereotypes because conflict sells advertisements. The media adores stories of prosecutors hiding evidence or defense attorneys inventing specious defenses out of thin air. Sensationalized story lines obfuscate the truth: the vast majority of trial lawyers are scrupulous professionals who zealously fight their case without demonizing their opponent.

Recently, our country has experienced an ugly turn in the public discourse. The proliferation of internet news means anyone can selectively reinforce their political opinions by relying on an outlet that shares their views. This "echo chamber" effect reinforces negativity and causes people who started out somewhere in the middle of the political spectrum to be pushed to the poles. Compounding the problem, outside forces are marshaling social media sites and internet "bots" in a campaign to inflame passions and sow division.

This polarization of public opinion is slowly corroding the foundations of our nation. Human beings are tribal and evolution has hard-wired us to cluster into groups. Every social clique has a belief system to which its members must hold. Adherence to the system becomes a litmus test for inclusion and any attempt to question or assess the system's taxonomy is evidence of insufficient dedication. Contrarian reasoning is a weakness that necessarily must be banished. The result is a lamentable situation in which disparate viewpoints are eliminated. Unchallenged opinions become unquestioned dogma and any hint of a differing analysis constitutes treason.

Just because our criminal system is adversarial in nature does not mean a lawyer must consider opposing counsel their personal adversary. In the courtroom, during the heat of battle, defense attorneys and prosecutors are going to disagree, sometimes vigorously. Outside of the courtroom, the parties should treat each other with cordiality and respect.

The same climate must exist for those with whom we disagree politically. We should stand firm in our beliefs but be willing to engage those who maintain an opposing view. We should constantly reconsider our position and be willing to adapt if the facts appear to so dictate, avoiding the demonization of our political opponents even if we disagree with their viewpoints.

If we cannot be civil to those with whom we disagree, I fear for our country.

\*\*\*\*

The first courtroom hearing in the Severance case was held in October 2014. Severance was wheeled into the courtroom because of his phantom ankle injury. At this point, I think he also planned on using a "bum ankle" defense, arguing he could not have committed the murders because his ankle made it impossible for him to walk. However, detectives had previously established his ankle was not a significant problem. Robra confirmed Severance had no issue walking before his arrest and the Secret Service officers at the embassy had seen him walking without any issues. The defense team ultimately eschewed the ankle defense.

Inefficacy as a defense did not stop Severance from insisting his ankle hurt and deputies were forced to push him around the courtroom in a wheelchair. The chair made for bizarre optics: grim-faced deputies escorting a Unabomber-lookalike like so many healthcare aides.

As the bailiff shouted, "All rise!" Judge Roush ascended the bench. The first order of business was setting a schedule. Roush told us we were not leaving the courtroom without selecting a firm trial date and that she "intended to keep it," overtly discouraging either side from seeking a continuance in the future. Roush also set a schedule for motions hearings, holding roughly one such hearing a month.

From the start, Judge Roush made it clear she was in charge of the conduct of the case. Chris Leibig objected to setting a date during the hearing and asked the judge to delay that decision. She was having none of that. "We are leaving today with a trial date," she thundered.

She soon announced we would commence on October 5, 2015, just a little short of a year away. We told the judge we needed five or six weeks of trial time, an exceptionally lengthy estimate. In Virginia, we are usually able to try a murder case to a verdict in one week.

One of my favorite sports anecdotes involves a hero from my youth, John Riggins, the MVP of the Washington Redskins' 1983 Super Bowl win. When Riggins scored a touchdown, instead of spiking the football or engaging in a wild dance, he would calmly walk over and hand the ball to the referee. In doing so, he epitomized an old football saying: "when you get to the end zone, act like you've been there before." This little nugget could almost pass for a philosophy of life.

I got the feeling Judge Roush had been to the end zone before. She was calm and comfortable with the spotlight on her. I immediately liked her style. The complexity and gravity of the case would not perturb her at all.

\*\*\*\*

There are thousands of movies and television shows that purport to realistically recreate a criminal trial. I have never seen an accurate representation, probably because obtuse legal arguments, the vagaries of the hearsay rule and lengthy citations to appellate cases do not make for compelling drama. Indeed, I am struggling with these issues as I write this book, trying to include enough of the legal framework of the case to construct an accurate picture without getting bogged down into a confusing morass of legal doctrines and obscure Latin phrases.

Pretrial motions, in which the parties raise issues that should be decided outside the presence of a jury, are full of those obtuse arguments and case citations. Because of this, motions practice is never depicted in T.V. shows and movies. This is unfortunate, because in the real world, the arguing of motions can be as important as the trial itself.

In my experience about 95% of pretrial motions are filed by defense attorneys. They attempt to attack and limit the prosecution's case, chipping away at the evidence to make the case more manageable. This state of affairs means the government spends months on the defensive, trying to fend off the cunning attacks of opposing counsel. My philosophy was we would not stand idly by and play defense. There were a number of motions my team needed to file, both to limit the defense's tactics and to prevent them from going too far afield.

The first substantive pretrial defense motion requested a change of venue. The defense team contended we could never seat an impartial jury in the City of Alexandria given the intense media attention and public fear related to the case. In rebuttal, we noted the law presumed the defendant could receive a fair trial in the City and the defense was engaging in guesswork when it stated the Alexandria jury pool was prejudiced against their client. At about the same time the venue motion was pending in our case, a federal judge denied a defense motion to move the Boston Marathon Bomber case, a decision we pointed out to Judge Roush.

Roush was not impressed. She agreed with the Severance team and granted the motion to change venue. Not surprisingly, she moved the trial to her home court, Alexandria's next-door neighbor. Fairfax is the largest county in Virginia, with roughly one million residents. It is also one of the most affluent jurisdictions in the United States.

Although I was not happy about the venue change at the time, in hindsight, Roush did us a favor by granting it. The decision to move the trial to Fairfax eliminated an appellate argument for the defense should we obtain a conviction. While Fairfax is substantially larger than Alexandria, the jury pool in both jurisdictions is similar: affluent, diverse and well-educated. We would not be fighting on completely unfamiliar ground.

Since our evidence was complex, I needed intelligent jurors on the panel. We ended up with one of the most intelligent juries I have had the pleasure of appearing before.

****

From the moment of his arrest it was clear Severance's mental health would be an issue at trial; the combination of his ungroomed appearance and disturbing writings would alert the jury something was not quite right with Charles Severance. As we entered the motions phase of the trial, I pondered whether the defense might raise the insanity defense.

All criminal defendants are presumed to be sane and the prosecution does not have to prove a defendant's sanity. If this were not the law, then in every single criminal trial, from drunk driving to murder, the prosecution would have to put on psychological evidence to establish the accused's mental soundness. Such a system would quickly prove unworkable.

Criminal insanity is what is known as an "affirmative defense." The defendant has to affirmatively produce evidence sufficient to establish he was criminally insane at the time of the offense. The simple fact a person has been diagnosed with a mental disorder does not, standing alone, mean the person will be found "not guilty by reason of insanity." To raise the defense, a defendant must establish he suffered from a mental disease at the time of the offense and that the disease was so severe it rendered him incapable of understanding the difference between right and wrong or caused an "irresistible impulse" in him to commit the crime.

These legal standards explain why the Severance defense team would ultimately avoid the insanity defense. For starters, Charles Severance knew the difference between right and wrong. He engaged in a significant amount of planning and premeditation in committing his crimes. He took significant steps to avoid detection. The mere fact he wanted to evade capture was evidence he knew what he was doing was wrong. There was no evidence of irresistible impulse, either; Severance had been able to resist the impulse to kill for over a decade and the level of premeditation involved established his crimes were not impulsive.

Had they raised insanity, Severance's attorneys would necessarily have been forced to concede he had committed the murders. A defendant who reaches for the insanity defense in effect waives the presumption of innocence because he agrees he committed the crimes. The case then becomes a battle of dueling mental health professionals debating whether the defendant should be found "not guilty" because he was "criminally insane" at the time of the murder.

The clinical precision with which Severance conducted his assassinations, the amount of forethought that went into his crimes and his desire and ability to avoid detection belied any notion he was criminally insane. I doubt Severance's defense attorneys seriously considered mounting the insanity defense. They were seasoned and sharp. They knew on these facts a jury would never find Severance not guilty by reason of insanity.

Furthermore, Severance himself would have angrily resisted any efforts made by his attorneys to question his mental state. In an interesting turn, one of the symptoms of Severance's illness was an unshakeable conviction he was perfectly sane. The Manifesto of Hate was full of angry references to psychiatry and psychology. Severance's website, MentalDisorder.com, was devoted to excited gibes at mental health professionals and his "Mental Disorder" board game was a sarcastic joke about psychology writ large. Throughout his life, Severance greeted anyone who questioned his sanity with venom and would have done so with his lawyers had they the temerity to suggest it.

As we will see, the defense team still found a way to inject Severance's mental health into the case, pursuing what I deemed the "insanity lite" defense.

# CHAPTER TEN

*"Introduce murder into a safe and secure neighborhood. It shudders with horror. Do it again and again and again."*

The best real-world example of the competing ethical pressures placed on a public prosecutor is criminal discovery, the process by which the parties exchange information about a case before trial. The Supreme Court has ruled the prosecution has an ethical obligation to provide the defense with all "exculpatory" and "impeachment" evidence. Exculpatory evidence is evidence tending to establish the defendant did not commit the crime or supportive of a lesser sentence. Impeachment evidence is anything that might be used by the defense to attack a witness' credibility on cross-examination.

During their investigation of the Dunning scene, CSI investigators had recovered a male DNA profile from the locking mechanism of the front door of the Dunning house; later it was determined to not be Severance's DNA. This is a clear example of exculpatory evidence. I will explain why the Dunning front door was the quintessential red herring, but there is no doubt the defense was entitled to know about it and we dutifully disclosed it.

For an example of impeachment evidence, I turn to Linda Robra. Robra arguably could have been charged with a crime known as a "straw purchase of a firearm." She bought two guns at the behest of a man she knew was a convicted felon and allowed him unfettered access to them. She had a defense—she always believed she was buying the guns for herself—but the possibility of charging her existed. In exchange for her truthful testimony, I agreed to provide her with immunity from prosecution. Arguably this gave her a reason to cooperate with the government and therefore constituted impeachment evidence. We disclosed the immunity agreement to the defense and Robra was cross-examined about it at trial.

Supreme Court jurisprudence establishes a prosecutor has an absolute duty to hand over to the defense the evidence most harmful to her case. To make matters more complicated, the defense has no reciprocal duty to provide the prosecution with all evidence in their possession that tends to incriminate the defendant. To the contrary, the defense is shielded from providing such evidence to the prosecution due to the defendant's Fifth Amendment right not to incriminate himself and the doctrine of attorney/client privilege.

I frequently teach young prosecutors about their ethical obligations. I stress that if they accept their job is to ensure justice is done, the duty to disclose exculpatory and impeachment evidence becomes a badge of honor. Prosecutors are duty-bound to rise above base self-interest. Despite working in an adversarial system, despite our duty to protect the citizenry and despite the natural human desire to "win" a big case, our role as a minister of justice demands we hand our opponent the very evidence that hurts our position. Given the huge amount of authority we wield, much is rightfully expected from us. Yet the prosecutor who faithfully exercises her ethical obligations can find nobility in her profession.

Young prosecutors often carp about a perceived "double standard," in that a defense attorney is ethically prohibited from turning over incriminating evidence to the prosecution while the prosecutor is required to hand over exculpatory evidence to the defense. I cannot deny there are two standards at play but I hold the difference exists because of the different responsibilities inherent in our offices: a prosecutor's duty is to obtain a just result while a defense attorney's is to obtain an acquittal at almost any cost. To the extent there is a "double standard," young prosecutors should embrace it as the mark of a higher calling.

The only way to ensure we had scrupulously honored our duty to provide exculpatory evidence was to turn over every substantive document in our possession; in total, several thousand pages of criminal discovery: every police report, every forensic analysis and all of Severance's writings. David Lord dutifully and methodically scanned the material onto more than 30 discs and handed them to the defense attorneys. By being completely open with discovery we avoided wasting precious resources fighting defense motions for access to information; despite the serious nature of the case and voluminous evidence, there was never a serious dispute on this subject.

I believed in the outstanding team of attorneys I had assembled. My attitude was straightforward: we would provide comprehensive discovery to the defense and still prevail.

****

One pretrial legal issue loomed above all others: would Judge Roush allow us to present all three murders together in one trial?

Under the "serial killer" provision of the Virginia Code, a person who commits two or murders within three years is guilty of Capital Murder for both crimes. Since the Lodato and Kirby cases had been charged as Capital Murder the applicable law was clear: these two offenses had to be tried together. The defense attorneys conceded the point but filed a pretrial motion arguing the Dunning case should be severed and tried standing alone.

My team had to convince Judge Roush the manner in which the three murders were committed was so unusual they must be related. In legal terms, we had to establish the offenses were "connected" or constituted part of a "common scheme or plan."

In the lengthy brief he wrote in opposition to the severance motion David Lord noted the term "common scheme" described "crimes that share features idiosyncratic in character, which permit an inference that each individual offense was committed by the same person." Factors the judge could consider included whether the offenses were committed in the same neighborhood, whether a weapon of the same description was used in the crimes or whether the perpetrator chose victims only of a certain gender or age group. Most of these factors went our way, but the defense vigorously contended the "10-year gap" destroyed any prospect the Dunning case was linked to the others.

The courtroom hearing on the severance motion did not start well for us. Megan Thomas argued for the defense team, deftly weaving case law and facts together to make a compelling argument the Dunning case was unrelated to the two more recent crimes. She said our position constituted "failed logic" and added sarcastically that, if the murders constituted a common plan, the "10-year gap" made it "one of the worst plans ever."

Judge Roush interjected and cited a new Court of

Appeals case helpful to the defense. When a judge interrupts an argument to bolster one side's position, the message to the opposing side is clear—you're not winning this motion unless you have a bombshell to drop during your rebuttal.

Luckily, we had a bombshell.

\*\*\*\*

The bomb I was about to drop was constructed from Severance's own words, revealed in thousands of pages of handwriting the police recovered throughout the investigation.

Until this point I had not publicly discussed the content and substance of the Manifesto of Hate. My ethical obligations prevented me from releasing Severance's writings to the press. When I quoted from the Manifesto during the severance hearing it was the first time the judge, the public or the reporters had heard his disturbing words.

I began my remarks by stressing the demographic similarities of the victims, the geographical proximity of the offenses and the forensic similarities of the firearms evidence collected at each of the three scenes.

After recounting these foundational arguments I dove headlong into the Manifesto. A courtroom filled with reporters sat in rapt attention. The words they were hearing were shocking and, as I recounted example after example of Severance's violent musings, I started to hear the muted tap of thumbs on haptic keyboards.

The gravity of Severance's own words, as I barked them in quick, staccato bursts, shifted the momentum in our favor:

**"Please purchase three North American Arms**

**.22 caliber mini-revolvers and 500 rounds of Subsonic ammunition. The five round stainless steel with the wooden grip is small and easily concealed."**

**"Thou shalt kill and vengeance is mine, saith the Lord. Hollow point and below the speed of sound is sweet music and very effective. Violence wins."**

I transitioned to Severance's motive for these murders: his anger at Alexandria's "law enforcement class" for granting full custody of his son to the mother back in 2001. Again, Severance's own words proved my point:

**"Murder is good. Court justice is bad."**

**"Can you forgive someone for kidnapping your son? Can you kill someone for kidnapping your son?"**

**"They kidnap and they die!"**

**"Thou shalt not kill is a lie. No god-fearing, self-respecting patriarch would not kill men and women who delight in terrorizing his family."**

As I initiated this barrage of selected quotes advocating murder Judge Roush stared down intently from her perch.

**"Murder on my mind and my mind on murder."**

**"The last scream of a victim echoes to eternity."**

Severance's own words established he was angry at the City of Alexandria and had been since the child custody decision went against him. They proved he was fixated on murdering Alexandria's "elites" and "law enforcement class" and obsessed with the exact guns and ammunition that constituted the hallmark of our assassin.

\*\*\*\*

I have often wondered how much more difficult our task would have been had Severance destroyed his Manifesto before the police located it. He was a very clever murderer, methodically planning his crimes so as not to be caught. He hid the guns and ammunition when he felt the police were on to him. Why, then, did he not destroy the writings, too? Why did he hold on to them?

The ideas Severance espoused in the Manifesto were his innermost thoughts. Although he created internet posts advocating the use of violence, he never mentioned the .22 mini-revolvers or Subsonic ammunition online. He never openly posted about murdering "elites" who "kidnap" your son on the internet. He never told Linda Robra Subsonic ammunition "makes sweet music." He never related his belief that "the last scream of a victim echoes to eternity" to his parents.

The only place Severance set these thoughts to paper was in the composition notebooks. I think Severance saw the Manifesto as a physical manifestation of his psyche. He necessarily had to keep his crimes secret. He couldn't share his successful "missions" with his parents. He could not post his most violent thoughts online because someone might suspect he was capable of acting on them. His only true confidant was himself. By writing in his journals, Severance found a singular release, all the more satisfying because he could go back and reread the pages whenever the mood struck.

There was another reason to keep the notebooks. They contained hundreds of ruminations directed to or written about the son the government had "kidnapped" from him. Severance only knew his son for a brief period while the boy was an infant. He had no contact with him after the courtroom goodbye years before, but the frequency with which he wrote about his child did not diminish with time.

Severance did not write love letters to his son, however. The missives in the Manifesto addressed to the boy are cruel exhortations to violence in which Severance hopes he will grow up to be an "effective predator" not afraid to resort to "violent means."

Here I venture into speculative armchair psychology, but Severance did not see his absent son as an independent human being. He considered the child an extension of his own ego, a *tabula rasa* who would grow up and become successful in a world in which his father had failed. Severance considered his son a doppelganger. The composition notebooks contained a decade's worth of entries about this alter-ego and were, therefore, a physical part of Severance. He could no more get rid of them than he could a limb.

So he held onto his notebooks. By so doing, he provided us with an in-depth view of the fractured mind behind the murders.

****

A judge will usually announce her ruling on a motion as soon as the attorneys are done with their arguments. That did not happen here. Judge Roush deferred, saying she would take the severance issue "under advisement," judicial shorthand for buying time to consider the correct legal outcome. She indicated she would issue a written opinion outlining her reasoning, an unusual exercise for a trial judge. She gave no time frame for its release.

Each day that passed without her opinion being issued meant it was more likely we would prevail. A judge deciding a pretrial motion in the defendant's favor does not have to give a detailed legal exposition because the prosecutor usually cannot appeal the ruling and no appellate court will be asked to review the judge's decision-making.

On the other hand, a motion that goes against the defense always presents a potential appellate issue. A good trial judge will create a detailed record of the legal reasoning on which she based a decision to deny a defense motion. Each day that elapsed was evidence the judge was working on a thorough written opinion. This, in turn, suggested the motion was going to go our way.

Judge Roush released her decision about a month after the hearing. In an exquisitely reasoned, 20-page opinion the judge ruled the three murders were sufficiently linked to be deemed parts of a common scheme or plan. The defense motion to sever the Dunning case was denied.

This was a huge win. The victims' families were extremely relieved. We were going to settle this matter, once and for all, in one trial.

****

As 2014 neared an end, another problem threatened to derail the trial process entirely: Severance's mental health. For weeks, the defense team had hinted they were having problems communicating with their client and had reason to question his competence to stand trial. If the judge agreed Severance was mentally incompetent, the trial would be postponed indefinitely. A lengthy delay in the trial would wreak havoc on the families and could cause significant problems for the prosecution.

A defense request for a mental competency evaluation is quite different than raising the insanity defense. Competency to stand trial looks at the defendant's present mental state: right now, in court. The insanity defense is retrospective, looking back at the defendant's mental state at the time of the crime. It is possible to have a criminal defendant who is competent to stand trial but who was insane at the time of the offense. Likewise, it is possible to have someone who is incompetent to stand trial but who was legally sane at the time of the offense. Of course, a defendant can be both incompetent and insane.

When considering a defendant's competency the court must determine whether he is so mentally ill that he cannot understand the nature of the proceedings against him or assist his attorneys in his defense. The only way the judge can make this determination is to have the defendant evaluated by a mental health professional. In serious cases, it is not unusual to have more than one doctor give an opinion. Although whether the defendant is competent is a legal decision made by the judge—and not a mental health decision made by a doctor—the judge relies heavily on the opinions of the mental health professionals assigned to conduct the evaluations.

If a suspect is deemed incompetent he is sent to a mental health facility to receive therapy designed to restore him to competence. In extreme cases, the treatment can include the forced dosage of psychotropic medicines. From that point forward, until and unless the doctors opine the suspect has been rendered competent—an event that can easily take years and, in some cases is never accomplished—the trial is in a state of perpetual limbo.

In Alexandria we are still locked in a holding pattern with regards to a 2001 murder. In that case, a mentally-ill man sliced the throat of an eight-year old boy who was playing in the street in front of his house. The alleged killer was caught, charged and then deemed mentally incompetent. He has remained in a secure psychiatric facility ever since, receiving restoration services. It is doubtful he will ever be brought to trial.

This was the exact state of affairs I wished to avoid. Since the defense team had not filed a motion for a competency evaluation during the first few months of the case, I was hopeful we might avoid one altogether. But a phone call from the defense attorneys in early December 2014 crushed that hope entirely.

Megan Thomas said: "We are having a very tough time communicating with our client. We fear he isn't rational and we believe he is incompetent. We are going to file a motion to have a doctor appointed to evaluate him."

Severance's competence to stand trial was ultimately evaluated by two doctors. The written reports submitted to the court by these mental health professionals remain under seal, so I cannot quote directly from them, but, by early 2015, Judge Roush had decided Severance was capable of making rational choices and therefore ruled he was competent to stand trial. Crisis averted.

With the issues of severance and competency decided and trial just about 6 months away, my trial team delved into the intricacies of crafting our trial plan.

****

I spent a significant amount of time trying to get into Severance's head. Believe me, it is a very dark place. I know more about the way he thought and operated than anyone outside of his parents and Linda Robra. Because I understood at least some of his thinking, I was convinced he was competent to stand trial. I was happy the judge agreed.

Severance's decision to commit murder was rational in that he knew exactly what he was doing. I use the term "rational" here to define someone who was making a conscious decision to commit murder, after thoughtful deliberation and consideration of the consequences. Severance knew the "law enforcement elites" would find his actions repulsive, but, in his mind, the murders were justified because of the injuries inflicted on him by these very same "elites." Severance's writings revealed an internal debate about whether the slights he perceived merited his taking up arms and instigating a violent "revolution" against the "law enforcement class" that had personally offended him. His actions establish his verdict on the question.

Severance consciously decided and meticulously planned to kill his victims. He took great pains to avoid being caught. Had he elected never to kill again after the Dunning murder, I doubt we would have ever solved that case.

The evidence suggested he walked around the victims' neighborhood, scouting out prospective targets in the weeks preceding each crime. He assembled an "assassination kit" comprising an easily concealed gun and ammo he thought would make less noise during an assassination. He wore latex gloves to make sure he would not leave forensic evidence behind. He apparently selected an escape route from the scene of each murder.

His acts of violence sprang from the same well of anger as the string of mass shootings our country is now suffering from on an almost monthly basis. Severance just chose to be cunning about how he carried out his crimes. Unlike many mass shooters, Severance did not want to go out in a blaze of glory. He wanted to continue killing until he had either "received satisfaction" or had ignited a political "revolution."

Severance's thinking was in many ways consistent with that of other high-profile mass murderers. There are strong similarities to the Ted Kaczynski "Unabomber" case, to include Severance's physical resemblance to Kaczynski, his reclusiveness and his anti-government political Manifesto.

I once attended a presentation by the detectives who worked the 2012 Colorado movie theater shooting and there are also similarities between Severance and the perpetrator of that crime, James Holmes. Online, it is possible to find copies of composition notebooks Holmes filled with ramblings about committing murder. When I read Holmes' writings I was immediately shocked at how evocative they were of Severance's Manifesto.

There are lessons to be gleaned from Charles Severance's distorted and violent worldview: lessons for law enforcement, lessons for prosecutors and lessons for society as a whole. I will discuss those lessons in the afterword.

****

I had never before lost a trial judge during the pendency of a case. I guess there is a first for everything. In July of 2015 we learned Judge Roush was being promoted to the Virginia Supreme Court and would therefore be unable to preside over our October trial.

I was not happy about this turn of events and not because Judge Roush was biased toward our side. To the contrary, there were a series of pretrial decisions Roush made with which I disagreed.

For example, after the police seized Severance's Ford Escort in West Virginia they brought it to Alexandria on a flatbed tow truck. Since the surveillance camera that captured the car leaving the Lodato scene was still in the same location on Braddock Road, Dave Cutting drove the Escort past the camera, allowing us to compare the resulting images with those from the date of the murder. Not surprisingly, the images were identical. Nonetheless, Judge Roush ruled these images were derived from an impermissible "experiment" and would not allow us to present them to the jury. I still respectfully disagree with that decision. Of course, she was the judge and that means she won the argument.

Judge Roush was exceptionally smart, ethical and thorough. Her integrity was beyond reproach. Although I disagreed with her on certain points there was no doubt her decisions were well-reasoned. She was in control of her courtroom. She was also very good at dealing with Severance, who often argued with his attorneys and who was prone to verbal outbursts in which he loudly referred to 18th-century historical figures. Judge Roush treated him with forbearance.

I was unhappy we were losing her. The victims' families were also upset. None of us knew who would be appointed as her replacement. It seemed unlikely we would get another judge who was as seasoned and intelligent.

Roush's departure posed another problem: a new judge might continue the trial date because they could not get "up to speed" on such a complex case in the 90 days left before October.

****

In early August we found out Fairfax County Circuit Court Judge Randy Bellows would be our replacement. Like Roush, Judge Bellows was a veteran judge who had presided over many serious cases. He began his career as a federal prosecutor, distinguishing himself in national security investigations. He had earned a reputation as an exceptionally smart and well-balanced jurist. Since I had never appeared before him, I did not know his courtroom personality was completely different than Judge Roush's.

During the first motions hearing in front of Judge Bellows, I was struck by his sphinxlike demeanor. He was quiet. He did not engage in witty banter. He sent the signal he was all business. When it came time to rule on a motion he read from a lengthy document containing a potent cocktail of case citations and impeccable legal reasoning. I was in awe of his intelligence. If we added up the IQs of all four attorneys on the prosecution team, Bellows would have bested our collective score.

An internet report suggested Bellows might wish to review decisions Judge Roush had made, such as her denial of the severance motion. While Bellows had the legal authority to do so, reviewing decisions already rendered would certainly delay the trial. Rehearing issues previously decided would have been particularly difficult for the victims' families, who would suffer renewed uncertainty over matters that had been settled in our favor.

Judge Bellows quickly allayed our fears. He announced he would not be reconsidering any of the legal decisions Judge Roush had made and intended to keep the October start date.

\*\*\*\*

As the calendar turned from August into September, Bellows had to rule on the most significant pretrial motion left: whether or not he would allow Severance's defense team to attempt to pin the Nancy Dunning murder on her deceased husband, Jim.

I had no desire to sit in a courtroom and hear Jim's name dragged through the dirt. I understood the original detectives had a duty to take a look at Jim. But I also knew there was no evidence Jim had anything to do with the crime. This, of course, explained why he had never been charged.

The fact that retired Alexandria police detectives may at some point have suspected Jim Dunning of participating in Nancy's murder was absolutely irrelevant. The defense could not put a detective on the stand and ask him "Did you think Jim Dunning did it?" any more than I could call Dave Cutting to the stand and ask him if he thought Severance was guilty. What a witness subjectively "believes" is not evidence and is inadmissible.

Despite the lack of evidence, the defense team would have been committing malpractice if it did not seek to implicate Jim Dunning, even if it meant hurting the Dunning family. The defense team's only job, indeed, their ethical obligation, was to obtain a verdict of 'not guilty.' If they could convince the jury Jim may have killed Nancy, they would inject a reasonable doubt into the jurors' mind and obtain an acquittal on that murder. If the jury bought my argument that all three murders were committed by the same person—but was also convinced Severance did not kill Nancy—there was a real risk of an acquittal on all charges.

Defense attorneys do not have to "win" their case. Since a criminal defendant is presumed to be innocent and the prosecution has the burden of presenting proof beyond a reasonable doubt, all the defense need do is inject sufficient doubt into the jurors' minds. Contrary to the way it is portrayed on television, a "not guilty" verdict does not necessarily mean the jury is convinced the defendant did not commit the offense. It often signifies the jury's belief the prosecution did not produce sufficient evidence to prove its case. Not guilty is not always a synonym for innocent.

It was clear the defense team would inject Jim Dunning into the case and I intended on doing something about it. David Lord wrote an exquisite pretrial motion arguing the defense should be precluded from implicating Jim because it did not have any evidence pointing to his guilt. If David's motion could stop the defense from going down this path it would be a huge tactical win for us and a relief for the Dunning family.

This kind of prosecution motion is usually denied because the trial judge is reluctant to prohibit an accused from exploring a defense. Therefore, I was pleasantly surprised when Judge Bellows granted our motion in late August. He specifically told the defense attorneys they could not mention Jim Dunning's name in their case. Thanks to David's incredible efforts we had prevailed on a motion I thought we had little chance of winning.

The next month the defense team asked Judge Bellows to reconsider his ruling. The judge acceded to the request and held a second hearing in September. This time the defense changed the manner in which they argued the motion and Judge Bellows changed his mind, opening the door to a defense attempt at placing the blame on Jim Dunning.

****

If it is true criminal trials are elaborate exercises in performance theater, then the stage was set. All pretrial motions had been heard and decided. The trial date of October 5th, 2015 had not changed. The estimate of five to six weeks had also not changed and turned out to be just about right. With a huge amount of help from our victim/witness team of Judy Holl and Lisa Bowman, we managed to get subpoenas out and travel arrangements set for well over 100 witnesses. My team put together an extremely complicated plan involving over 300 exhibits and 2000 documents. We prepared detailed PowerPoint presentations for opening statement and closing argument and lugged more than 50 binders of documents over to Fairfax.

The pretrial part of the case was over. It was show time.

# CHAPTER ELEVEN

*"Add violence and increase uncertainty among status quo utopian oppressive elites. Emotionally disturb them with violence. Nightmares and day-dreams of terror."*

In the weeks before the trial commenced I would occasionally run into citizens who wanted to share their thoughts. People I barely knew would drop observations in casual conversation such as: "you've got the wrong guy" or "maybe Jim Dunning paid Severance to kill his wife." Sometimes I would hear a slightly more optimistic version: "You may get him on Lodato but there is no way you're getting a conviction on Dunning." My favorite was the following chestnut: "You don't have any evidence that Severance did it, do you?"

Could someone really think I indicted the most serious case of my career without any evidence?

The offhand manner in which these pronouncements were made was a lesson in human nature. Decent people felt it appropriate to approach me, the architect of the case, and dismiss my decision-making with the sweep of a hand. All of this, of course, from those who <u>*did not know the evidence,*</u> which we had purposefully kept out of the public eye.

Now, I don't think these inquisitors were intentionally trying to make me angry. They just did not realize that in expressing their opinions they were, in effect, personally insulting my competency and judgment. It is just a facet of human nature to confidently hold forth on topics about which we know very little.

I am guilty of the same sin. My favorite football team, the Washington Redskins, is never any good. The Skins always hover around .500 and cannot break into the top echelon of the NFL. Every summer, Washington fans are optimistic about the latest free agent signing and every December the same fans are saying: "there's always next year."

I am one of those fans and I admit I routinely second-guess the head coach, Jay Gruden. I bemoan the lack of a run game, question why certain plays are called and frequently criticize the team's personnel decisions.

The reality is Jay Gruden probably knows just a little more about professional football than I do. On reflection, it's amusing how I so confidently question Gruden's decisions. Do I really think I would be a better football coach for the Redskins? Obviously not; the rational part of me realizes my criticism is ill-informed. But that doesn't stop me. If I ever had the pleasure of meeting Coach Gruden, I'm sure I would give him my opinion on some roster decision about which I know nothing.

By the way, Jay, if you were wondering, I was okay with letting Cousins walk.

****

The Fairfax County courthouse lies just about 20 miles west of Alexandria. The change in location made things complicated as we had to move our office to a different facility. We trucked reams of documents over to Fairfax along with a litany of hardware like computers, printers, routers and tablets. My counterpart in Fairfax was kind enough to give my team some space in a conference room so we might have a "home base." We quickly dubbed it our "war room."

Luckily, we had more than just the four attorneys working on the case. The trial team was rounded out by several amazing non-lawyers: my office administrator, Donald Harrison-Wright, my Victim/Witness Director, Judy Holl and Judy's most senior victim advocate, Lisa Bowman. Television shows tend to focus on police detectives and lawyers and never depict how crucial other disciplines are to a successful trial.

I consider Donald much more than an office manager. Throughout this case, he kept us on schedule. He was in charge of all our numerous IT and audio/visual needs. He helped us organize and present the immense amount of digital evidence we had in this case: photographs, documents and videos. He deserves a huge amount of thanks for his work.

As the title Victim Advocate suggests, Judy and Lisa focused on working with the victims' families. The relationship between a prosecutor's office and the family of a murder victim is vital: if the family does not trust the prosecutor and is not informed about the progress of the case, they feel their needs are not being met. The trial can easily become another source of frustration and anger.

A prosecutor who wants a victim's family to trust her must always be scrupulously honest. She cannot sugar coat things; if it appears that a motion is going to be decided adversely, she must explain why and what it means to the case. Being upfront with a family means a huge time commitment for the prosecutor as she meets with the family regularly to update them. That time commitment doubles when the case is exceptionally complicated and it trebles when there is a large number of family members invested in the case.

In the Severance case we had an exceptionally complicated case and a large number of victims. With three victims' families we sometimes had over 30 victims in the room during our pretrial meetings. A lot of preparation went into them and Lisa and Judy were instrumental in putting it all together.

In the pretrial phase of the case I gave the families a significant amount of my time. I met with them before every hearing, explaining what the defense was arguing and what our counter-arguments would be. Afterward, I met with the families again and detailed what had transpired in court. Given the complexity of the issues and the number of questions, these meetings often ran several hours in length.

Once the trial commenced I could no longer give the families as much attention. I had to focus on trying the case. Standing on your feet in a courtroom all day is exceptionally tiring; at the conclusion of each day I was exhausted and usually in no shape to meet with anyone. I relied on Judy and Lisa, two caring advocates who exhibited a vast store of energy. Judy and Lisa would meet the families every morning, get them to the courtroom, stay with them during recesses and lunch breaks and help them avoid being accosted by aggressive reporters outside of the courthouse. These unsung heroes have my respect and admiration.

\*\*\*\*

D-day had arrived: October 5, 2015. The initial phase of a trial is jury selection, usually referred to as *voir dire*, an Old French term which, by way of Latin, literally means "to speak the truth." The idea is the prospective jurors are going to tell the truth about their opinions so those incapable of being impartial can be identified. In reality, it is very difficult to get prospective jurors to be open and answer questions. Human beings are naturally reticent in public settings.

Given the attention the case had received and the estimated length of the trial, Judge Bellows ordered 150 prospective jurors to be called to the courthouse, anticipating a large number would be unwilling to serve five to six weeks. Bellows planned on seating a total of 16 jurors: 12 would comprise the jury while four would serve as alternates who would be present for the entire case but released before deliberations unless we "lost" a juror during the trial.

Jurors can be "lost" for any number of reasons: sickness and failure to comply with the Court's orders are among the most common. Having four alternates meant we could lose as many as four and still have the required number of 12 to deliberate and return a verdict.

If we somehow lost a fifth, the only recourse would be for the Court to declare a mistrial and start over again.

****

I struggle with the question of whether the American jury system is well conceived or not. On one hand, the entire structure seems ludicrous. In a murder trial, we randomly take 12 citizens off the street and ask them to serve as arbiters of the most serious and grave criminal charge. They are given no training. The only criteria are that a juror be at least 18 years of age and be a citizen of both Virginia and the locality in which the trial is being heard. We expect them to abide by the legal principles given to them by the judge and to lay whatever preconceived notions they have at the door to the jury room. One could argue this system is a recipe for disaster.

On the other hand, juries usually get it right, particularly in murder cases, and it is true that if a prosecutor can convince 12 perfect strangers to agree the defendant has committed a crime, society can have some confidence in the conviction. The ancient architects of the jury system had a method to their madness.

If asked, most prospective jurors will say they are ambivalent about serving because of scheduling concerns. They will tell the judge they are needed at work, their children have a school project or they have a scheduled vacation.

While these citizens are telling the truth, I don't think scheduling concerns are the real reason most are reluctant to serve; it is the job description that makes people wary. Many murder jurors chafe at the strain imposed on them by their service. They ask themselves serious questions: What if I help acquit someone who committed murder? What if we convict someone who is innocent? Do I want to go into a small room and argue with 11 strangers? Can I really sit in judgment of another person? Could I put someone in prison for life?

In every trial, I tell the panel that being a juror is a tough job and there is no shame in admitting it's not the job for them. I ask them if they have any moral, religious or ethical objections to judging another human being. I explain this is serious business and the time to let us know about their concerns is during *voir dire*, because once they are back in the jury room deliberating on the case, it's far too late.

Citizens exposed to criminal trials through T.V. or podcasts may *think* that serving as a juror in a murder case may be fun only to realize it is extremely difficult after having been selected. One of my primary goals in *voir dire* is to make sure the panel understands a trial is not a television show. They must realize that if they are selected, they will be required to make difficult decisions about the credibility of the witnesses, the strength of the evidence and the guilt of the defendant. My job is to impress upon them the gravity of the situation.

The estimated length of this trial meant a large number could be eliminated because serving would constitute an undue hardship on them. Judge Bellows brought the jurors into the courtroom in groups of 25 to ask if they could serve for six weeks. By lunch on Tuesday, October 6, we had already whittled down the original group of prospective panelists from 150 to exactly 75.

****

Next, the judge brought the 75 remaining prospective jurors into the courtroom and asked them a simple question: "Please raise your hand if you have any familiarity with this case, such as reading about it, seeing it on the television news or the internet or talking about it with your friends or family." Forty-five hands went up. Well over half of the pool would need to be individually questioned about their exposure to the case.

Having heard about the matter at issue is not an automatic disqualifier for a prospective juror. The dispositive question is whether the juror can be fair and impartial despite what they may have heard. We want intelligent citizens to serve. Given the intense media attention that had been devoted to the case, it would have been impossible to find 16 intelligent jurors who had never heard of Charles Severance.

Judge Bellows brought each juror into the courtroom individually and asked a series of questions: "What have you heard about the case?" and "has what you have heard about the case caused you to form an opinion about whether Mr. Severance is guilty?" After hearing the juror's answers, Bellows allowed the prosecution and defense to ask questions.

I had never gone through such a thorough, time-consuming *voir dire*, which ended up taking three full days. In prior murder trials I was usually able to seat a jury on the first day, often by lunchtime. But I am not complaining. By going through the jury questioning in such a painstaking manner Judge Bellows created an outstanding record of what had transpired during jury selection

"Making a record" is a term of art in a criminal trial. Trial courts work by the "adduction"—the bringing forth—of evidence in the form of witnesses and exhibits. If a defendant is convicted of a crime, they invariably assert their right to appeal the conviction. Appellate courts do not hear testimony from witnesses and an appeal is not a "re-trial" where both sides put on evidence.

Instead, an appellate court decides whether the trial court honored the applicable law. In making this decision the appellate court relies on written transcripts of what was said and done during the trial. These written transcripts are called the "record" of the case. In the Severance trial, the record marshalled by Judge Bellows was just about 7300 pages in length, the equivalent of 25 modern novels.

Most criminal appeals are unsuccessful, but in many that are granted the problem starts with a deficient trial record. In these cases the record created by the judge is lacking in the amount of detail the appellate court needs to fairly decide a legal question. *Voir dire* is one of the areas frequently targeted on appeal and also one in which the trial record is often scanty. By going through this lengthy process of "making a record" Judge Bellows was helping the appellate court to decide any future appeal.

****

Prospective jurors get excused from serving on a jury in one of two ways. They are either "struck for cause" or are subject to a "preemptory strike." "Struck for cause" means a juror is removed because the judge determines they cannot serve fairly or impartially as a matter of law. A juror may be struck for cause if they have a medical condition that makes it impossible to understand the proceedings, if they are related to a witness by blood or marriage or if they have been so influenced by pretrial publicity they have already decided the defendant is guilty.

The prosecution and the defense get "preemptory strikes" as well. Both sides can strike six jurors for almost any reason. The only restriction on the use of preemptory strikes is neither side may strike a juror solely based on the juror's race or ethnicity.

We started with 150 possible jurors. Half of this number were struck by the judge "for cause" before we got to the question of pretrial publicity. That issue caused the judge to strike another 19 "for cause" because they had already formed an opinion about the guilt of the defendant. We were now down to 51.

The next step was to reduce the number to 28 finalists on whom the prosecution and defense could employ their "preemptory strikes." Once the 12 preemptory strikes had been exercised, we would have culled the pool to 16: a 12-person jury and the four alternates who would sit through the trial but be dismissed before deliberations if unneeded.

**\*\*\*\***

Although he does not want anyone to know it, Jimmy Entas is exceptionally smart, having graduated from the College of William and Mary's Marshall Wythe School of Law. He clerked for a federal judge after law school and is an accomplished legal writer.

Jimmy cultivates a persona reminiscent of Detective Martin Riggs from *Lethal Weapon*. Entas says what is on his mind and has no issue with speaking truth to power. I have a very strong suspicion Jimmy prefers people thinking he's a loose cannon. It's a defense mechanism that protects him from showing the thoughtful person lurking behind the mask. If you think he's a little unbalanced, that's just fine with him.

Inside of the courtroom, however, Entas is in his element. He served as a prosecutor for over 20 years and had a great deal of experience trying murder cases. He had honed an aptitude for connecting with victims. His strengths and capabilities made him the right person to conduct the Commonwealth's *voir dire.*

Jimmy's prefatory comments hit the perfect tone: "It is my privilege to represent the Commonwealth of Virginia and the City of Alexandria in the case you are about to hear. The Commonwealth is attempting to hold the defendant accountable for his actions. Specifically, for killing three Alexandria citizens: Nancy Dunning, Ron Kirby and Ruthanne Lodato, and for shooting and injuring a fourth, Jeanette."

These initial words were the jurors' first glimpse of what kind of people the prosecutors were. In television shows and movies, we are often portrayed as ambitious, vainglorious climbers who burnish our own careers by putting bad guys in prison, regardless of the cost. Many jurors enter the courtroom with this stereotype of the "central casting" prosecutor. We needed Jimmy to push back on the stereotype.

Jimmy reiterated it was our privilege to represent the Commonwealth in such a grave case. This was absolutely true and had the benefit of adding a note of humility to his opening words.

Entas emphasized the Commonwealth's goal was to hold the defendant accountable for his intentional actions. Few would argue with the notion that a person should be held to account for their intentional acts. By using this formulation, Jimmy was signaling we were not seeking vengeance. To the contrary, we were dispassionate and calm, wanting only to hold the defendant responsible for his conscious decisions.

\*\*\*\*

Entas explained that, if selected, the panelists would be instructed by Judge Bellows as to what the law applicable to the case was. He noted they would have to set aside their own personal ideas about what the law should be.

Detailed testimony about guns and ammunition was going to be a significant part of our evidence but could be difficult to understand for the uninitiated. It was crucial we seated at least one juror who had some familiarity with firearms. Therefore, Jimmy asked the panel about their views with regards to guns, learning several had extensive experience.

Jimmy ended his questioning of the panel with a flurry of crucial points. He asked the jurors to remember the concept of a "fair trial" did not apply only to the defense and that the prosecution gets the same protection. A person who is so prejudiced against the government that she cannot be fair to the government should not serve as a juror in a criminal case.

Finally, he raised the issue of the legal standard applicable to determining guilt: the requirement the prosecution must prove its case "beyond a reasonable doubt."

Defense attorneys routinely highlight the fact that the "beyond a reasonable doubt" is the highest legal standard countenanced by our system of law and much higher than other standards such as "preponderance of the evidence" or "clear and convincing evidence." They rightfully point out it is the prosecution's burden to prove the case to this standard and, since the defendant is presumed to be innocent, any "close calls" must go in his favor.

Prosecutors accept the "reasonable doubt" standard is very high. However, smart ones point out two salient facts to jurors: first, "beyond a reasonable doubt" is not the highest possible standard that *could* be imposed by the law, and, second, by its very definition, it allows a juror to convict even if he harbors some doubt about guilt, so long as the doubt is "unreasonable."

Entas asked the jury: "Some people feel the burden (on the prosecution) should be even higher. That, for instance, it should be proof beyond a shadow of a doubt or beyond all possible doubt or even to a moral certainty. Does everyone understand the only way you could be convinced beyond all possible doubt is if you personally observed the crime and were a witness? But if you were a witness, you could not serve as a juror because you would be part of the case?"

"Is there anyone here who would hold the Commonwealth to a legal standard higher than that required by law?"

Hearing no problematic answers, Jimmy thanked the jurors for their time and sat down.

****

After Jimmy was finished the defense got its chance to question the panel. Any smug feelings of satisfaction I might be harboring about the prospective jury quickly started to dissipate as Megan Thomas rose to speak.

Thomas started by addressing a concept she called the "rooting interest." She observed most citizens instinctively identify a little more closely with either the prosecution or the defense. She employed a clever analogy, pointing out that as a University of Florida graduate, she would be more emotionally attached to a televised Gator football game than one involving two schools she had not attended.

The fact a juror may identify more closely with one side over another is not, in itself, sufficient to strike "for cause." The pertinent question is whether the person is so predisposed to one party he cannot be fair to the other. By bringing up this issue in a very direct way, Thomas was able to get the panelists to question their own ability to sit impartially.

Thomas then assertively went into the legal concepts that favor the defense. She raised the burden of reasonable doubt, the presumption of innocence and the fact the defense does not have to present any evidence at all if it so chooses.

One of the secrets of *voir dire* is to softly raise issues you recognize could hurt your position so as to lessen the impact on the jurors. Thomas waded into one of the big problems she had going into the trial: Severance's Manifesto of Hate. The defense feared these awful writings would immediately turn any jury against Severance.

Thomas was brutally honest. She admitted Severance had written the documents and she characterized them as "vile (and) horrific." She admitted her client made frequent use of the "N-word" and the words "whore" and "faggot." She admitted Severance wrote these words in anger and intended them as "slurs."

Many attorneys would have run the other way and avoided the writings, allowing the jury to be surprised by them when the prosecution admitted them into evidence. By being the first to raise this issue, Megan Thomas decided to cut against the conventional wisdom and thereby displayed her brilliance.

By letting the jurors hear about her client's hate-filled writings from her own mouth, in her own words, Thomas absorbed some of the sting of the Manifesto.

She could not, however, completely inoculate the jurors from his venom.

**\*\*\*\***

The remainder of the defense *voir dire* was straightforward. Thomas asked the jurors if they were related by blood or marriage to law enforcement officers. She asked whether anyone on the panel had previously served on a jury.

Severance's attorneys had never raised the insanity defense and, because of notice provisions in the Virginia Code, could not do so at this late date. However, the defense team was sharp and had devised a clever way of getting Severance's mental health before the jury. I could sense Thomas was lightly dipping into this topic, providing some foreshadowing of a defense trial theme.

The moment the jurors saw Severance they would have known there was something going on with his mental health. Severance had refused to shave his beard or cut his hair for trial and when the deputies wheeled him into the courtroom in his Hannibal Lecter-style wheelchair his disheveled appearance was visually arresting. When a witness was on the stand, Severance would usually glare directly ahead, unmoving and with his jaw clenched.

Severance engaged in several angry outbursts during trials. To the extent the jurors observed this behavior—sometimes it occurred when they were not in the courtroom—it cemented the conclusion Severance was "off." Usually these diatribes contained inscrutable arguments about the Constitution. At different times he engaged in angry exclamations about both his attorneys and the prosecutors. We learned he had coined a nickname for the prosecution team, calling us the "Four Horsemen of the Apocalypse."

I'd like to think I was Conquest.

Despite the hard work the experienced defense team put in on his behalf, Severance openly disparaged his attorneys and was uncooperative. He would often refuse to discuss his defense with his lawyers and routinely told Judge Bellows he did not want Chris Leibig to represent him. Every time he was wheeled into the courtroom, the fishbowl eye of the camera would be watching, hoping to catch Severance screaming or giving an obscene gesture.

Since Severance's mental issues were patent the defense attorneys would have been irresponsible if they did not try use them to his benefit. They had to convince the jury Severance was harmless.

If the tactic was successful, the jury might even begin to feel pity for Severance.

# CHAPTER TWELVE

*"Please purchase three North American Firearms*
*.22 MINI-revolvers and 500 rounds of subsonic*
*low velocity cartridges. The five round stainless*
*steel with wooden grip revolver is small and easily*
*concealed."*

Attorneys spend a lot of time debating what "type of juror" they want in a given case. Should they use their preemptory strikes on young people, who have little life experience? Should they strike older, retired panelists? Should the prosecution strike social workers and teachers who are likely more inclined to see the best in people and be sympathetic to a defendant? Would either side want a lawyer on the jury? As my experience has grown, I've become convinced such stereotyping simply does not work.

Jury selection is a crapshoot. The attorneys do not get hours to interrogate each juror and are necessarily left with a sketch of what kind of a person sits before them. Attempts to select jurors based on class characteristics such as age or occupation are lawyerly attempts to bring structure to a chaotic process. Creating complex selection criteria for jurors makes an attorney feel like he is guiding what is an uncontrollable process.

In my opinion, the only stereotype that tends to hold true is the prosecution does not normally want very young jurors, say under the age of 25. Young jurors do not have a lot of life experience. Most have never been required to face the difficult decisions that come with maturity. Since they have necessarily just started their careers, young adults usually have not progressed to a higher level of responsibility or supervision.

Those with little experience making stressful decisions cannot be expected to respond well when under the pressure of a high-stakes murder trial. I have personally tried murders in which young jurors started to crack under the pressure once the case was handed over for deliberations. In one case, a panelist suffered heart palpitations and had to be rushed to the hospital.

During *voir dire*, I focus on accomplishing three things: first, making a good impression with the jurors, convincing them the prosecutors are honest and humble; second, giving an overview of our case, finding ways to emphasize the strengths of the evidence while exposing the jurors to any weaknesses I perceive; and finally flushing out "wackos" and conspiracy theorists on whom to exercise preemptory strikes.

Due to the amount of time Judge Bellows allowed for juror questioning we had more information about the panel in this case than in any other I have ever tried. This allowed us to be more intelligent in exercising our strikes.

We tried to remove younger people from the panel but, given the limited number of strikes, three made the final cut. I was pleased to see two jurors had served in the military, insuring both had a familiarity with firearms and would better understand our evidence.

****

The final step of jury selection was choosing the four alternates. The jurors themselves could not be allowed to know who had been selected. If they were, the four alternates would expect to be dismissed and might pay less attention. To keep the identities secret, Bellows excused the entire panel of 16 from the courtroom. He indicated he would tell the lawyers who the alternates were but would not openly identify them until the end of trial.

Judge Bellows assigned each juror an identifying number, wrote the number on a scrap of paper and threw the 16 scraps of paper into a box. He then randomly selected the numbers of the four alternates.

Severance interrupted before Bellows could finish the selections. Severance feared the judge would manipulate the process and intentionally pick alternate jurors he did not want on the jury. Severance angrily asserted he had a right to "inspect the box" into which the juror numbers had been placed.

This unusual request illustrated Severance's suspicious mindset. Judge Bellows handled the situation calmly and allowed Severance to inspect the box and the paper scraps. He also offered to let me inspect these items as well, but since I trusted the judge, I tried to inject a little bit of levity by saying: "The Commonwealth waives its right to examine the box, your honor."

No one laughed. Lawyer humor isn't funny.

After Severance had completed his inspection of the box, the judge drew the numbers of the alternates. He allowed both sides to see the selected numbers and placed the names under seal until the conclusion of the case.

****

After a jury is seated, the next phase of a criminal trial is the presentation of opening statements, which the popular media sometimes inaccurately refers to as "opening arguments." Lawyers are not allowed to actively argue their respective cases during opening. Opening statements are supposed to be recitations of the facts each party will establish, along with an overview of the witnesses the party intends to call.

The reality is both sides engage in some argument because it is the first chance to present the case to the jury. Either side may object to the other's opening statement if it goes too far. The trick is to focus on the facts and to keep argument to a minimum so the other side does not object. No lawyer wants the judge sustaining an objection during his opening statement. It tends to make a bad first impression with the jurors.

David Lord presented the prosecution's opening statement. David was the best person for this assignment because had a unique ability to present facts in a linear fashion. David does not engage in needless theatrics, hyperbole or dramatic flourishes. He dispassionately and methodically presents the case and leads the jurors' collective mind to a logical conclusion.

David began by focusing on Severance's victims. Since the jurors' only prior exposure to a murder trial had come from television, David wanted to remind the jury three real, flesh-and-blood people had been murdered. David used an audiovisual presentation to emphasize his opening and the first slides included in-life photographs of Nancy Dunning, Ron Kirby and Ruthanne Lodato.

As I discuss the trial, I will use bold type whenever I am directly quoting words spoken inside of the courtroom or citing passages from Severance's Manifesto. David concluded his prefatory remarks by saying:

**"Three lives united over the course of a decade by a common tragedy. All three of these murders happened in the same neighborhood, within rough-**

**ly one mile of each other. You're going to hear that the defendant, Charles Severance, used to live on the outskirts of that neighborhood. When he lived there, he lost custody of his infant son. He blamed the Alexandria courts and law enforcement. That hatred led him to commit these three murders. It devastated three families and the community."**

David planned on grabbing the jury's attention by reciting some of Severance's hateful writings. He utilized the audiovisual capabilities of the courtroom and put the documents on a video display. The jury box was equipped with monitors and I noticed the individual jurors were transfixed by the hateful words suspended electronically in front of them.

Humans are hardwired to respond to ocular stimuli and having a visual representation of evidence helps burn an image into the jurors' brains. The need for visuals is even more necessary in the digital age, where everyone is connected to the internet and is constantly bombarded with information. Jurors subconsciously expect lawyers to provide an A/V presentation. A modern attorney who does not use visual media to emphasize evidence is committing malpractice.

David slowly shuffled through the slides he had created, reciting the written words visible on each one and allowing the jurors time to read along with him:

**"Introduce murder into a safe and secure neighborhood. It shudders with horror. Do it again and again and again."**

**"The last screams of a victim echo to eternity."**

**"It has nothing to do with business. Everything is personal. They kidnap and they die."**

**"Violence in utopians is the new role of law and**

**order. Reverse roles and become the enforcement class only by violent means... The operative word is violence. Violence wins."**

As the words flashed on the screens before them I saw two jurors physically recoil, sitting back in their seats. One juror's mouth was agape in mute horror.

****

After shocking the panel with selections from Severance's writings, David turned to sketching out how we were going to present our case. David told the jury about Jeanette and the composite sketch she had helped to create. He explained the firearms evidence and the surveillance video that caught Severance's red Escort fleeing the Lodato scene. He talked about Severance's motives for committing murder. Wherever possible, he recited a passage from Severance's writings for emphasis.

Prosecutors cannot create their evidence. We are necessarily forced to play the hand we are dealt. In serious cases we are often required to present credible explanations for the absence of incriminating evidence.

I once attended a trial advocacy course in which the instructor taught that prosecutors should never admit a weakness in opening statement for fear the jury will believe the entire case is flimsy. This is definitely the wrong approach. Above all else, a prosecutor must establish credibility with the jury. The jury does not have to like the prosecutor personally, although it helps. The jury must, however, *trust* the prosecutor. There are always holes in the evidence. No major case is ever "open and shut." Pretending otherwise necessarily means avoiding the obvious.

The prosecutor who, during opening, briefly raises

and then provides a credible explanation about a weakness in the evidence reaps an additional benefit: "stealing the thunder" of the defense attorney who is certainly going to raise that very weakness during her statement. With that in mind, David turned to addressing the issues in our case.

The main problem confronting us was the lack of incriminating forensic evidence at the crime scenes. The police had diligently searched the three homes for Severance's DNA and fingerprints but had come up with nothing. We anticipated the defense making a great deal of noise about this throughout the trial.

David explained the prosecution would call a number of experts to explain that in real criminal investigations it is very unusual to find the suspect's DNA or fingerprints at a crime scene. David foreshadowed our evidence, giving the jurors a taste of what was to come so they would be prepared when our expert witnesses began their testimony.

****

Joe King is a cerebral attorney, projecting calm and measured thoughtfulness when he appears before a jury. For the same reasons that David was the right choice to present our opening statement, King was the right one to present the defense version.

I was interested in hearing King's statement because I had little insight into the defense strategy. In an effort to maintain a tactical advantage, defense attorneys often obscure their theory of the case. The defense is required to provide the government almost nothing about its trial plan. The prosecution usually does not know what defense theories will be presented until defense counsel gives their opening statement. Defense attorneys are given more leeway to play their cards close to the chest.

My team had gleaned some idea as to where the defense was going because of the immense amount of pre-trial litigation. For instance, we knew the defense was planning on implicating Jim Dunning in Nancy's murder. But for the most part we were in the dark about what the other side was going to argue. King's opening promised to reveal more about our opponents' tactics.

Defense attorneys tend to be ambiguous during opening statement. The defense wants the focus to remain on the government's case and does not want to encourage unrealistic expectations. Furthermore, the defense is often not certain how the government's evidence will play out. Defense attorneys usually wait to see the prosecution's case before committing to a definite course of action. Since the defense does not want to promise the jury something they cannot deliver, defense opening statements tend to be filled with more rhetoric than facts.

That was the case with Joe King's opening statement. Instead of delineating the testimony the defense would put before the jury, Joe deftly used his time to introduce several themes: the prosecution's case was founded on circumstantial evidence, the police had conducted a shoddy investigation and had "rushed" to arrest an eccentric gentleman just to calm the public's fears.

King's very first line was an argument: "the evidence will show, time and time again, that the Commonwealth has jumped to conclusions." He alleged there was a "dearth of evidence" incriminating Severance. He said his client's "historical writings" about "frontier history" had been misinterpreted. Lots of argument and very few facts.

Much of King's opening was technically objectionable because it was argumentative, but I made a conscious decision not to object. For one thing, I wanted to hear what he had to say and I understood some argument was inevitable.

I also adhere to a rule of courtesy: unless the defense attorney's comments are completely unreasonable I will not object during opening statement. I am even more loathe to object during closing argument. I have a healthy professional respect for opposing counsel. In a murder case, I expect the defense attorneys know what they are doing and will keep their remarks largely within the bounds of propriety. My commitment to professional comity was heightened in the Severance case where I personally knew all three members of the defense team. I certainly understood they knew how to try a case.

The other reason I do not object during arguments is tactical. If I interrupt and object I am signaling the jury that the defense attorney is seriously hurting my case. Worse yet, judges are likely to give experienced attorneys a degree of latitude and an objection may well be overruled, a sure way to diminish your standing with the jury and emphasize the strength of the defense attorney's argument.

\*\*\*\*

Defense attorneys always try to "humanize" their client, hoping the jurors will see him as a person and not a violent monster. Given the venom spewed by their client, the defense team admittedly had a hard job in trying to humanize Charles Severance. Joe King gamely tried to do so, first by recounting Severance's upbringing. King mentioned Severance's parents and siblings, all of whom were decent, well-adjusted people. He recounted portions of Severance's childhood and his education.

King then delved into Severance's odd beliefs and raised Severance's obvious mental illness. He explained Severance's friends and families had noticed unusual behavior for quite some time. He told the jurors they would about hear Severance's issues and how his disorder might explain his violent ideation and unusual actions.

The defense was going to rely, in large part, on expert testimony about Severance's mental health. This would provide the defense an alternative explanation for the Manifesto of Hate and for other suspicious behavior exhibited by their client, such as the request for asylum at the Russian embassy.

King finished by arguing that when Severance drove to West Virginia in March 2014 he was conducting "historical research" about Native Americans and not, as the prosecution asserted, fleeing from the police. King's last words accused the government of rushing to judgment and "jumping to conclusions" in charging an eccentric gentleman with murder.

King abruptly sat down, signifying that opening statements were complete.

Judge Bellows looked directly at me and curtly said: "The Commonwealth would like to call its first witness?"

It was more of a statement than a question.

# CHAPTER THIRTEEN

*"Thou shalt murder and vengeance is mine saith the Lord."*

Psychologists have established that people listening to a presentation tend to remember the very first and very last pieces of information they hear. In my business this is referred to as "primacy and recency." Crafting a trial plan is an art and good prosecutors make sure they start off a trial on a high note.

We began with the Lodato murder because the evidence directly linking Severance was strongest for this crime. There was an eyewitness to the crime itself, the caregiver, Jeanette, who might even be able to identify Severance as the killer. We were calling two citizens who had observed Severance in the Lodato neighborhood before Ruthanne's murder. We had surveillance video showing Severance's car leaving the scene just two minutes after the murder. This was the core of a persuasive case.

David Lord called the first eyewitness, a neighbor who lived in the same neighborhood as the Lodatos and had a habit of walking her dog during the early morning hours. She testified that on at least three mornings in the month before Ruthanne was killed she saw an unusual man walking around the neighborhood. The man looked out of place and the neighbor formed a distinct mental image of him. On the stand, she described him as having a "full, gray beard, messy hair" and wearing "sort of a baggy tan jacket." She said the man made an impact on her "because of his eyes… they were vacant."

Charles Severance had a penchant for staring vacantly into space. When he was arrested for the Alexandria firearms charge in 1997, he sat in his truck staring straight ahead in what could only be called a "vacant manner" until he was pulled from the car and handcuffed. When the Virginia State Police arrested him in February 2004, the trooper remembered him sitting rigidly in the car, staring straight ahead. Throughout the entire trial Severance spent most of the time vacantly staring straight ahead, unwilling to look at the witnesses testifying in the chair to his left.

When Severance was arrested and his booking photo released to the media, the neighbor recognized him at once and called the police. David Lord asked her whether she saw the same man in the courtroom and she confidently identified Charles Severance as the person that had been walking around the Lodato neighborhood in the weeks immediately preceding Ruthanne's murder.

So far, so good. But Jeanette was next. Given the extreme anxiety she had about the trial her testimony might not go as well.

****

If this story has true heroes, one of them has to be Jeanette. In all of my years as a prosecutor I have never dealt with a victim who was traumatized as extensively by a crime. Neither have I seen a victim overcome that trauma and find it within herself to change the very course of the trial.

Back in February of 2014, before Charles Severance altered her life forever, Jeanette was going about her daily routine. Jeanette truly enjoyed working for the Lodatos and felt a real sense of belonging to the family. She had formed bonds of affection with Ruthanne, Norm,

Mary Lucy and the three Lodato girls.

Charles Severance changed everything in an instant, ripping Jeanette from a safe world in which love and happiness abounded and throwing her into one dominated by horror and violence. Severance walked into Jeanette's life without warning, murdered her friend, almost killed her and then calmly strolled away, leaving her bereft and shaken.

Jeanette was an intensely religious person and Severance's despicable actions had her questioning even her faith. In one early meeting I had with her, she grabbed the crucifix on a black cord around her neck and started to wail. She threw her head on the table before her, pounded it with her fists and howled: "Why would God let this evil man do this!?"

I don't think she expected me to answer the question. I'm glad she didn't, because people far more intelligent have pondered it and been left with unsatisfying responses. That question is unanswerable. Why is there so much sadness and violence around us? Why would an omnipotent, omniscient God allow monsters like Charles Severance to lurk amongst us? Indeed, with so much evil in the world, how is it we were not wiped off the face of the planet ages ago?

Jeanette's lamentations revolved around what is known as the "problem of evil." It is a problem theologians and philosophers have struggled with since time immemorial. It is a problem definitively illustrated by Charles Severance's murderous rampage.

How could a human being so viciously murder three people without facing immediate divine retribution?

\*\*\*\*

I have been in law enforcement for over 20 years. I deal with the worst humans can do to one another. I have seen dozens of bodies, some in an extreme state of decomposition. I have observed mutilated human corpses, to include one case in which the dismembered torso of a murder victim was stuffed into a suitcase. I have formed defensive mechanisms to cope with the misery. The usual method is to detach myself from what I am experiencing. When I look at gruesome crime scene photos, I try to imagine I am looking at fake gore from a Tarantino movie. A person can only take so much evil.

When I first interviewed Jeanette and watched her quickly become inconsolable, the horror of what Severance had done began to sink in. The visceral reaction to reliving the most horrible day of her life affected me physically. When she repeatedly wailed the words "why, God, why?" my heart sunk.

Comforting a grieving victim is one of the most difficult parts of a prosecutor's job. Unfortunately, we often unintentionally make things worse because our job requires us to discuss the terrible things the victim has experienced. I was tormenting Jeanette by taking her back to the most harrowing day of her life. Yet I had to try; I needed to know what she remembered.

Not only did I need her to talk with me about the crimes, I needed Jeanette to testify. She would be forced to walk into a courtroom filled with strangers. Reporters would transcribe every word she uttered. She would have to face the man who had killed her friend and shot her. She would then be cross-examined by a seasoned defense attorney whose only goal was to discredit her testimony. Defense attorneys aren't paid to be nice.

Honestly, I did not think Jeanette would find the

necessary strength inside of her.

I was wrong.

****

David Lord volunteered for the responsibility of handling Jeanette's direct questioning. That David sought this assignment is testament to the kind of person he is. He knowingly accepted an extremely tough job and did so with avidity.

On Thursday, October 8, at about two p.m., Jeanette entered the courtroom and was sworn in as a witness. She started by telling the jury she had worked for the Lodatos for roughly two years prior to the murder. It was her job to take care of Ruthanne's mother, Mary Lucy, preparing her meals, helping her bathe and getting her dressed. She explained she was from Ghana and that English was not her first language.

Turning to the day of the murder, Jeanette said she was helping Mary Lucy do her hair when she heard the front doorbell ring. She remembered a male voice saying something, although she could not hear what it said. As Jeanette narrated what happened next, her voice dropped to a whisper and a hush fell over the courtroom:

**"Then I heard a noise and a scream... I dashed to the door to see what had happened.... I ran through the kitchen and there was this man... I fell down... Then I heard a boom... and I felt pain... I started screaming very hard."**

Jeanette was visibly upset. She sat back in the witness chair, recoiling from the memory of the worst day of her life. Her face showed revulsion but she was not sobbing inconsolably. She was coherent and answering the questions put to her.

She continued, now giving more detail. She described her assailant:

**"A white man, between 50 and 60. A slim man. (His beard) was trimmed... (with) gray hair mixed with white."**

Sounded like Severance to me.

She was also able to describe the gun. Jeanette said she saw the shooter was **"holding something round in the sleeve."** From her hand gestures it was clear that what she was describing was a round gun partially concealed in the sleeve of a coat.

The slide of a semiauto pistol is square in shape. A round barrel is indicative of the cylinder of a revolver. If the killer was able to hold this revolver inside of his coat sleeve and thereby conceal it, the gun had to be very small. Jeanette's testimony supported our position the murder weapon was a mini-revolver.

Jeanette testified the gunman shot her twice, once in her left forearm and once in her side. The second shot caused a small wound but did not penetrate her chest cavity. The gunman then stopped shooting and left the house, walking calmly out the front door without saying a word.

Injured and bloody, Jeanette was able to get up and flee through the back door of the home. She told the rapt jury she went to a neighbor's house and asked him to call 911. Despite the danger to herself, and despite the fact she had been shot, her sense of duty to Mary Lucy compelled her to go back into the home. Jeanette returned and rescued the elderly mother, walking her to the neighbor's house to wait for the police and medics. Incredibly, Jeanette then went back to the house again, this time to help Ruthanne.

The personal courage she showed that day is an illustration of the tenacity of the human spirit. Jeanette, a simple woman who focused on her friends, her work and her religion, was not trained to respond to emergencies. She had no experience in dealing with violence. For most, being shot by an unknown intruder would be enough to convince them to flee the house and wait for the cavalry. But not Jeanette. Her friend Ruthanne needed help.

As Jeanette re-entered the home she saw Ruthanne lying on the floor, still alive. Concurrently, the first police officers arrived on the scene, summoned by the neighbor's call to 911. The officers entered the house and began to help Ruthanne. They figured out Jeanette had been wounded as well and started to dress her wounds. Soon, she was taken to an arriving ambulance.

Jeanette moved on to what happened in the aftermath of the shooting. She told the jury how the composite sketch was created, relaying that a police sketch artist had come to her hospital room to work on it with her. The process took a couple of hours and resulted in the sketch released to the public. She identified a copy of the composite which was admitted into evidence.

An open question remained: whether Jeanette would be able to identify Severance in court? We did not know the answer because, as of yet, Jeanette had never been asked if she recognized him. Jeanette intentionally did not seek out news coverage of the investigation and, to avoid defense allegations we had influenced her into making an identification, we had studiously avoided showing her photos of Severance.

The victims' families, the media and probably the jury were eagerly awaiting the answer.

So was I.

**\*\*\*\***

Throughout Jeanette's testimony, Severance sat in his chair staring directly in front of him. He barely moved. He never looked at the judge or Jeanette. He just focused straight ahead, stone-still.

To give Jeanette the best possible chance of making an in-court identification, we wanted Severance to look directly at Jeanette. She needed to see his face straight-on. David Lord asked Judge Bellows to order Severance to look at Jeanette before she was asked to identify him.

If Jeanette was able to identify Severance from the stand it would be a huge turning point in the trial. Megan Thomas fought our request vehemently, arguing that forcing Severance to look at Jeanette would be a violation of his constitutional rights. Thomas suggested that, instead, Jeanette could come down from the stand and walk over to where Severance sat, positioning herself just feet away from a killer before the crucial attempt to identify was made. I feared Jeanette would be petrified and unable to positively identify Severance as the killer.

Thankfully, Judge Bellows adopted our position and ordered Severance to look directly at Jeanette. Although he had been combative throughout the early portions of the trial, Severance surprisingly complied with Bellows' order without so much as a whimper. As Severance turned his head to face the only eyewitness to his crimes, David asked Jeanette the question we had all been waiting to hear:

**"Ma'am, I would like you to look to your left and tell me if you have seen the defendant before?"**

Jeanette took a deep breath. She exhaled audibly

and slowly rotated her neck. Her eyes locked on Severance and grew wider. Severance squinted narrowly and did not blink at all, turning up the intensity in an effort to mesmerize the woman he had unsuccessfully tried to murder.

Charles Severance was trying to frighten Jeanette through the sheer power of his gaze. He thought he could terrify her so much she would be unable or unwilling to identify him from the stand.

Jeanette raised her left hand to her chin, pondering the question that had been posed. She nodded her head for a second, following the nod with a simple and quiet statement of fact: Severance **"looked like the man"** who had shot her. As soon as she said this, she turned her head sharply to the right and covered her eyes with her hands as though she had just witnessed a ghastly car wreck.

Jeanette's identification of Severance was not emphatic. Saying the defendant "looks like" the killer is different than saying the defendant *IS* the killer.

In the real world, though, prosecutors cannot script a witness' testimony. The fact that Jeanette had been able to come into the courtroom, take the stand, cogently answer David's questions and softly identify Severance as the killer was a minor miracle. We could live with it. There was no use in David pushing Jeanette for a more definite identification.

One of the few things television gets right is the way a prosecutor ends his direct examination. David succinctly said, "no further questions" and sat down.

\*\*\*\*

Cross-examining a witness is one of Megan Thomas' many strong suits. She is quick on her feet and more than willing to engage the witness in a back and forth series of lightning-quick questions. Thomas is prone to making argumentative asides to a witness in an effort to rile them up. She thereby increases the chances the witness, in a moment of high dudgeon, will say something helpful to the defense. If Megan Thomas smells blood in the water, like a Mako shark, she goes on the attack. I would not want to be subject to one of her cross-exams.

A combative attitude works well on cross if the witness is intentionally refusing to answer a question or is trying to shade his answers. The technique does not work as well with someone who is being honest and doing their best to answer truthfully. The more sympathetic a witness is, the less effective a frontal attack on their testimony. Few witnesses could be more sympathetic than Jeanette. No one would believe she was intentionally lying.

Thomas understood this and tempered the tenor of her questions during Jeanette's cross-examination. In a soft voice, Thomas had Jeanette go through the day of the murder yet again, asking her questions about the many details. She got Jeanette to admit the whole thing happened "very fast," a point the defense could use to argue Jeanette did not have enough time to see the shooter very well. Jeanette agreed she was in extreme pain after she was shot and was terrified throughout the events: factors that could help convince a jury Jeanette's soft identification of Severance was doubtful.

Thomas then tried to get Jeanette to say the gun the killer had used was black. North American Arms mini-revolvers are stainless-steel. If the gun used was black, then it probably could not have been one of the two firearms Linda Robra bought for Severance.

Defense attorneys are taught to lead witnesses, thereby getting them to agree with one-sided statements of fact. Many witnesses not used to the pressure of being cross-examined go along for the ride. Much to her credit, Jeanette did not blithely agree with Megan's assertions. When Thomas asked the leading question: "So, what you saw was a black gun?" Jeanette agreed she saw "something black." But she did not agree the gun itself was black. She held her ground and told the defense attorney she "saw something" both "black" and "round."

Jeanette's English was passable, but she was not fluent. She had a difficult time elaborating on certain details. By describing something that was "black" and "round," she was trying to describe the muzzle of the gun—a small, black round hole from which she saw "fire" emit as Severance shot her. Jeanette was not saying the gun itself was black.

Thomas then returned to the million-dollar question. She pointed to Charles Severance and, adopting a strident tone, directly asked Jeanette:

**"You're not certain, sitting here today, that this is the man who shot you, right?"**

Jeanette looked at Severance for a second, then back at Thomas. She sat impassively. From my perspective, time seemed to stop. Jeanette again dropped her chin and for an instant it appeared she would meekly agree she was not certain.

But Jeanette had a quiet courage inside of her. She raised her head and looked directly at Severance.

Then she said, flatly but emphatically: **"Yes, it is."**

Thomas responded with a follow-up she probably should not have asked: **"You can say that with certainty?"**

Jeanette replied confidently with one simple word: **"Yes."**

I almost fell over in my chair. Score one point—no, score one thousand points—for the good guys.

****

As Jeanette got off the witness stand Judge Bellows called a recess. The amazing turn of events I had just witnessed, with Jeanette directly identifying Severance as the killer, was not lost on the reporters in the courtroom. They quickly filed out into the hallway, fingers flying at electronic keyboards, vying to be the first to tweet: "Surviving victim identifies Severance as murderer!" Within seconds it was all over the internet.

I used the stairs to quickly descend to our "war room" on the first floor of the courthouse, bypassing the elevators that were packed with the media and other observers. I was overcome with emotion about what had transpired and I did not feel like talking to anyone.

I arrived at the war room well ahead of the rest of the trial team. I shut the door and fell to my knees and thanked God for what had just transpired in the courtroom. I was overwhelmed by emotion. My first impulse would not normally be to thank my creator, but without thinking I assumed an orans pose and prayed. Once again, in a moment of stress I had instinctively reached out to a higher plane.

When I had first tried to talk to Jeanette about the case she had broken down into fits of inconsolable sobbing. Now she had entered a courtroom, looked directly at the man who had ruined her life and murdered her friend and summoned the courage to confidently identify him in court. She had withstood the crucible of cross-examination and completely changed the tenor of the trial.

For months I had stayed awake at night worried about our prospects. What had just occurred changed everything. Now, near the conclusion of day four of trial, my confidence was growing.

As I knelt and thanked God that afternoon, emotion overcame me. My eyes began to well with tears. And they do again now, as I write these words and remember the day two years, one month and 27 days later.

\*\*\*\*

After the trial was over, Monday-morning quarterbacks criticized the defense team for pressing Jeanette about her identification of Severance during cross-examination. These people, most of whom have never tried a criminal case, held forth bloviating that it was a mistake to give Jeanette a chance to shore up her identification of Severance.

These astute observers weren't aware Jeanette had testified in a pretrial hearing and that her demeanor therein would have led any real trial attorney to the conclusion she was susceptible to cross-examination. Given Jeanette's fear and her struggles to express herself, she appeared to be someone who could be "easily led" by the defense attorneys. I feared she would prove to be what I call a "malleable witness;" one who could be shaped, agreeing with whatever facts the defense attorney concocted.

The defense attorneys accepted a calculated risk by asking Jeanette whether she was certain about her identification. If Jeanette's response to the defense's line of questioning had been "no, you're right, I'm not certain it was him," then the quarterbacks would be praising

Severance's lawyers to high heaven as take-no-prisoners attack dogs. The Severance team took a chance—one that backfired on them. This sort of thing happens to all litigators. It's part of the unscripted, rough-and-tumble of trial work.

What cannot be denied is this backfire was more impactful than most. The one person in the entire world who had seen the Alexandria Assassin committing his crimes had just confidently and repeatedly identified Severance as the murderer.

****

We next called a woman who ran a house-cleaning business and had a cleaning team working near the Lodato residence on the morning of the murder. As she returned to pick her team up from the home, she took a left off of Braddock Road, near the surveillance camera that would catch Severance's car leaving the Lodato scene. After the turn she traveled north on Valley Drive, a minor artery running through the neighborhood. About two blocks from Ruthanne's house she saw a red car coming toward her, southbound on Valley. She watched the car run the stop sign and was afraid it was going to hit her. Fearing a collision, she paid close attention as the car passed her. This is how she remembered what she saw:

**"I made a stop and (this man) was coming with speed. He was supposed to make a stop… it was an old person. I turn my face and see this person… (with) a long beard and long hair."**

She then identified Severance as the person who was driving the car that day. She also identified his car as **"red/orange"** with a **"rusty"** hood. For good measure, she agreed that as he passed her, the defendant was "staring straight ahead."

On cross, the defense established that the woman only identified Severance after seeing his photograph on television after his West Virginia arrest. This is a common problem for prosecutors in big cases. The media is an image-driven institution and as soon as a "person of interest" is identified, the media wants a mugshot of the person to put on the news. Once that photo is published, any witness who thereafter comes forward will be accused of conforming their memory of the suspect's face with that of the published photo. For this reason, I rarely agree to release mugshots to the media.

Inconveniently for the defense theory of television contamination, the witness had also identified Severance's car. She described the car's color and the rusty hood, two specific facts that comported perfectly with Severance's Escort. While Severance's car had been briefly depicted on T.V., its rusty hood was not visible, eliminating the possibility the witness had somehow been exposed to this very specific fact.

Our first three witnesses had identified Charles Severance from the witness stand. One saw him casing the neighborhood in the weeks leading up to the murders. Jeanette identified him as the murderer himself. The third witness identified Severance fleeing right after the murder.

Chris Leibig and Megan Thomas had done a good job cross-examining the witnesses and had scored some points against each individually. However, the defense was running up against what I call the "Rule of Three."

The "Rule of Three" refers to the number of witnesses who are testifying to a particular fact. A defense attorney can usually score points against one individual eyewitness. It is relatively easy to convince a jury a solitary witness is either lying or mistaken about an identification.

The defense attorney's job gets a lot harder when a second witness identifies their client. The job gets to be almost impossible if three independent witnesses concur in the identification. It is extremely difficult to convince a jury that three different people, who do not know each other and who do not know the defendant, have all come into court and pointed to the wrong person.

When I have three witnesses separately testifying about a salient fact I am confident the jury is going to accept it as proven. I think of it this way: the defense attorney may poke a small hole in each witness' individual testimony—on the "micro level"— but she is going to have a hard time explaining how three unrelated people all are lying.

Our three witnesses posed a "macro level" problem for the defense attorneys. How could they explain away three strangers all walking into a courtroom and confidently pointing the finger at their client?

****

After the eyewitness testimony started off our case on a strong note, we edged into the crime scene testimony. We called the experts David had referred to in opening to explain that, in the real world of criminal investigations, it is surprisingly rare to recover incriminating DNA or fingerprints from a crime scene. Experts testified that a criminal's DNA is less likely to be found in cases where he wears gloves, does not touch the victim or is only at the crime scene a short time. In all three of our murders these factors were in play, significantly decreasing the chances the killer left a DNA signature or a latent print behind.

However, the police had an obligation to attempt to recover DNA and prints. If they did not thoroughly search for forensic evidence they could be accused of shoddy police work by the defense. In the Lodato case, for instance, the police examined the front door of the home, the doorbell and the walls of the entryway to the home, looking for DNA or fingerprints. None of these methods revealed any useable evidence.

Consistent with our ethical obligations, we disclosed every failed police attempt to locate incriminating forensic evidence, handing the defense a potent weapon. Each crime scene search that failed to reveal Severance's DNA provided the defense attorneys with a great argument to a jury that may have unreasonable expectations due to the CSI effect. Worse yet, any DNA or fingerprint that was recovered from any of the scenes and subsequently identified as not being Severance's further muddied the water.

Let me provide a specific example. In a murder case, it is standard operating procedure for the police to take fingernail clippings from the victim's body and then examine the clippings for the presence of DNA. A person who is being attacked might attempt to defend themselves, flailing their hands and thereby contacting the attacker. This could, conceivably, result in the attacker's DNA being deposited under the victim's fingernails. Now, the possibility an attacker's DNA would be found under the victim's fingernails is very remote. But the police have an obligation to try everything to identify the murderer.

In the Lodato case police crime scene investigators

completed this process. After the lab analyzed Ruthanne's fingernail clippings, it informed us that a male DNA profile was located under Ruthanne's fingernails. Further analysis revealed it was not Charles Severance's DNA.

Even though there was no evidence Ruthanne had ever touched the shooter—and, therefore, no reason to think it was the shooter's DNA the lab recovered—the reader can quickly see the presence of an unknown man's DNA under Ruthanne's fingernails would give the defense a cudgel with which to crush our case. When I learned an unknown man's DNA had been located in the fingernail clippings, I had nightmares of an indignant Megan Thomas thundering to the jury: "our client's DNA is not at the scene, but another _unknown_ man's DNA is! There is your killer, ladies and gentlemen!"

We ended up being extremely lucky. Oakley submitted Norm Lodato's DNA for comparison to the "unknown" profile from Ruthanne's fingernails. The lab subsequently determined the unknown profile was Norm's DNA. Problem solved.

Consider for a moment if it had not been Norm's DNA. Ruthanne had a home business at which she taught local children how to play the piano. She had contact with hundreds of male students, their fathers and their grandfathers. It was possible the unknown male DNA could have come from any of them. It would have been impossible to figure out whose DNA it was. We would have been left with an "unknown male contributor," and the defense would have pounded the jury over the head, arguing time and again the "unknown" DNA was that of the real killer.

The lack of incriminating forensic evidence constituted a very large "gremlin" in our case. A huge part of our trial plan was providing a compelling explanation as to why it was not surprising to find no forensic evidence incriminating Severance at the scenes. Attempting to explain the absence of evidence is not the type of thing portrayed on television. Reporters don't think it makes for interesting copy. In the real world, however, explaining the weaknesses of your case is an indispensable art.

We called several forensic scientists to discuss the vagaries of DNA and fingerprints. These experts testified that in criminal investigations locating any incriminating DNA and fingerprints is the exception, not the rule. The witnesses revealed DNA and fingerprints do not "float through the air" and that any number of environmental factors, such as temperature, humidity or direct sunlight can affect the deposition of such forensic evidence. In many cases, small bits of DNA or partial fingerprints are recovered, but prove to be too scant for scientific comparison to the suspect. Finally, the experts agreed that if the killer was wearing latex gloves like those found in Severance's car it would be almost impossible to find his DNA or fingerprints.

The Lodato case provided a powerful example of these principles. The evidence established the killer pushed the doorbell button at the front door of the Lodato home. We knew this because Jeanette heard the doorbell ring right before the shooting started. Aware the killer rang the bell, the police completed an extensive examination of the doorbell and the area surrounding it for DNA or prints.

Absolutely no DNA was recovered. Not Severance's. Not anyone's. There was one location that, beyond any doubt, the killer had touched: the Lodato doorbell. No DNA whatsoever was found there. This simple example illustrates how much of a crapshoot crime scene investigation can be in the real world.

A lack of incriminating forensic evidence did not establish that Severance was innocent. Nor did it establish he had not been at the crime scenes.

The absence of evidence is, most assuredly, not evidence of absence.

****

In today's technology-laden world, it is almost impossible to commit three assassinations in broad daylight and not get captured on video. The footage of Severance's car driving away from the Lodato home was a huge part of our case. We knew the defense would have a hard time explaining it away.

Marc Birnbaum's methodical courtroom persona made him perfect for the task of getting the video authenticated and admitted. Marc began by calling the Braddock Road homeowner to explain that he had the cameras installed because his car had been broken into. The owner had personally installed the eight-camera system, which recorded to a DVR he regularly checked. The owner confirmed the system's internal clock was functioning properly on the date of the murder. For good measure, he said he had never had any trouble with the clock.

The images of Severance's car driving past the cameras bore a time stamp just two minutes after Ruthanne was shot. If we could not conclusively establish the time of the video it would lose its efficacy. We could not leave the accuracy of the time stamp solely to the camera's owner. Marc had to shore it up.

Marc corroborated the time by calling Detective Dan Gordon. Gordon, an Army veteran, is a physically imposing man. At first glance, one would expect him to perhaps be an NFL lineman. Close-cropped red hair and youthful features conceal both his true age and the years he spent in the military before joining the police department.

Although he has now been promoted to sergeant, during the Severance investigation Gordon was a detective on the Alexandria Police Department's Electronic Surveillance Unit. This unit is tasked with a number of technology-related duties such as examining cellphones. Gordon's job was to download the video footage from the surveillance camera's DVR and to capture both still images and a slow-motion version of the video to play for the jury. Additionally, he was tasked with double-checking the accuracy of the system's internal clock.

Gordon was outstanding on the witness stand. He took the time to discuss the intricacies of video technology. He explained how he had downloaded the data from the DVR and created both a regular speed video and a $1/8^{th}$ speed video that more readily revealed the details of the Ford Escort. Marc asked Gordon to explain how he checked the DVR's time-stamp. He related that before downloading the video, he turned on the camera system and checked the time displayed by the system with that of his department-issued cellphone. Gordon testified his phone's internal clock was updated remotely by computer and had never, to his knowledge, been inaccurate. He said the time stamp displayed by the DVR system was the same as the time on his cellphone "to the minute." Gordon's testimony removed all doubt: the time displayed on the video was correct.

After Dan finished his testimony, Chris Leibig engaged in a last-ditch defense effort to keep the video from being admitted. The stridency he used in arguing his point made it clear he realized the significance of the surveillance tape. Birnbaum responded to Leibig with a well-reasoned rebuttal and Bellows dutifully admitted the video.

Birnbaum played the tape on the courtroom A/V system and soon the jury saw Charles Severance's car driving away from the Lodato scene, just minutes after Ruthanne's murder. While the jurors could not read the license plate, the similarities between Severance's car and the car in the video were too numerous for the defense to explain away. The make, model and color were identical, as was the dent in the rear quarter panel.

So was the sticker on the rear bumper, just to the right of the midline.

****

While the similarities between Severance's car and the car in the surveillance video were striking, we had to eliminate any doubt.

Marc Birnbaum called Dave Cutting, who had recently been promoted to Detective Sergeant, to identify a series of photographs of Severance's car taken in Wheeling. Marc used the courtroom system to display the photos in turn, giving the jurors several seconds to inspect each one before moving on. Since the photographs were admitted as evidence the jurors would have plenty of time to review them during their deliberations.

The photos prominently displayed the distinctive wheels on Severance's car and the dent in the left rear quarter panel. Finally, Marc showed a series of pictures detailing the shocking bumper sticker affixed to the rear of the car. The round sticker that displayed the words "Assassination City Derby" around the cylinder of a revolver.

It turned out the sticker was the logo of a roller derby team in Texas, but I don't think Charles Severance was a fan of the sport. When you want to slyly broadcast to the world your intent to commit murder with a bumper sticker depicting a revolver, your choices are somewhat limited.

The bumper sticker removed any remaining doubt as to whether it was Severance's car. Although the jurors could not make out the words on the sticker in the Braddock Road surveillance footage, they could easily tell it was the same size and shape as that on Severance's vehicle, and it was in the exact same location.

To ram the point home Cutting and I engaged in a little courtroom theatrics. I had asked Dave to physically remove the Escort's bumper from the chassis. Now, I had the bumper itself brought into the courtroom and admitted as an exhibit. Cutting came down off the witness stand and stood next to the bumper, replete with its sticker, highlighting it for the jurors. In effect, we hit them over the head with this evidence, repeating it for effect through a combination of witness testimony, videos, photographs and, ultimately, the spectacle of the bumper itself being brought into the courtroom and placed directly in front of the jury box.

To close the circle Birnbaum called a design engineer employed by the Ford Motor Company who opined that the vehicle depicted in the surveillance video was a 1997-1999 Ford Escort station wagon. The engineer also raised the unusual color of the car and the aluminum wheels which helped him to identify it conclusively as an Escort. These details mirrored Severance's car to a tee.

Our reinforcing evidence had established, beyond any doubt, that Severance was driving away from Ruthanne Lodato's house just minutes after her murder. An inconvenient fact for the defense, indeed.

We turned now to linking Severance to the Kirby and Dunning cases. To do so, we would have to expose Severance's motives for murder.

****

Charles Severance was a man obsessed with perceived slights and insults. He would take almost anything said about him out of context, construing it as a direct attack on his character. He never forgot the injuries he perceived, either. His anger would fester and grow, unabated in intensity.

Severance's mental issues were markedly different from what most would expect from a "deranged serial killer." He was extremely intelligent and very calculating. There was no evidence Severance suffered from "command hallucinations," disembodied voices urging him to commit violent acts. Likewise, there was never any reason to think he suffered from "bizarre delusions," such as believing aliens were controlling his brain or that his victims were computer-generated avatars.

The prosecution has no legal obligation to establish the motive behind a murder. In my experience, though, juries expect the prosecution to provide the motive. People want to know why a homicide was committed. Failure to establish motive can be fatal to the government's case. I spent countless hours getting into Severance's belief system so I could cogently explain the web of resentment and paranoia that motivated him.

My descent into this darkened mind was assisted by the FBI's Behavioral Analysis Unit(BAU). Numerous discussions with BAU members helped flesh out the story of Severance's thinking. BAU's groundbreaking work has helped law enforcement to identify suspects in countless cases. BAU provides a second service that is unappreciated—helping prosecutors distill the complex schemes of a disturbed mind into a compelling narrative a jury can digest.

****

Severance's motives were complicated. His political theories played a part, as did his feelings of envy for the neighborhood in which the murders took place. Shockingly, his fascination with the British General Braddock and western encroachment into the Ohio River Valley also contributed. But the underlying motive, the real spark that lit the kindling of Severance's anger, was the custody dispute over his son.

Most people would understand a person being extremely angry over a bitter child custody dispute. However, the same people would likely expect the anger to abate during the passage of 13 years. There was a danger the jurors would reason: "Okay, Severance was really mad when the court took his kid away—but that was way back in 2001. No one would remain angry enough to commit murder for 13 years. It just doesn't make sense."

Perhaps most would become less angry, but not Charles Severance. To the contrary, his anger increased as he stewed over what he felt were a series of personal insults and slights. Luckily for us, Severance had repeatedly written about his fury over the custody dispute, both in his composition notebooks and in his internet postings.

As Severance put it: **"My mind on murder and murder on my mind."** Later, the defense team tried to convince the jury this line was just their client quoting rap lyrics; an argument that did not seem to sway the jury.

Another quote was even more difficult for the defense to explain:

**"Suffering father's scheme is rife with murder and greed."**

****

In July 2013, about three months before the Kirby murder, Severance sent an email to a reporter who had written an online article. A police computer investigator recovered that email from one of the computers seized from Robra's home.

The email says, in its entirety:

**"I've been nudging and trolling for over a decade and nobody has noticed. Violence wins. Assassinate because it is in the best interest of the child. Tomahawking a homestead in the backwoods of America."**

There is quite a lot of meaning packed into this short email. At the outset, the reference to "nudging and trolling for over a decade" is a coded reference to the approaching 10-year anniversary of the Dunning murder. The line "nobody has noticed" reveals Severance felt his first murder had not produced the intended outcome. As a result, he had unfinished business to which to attend. Severance's pet phrase "violence wins" speaks for itself.

As he had in hundreds of other missives, Severance used the phrase "the best interest of the child" in the

2013 email, echoing the legal standard by which custody disputes are decided. In Severance's custody battle, the Alexandria judge decided it was "in the best interest of the child" for the mother to be awarded sole custody. Severance seized on that phrase. He appropriated the legal standard used to take his son from him as a sarcastic, oblique reference to his own violent motives. He planned on showing the "law enforcement class" what "the best interest of the child" really was.

Charles Severance did not solely blame the judge who ordered him not to contact his son or the deputies who guarded his final visit with the child. In Severance's mind, all of the City of Alexandria was to blame because the City was rife with "elites." The citizens of Alexandria constituted a corrupt "law enforcement class" that sought to oppress "strong, god-fearing patriarchs" like Charles Severance.

Soon after the custody decision, Severance became bent on revenge. For several reasons, he did not plan on killing those who were directly responsible. First, Severance wanted to get away with murder. He did not want to go to prison and he lacked the physical courage to "go out" in a firefight with the police officers he hated. Second, Severance considered himself a genius. He was convinced he was smarter than those who would be tasked with solving his murders. By killing people who *symbolized* the things he despised—as he put it, the "utopian, *status quo* elites"—Severance could sit back and watch the "law enforcement idiots" struggle to figure out who was doing the killing and why. This would be far more satisfying. It would prove he was smarter than everyone else.

By killing people who were at most tangentially related to him, Severance was engaging in what he called "aversion therapy." This is an actual clinical term in the field of psychiatry, describing a technique in which a patient is encouraged to give up an undesirable habit by associating it with a negative stimulus.

Nancy Dunning's murder was an example of Severance's "aversion therapy." Severance had his son taken away from him. He blamed Sheriff Dunning for this, apparently because Dunning's name was on a protective order served upon him and because Dunning's deputies were present guarding his son during his last goodbye.

By killing Dunning's wife Severance was, in effect, saying: "See how it feels to lose a loved one? Now maybe you'll stop taking children away from their proud, patriarch fathers."

****

On day 11 of the trial Severance's former girlfriend, Linda Robra, was called to the stand. I began Robra's direct examination by asking her to explain how she met Severance. She said their first encounter was a "swing dance" at a local hotel in March of 2011. By the end of that month, Robra had allowed Severance to move into the townhome she owned in Ashburn. Why Robra would allow Severance, an aimless drifter, to move in with her this quickly remains a mystery, but I think the explanation is simple: Severance was adept at manipulation and, in Robra, he met someone who was amenable to being manipulated.

Robra testified Severance always kept his beard neatly **"groomed by washing and trimming"** it. Her testimony clashed with courtroom reality; Severance's beard during the trial was bushy and unkempt.

Throughout the time Severance lived with Robra, he never worked. He was supposed to pay $400 a month in rent but, in the months before his arrest, Severance stopped paying, causing stress on the relationship. I asked Robra about the unusual dynamic she had with Severance. She admitted there was originally a romantic component to it, but it morphed back into a more roommate type of relationship over time. Although Severance slept with Robra on occasion, he would more often sleep in a separate bedroom.

Robra gave some details about how Severance passed his free time. She discussed his penchant for role-playing games, indicating he would spend significant time at a storefront "game parlor" in which he would engage in RPGs with a group of acquaintances. Robra had once played "Mental Disorder," the game Severance himself created and sold on his website of the same name.

Severance would often bring up the Alexandria custody dispute in his conversations with Robra. She admitted he blamed Alexandria's law enforcement community for **"taking away"** his child and remained angry about a protective order that had been served on him by the Alexandria Sheriff's Office in 2001. She agreed he **"was not fond"** of the Alexandria court system.

We then delved into Severance's musings on violence. Robra said he often watched the news and that when a story would come on about a deputy or police officer being shot Severance **"would think this was a good thing."** He found stories of police officers or soldiers being killed **"pleasing."**

I then got her to discuss Severance's views on history, in particular his views about white settlers moving into the Ohio River valley in the late 1700s. She said he was fascinated with this time frame, in part because there was **"a lot of killing."**

Robra said that when discussing the conflict between settlers and Native Americans, Severance often used the phrase "Tomahawking a Homestead in the Backwoods of America."

****

"Tomahawking a homestead" may seem an obtuse phrase to the reader, but I cannot overstate its significance to Charles Severance. He routinely used those exact words, usually as a farewell, both in his voluminous writings and in verbal conversations. He wrote it on postcards, on his website, in his internet postings and over and over again in the Manifesto. What did Charles Severance mean by his regular use of this unusual phrase?

On its face, it would seem to refer to the method by which Ohio Native Americans fought back against the white settlers trying to impose Western law and order. The Native Americans would find a secluded settler's homestead and then beset it, killing everyone inside. Like many other insurgencies throughout history, the Native Americans could not win a traditional military war with the invaders, so they adopted guerilla tactics. They hoped that by terrorizing individual homesteads they could convince the white man to leave the Valley they had called home for generations. In a way, the Native Americans were practicing a form of "aversion therapy," and this is exactly why their methods received Severance's strong approbation.

Severance imagined he was engaged in a guerilla war against an oppressive and haughty opponent, an opponent who wanted to impose its form of law and order on a "proud patriarch." Severance's repeated use of the "tomahawking" phrase was a metaphor for his murders. It allowed him to indirectly take credit for the crimes, doing so in an obfuscated manner which would prevent anyone from divining what he was talking about.

I asked Robra what Severance meant by his "tomahawking a homestead" tagline. Her response was not what I was expecting. She replied: **"it's where you would use a tomahawk to mark the trees on the boundary of your homestead to stake your claim."**

This response was outrageous. Robra had never previously mentioned this interpretation of the phrase and it was a naked attempt to protect Severance. In prosecutor parlance, Robra was "spinning me"—answering my question in a way intended to hurt my case. I felt my blood begin to boil.

I could not let her get away with that throwaway line. I needed her to tell the truth. I used my most authoritative voice, replete with a touch of anger, and repeated the question.

She looked at me for a second. Quiet filled the courtroom. Robra looked down and gulped.

Then she said, *sotto voce*: **"It was also that you would protect your homestead. So, if there was a threat to you or your family, then you were entitled to kill those people."**

****

After allowing these words to linger in the air for a minute, I moved on. Robra said Severance often railed against **"nefarious, status quo elites."** She admitted he was extremely angry at this group of elites and that Severance's anger **"all seemed to relate back to the**

**custody issue."** Severance often said: **"certain people deserved to be shot."**

In a pretrial meeting Robra's recollection of what Severance had said regarding people being shot was slightly different and far more alarming. I sensed she was spinning me again, so I directly challenged her, asking: **"Do you recall if he ever used the word murder in this context?"**

As the word "murder" left my lips, Joe King jumped to his feet and objected, asserting I had asked a "leading question." A lawyer conducting a direct examination is not allowed to "lead" his witness to a specific answer. Direct questions are required to be open-ended and allow for a variety of responses. If a prosecutor wishes to establish that a traffic light was a specific color at the time of an accident, she cannot, on direct examination, ask a witness: "Now, the traffic light was red, wasn't it?" because she has suggested the very answer she is seeking. She must use an open query such as: "What color was the traffic light?"

In contrast, leading questions are always allowed during cross-examination. Leading questions are allowed on cross so the questioning attorney may attempt to impeach the witness' direct testimony.

Whether a question is leading or not is usually in the eye of the beholder. Judges are often too quick to sustain defense objections to supposed leading questions. In this instance my direct question was not technically leading because Robra could have answered it in several ways. The question posed did not suggest which of those alternatives I preferred.

Joe King raised the objection because the truthful answer to my question would be very damaging to the defense. King had to stop Robra from answering.

Judge Bellows quickly overruled Joe's motion, handing me a dual victory because the objection only served to emphasize Robra's ensuing response: **"Yes, he did… He didn't like government in general."** When Severance would talk about the custody dispute, it was **"very upsetting for him. He would say that the legal system was not a very good system."**

Then the payoff line: Severance often said: **"those people"**—those responsible, in his mind, for the custody decision—**"should be murdered."**

\*\*\*\*

Having established Severance was consumed by the custody dispute, I wanted to discuss the guns. Robra admitted she knew Severance had been convicted of a felony and could not purchase firearms. She said he was very angry about his gun rights being taken away by the government and often raised this is a separate justification for hating the **"law enforcement class."**

Robra told the jury she felt comfortable around firearms and owned two .38 revolvers before ever meeting Severance. Soon after Severance moved into her house, he started telling her she needed to buy a smaller gun because the .38s were **"too big"** for her hands. He said he **"used to own a really good, small"** gun he suggested she buy because it would be easier for her to fire.

Severance was telling her the truth. He had previously owned a .22LR North American Arms five-shot mini-revolver. He purchased the gun in 2003 and used it to murder Nancy Dunning.

Robra did not immediately agree to buy the mini-revolver. Undeterred, Severance kept bringing up the subject with her. He printed out pictures of the mini-revolver from the internet and wrote notes about exactly which gun and ammunition he wanted Robra to buy. Soon, his request had morphed. Severance now asked her to purchase two identical NAA mini-revolvers, ostensibly because Robra owned a second house and needed one weapon for each home.

Severance's urging ignored the fact a .22LR five-shot mini-revolver is an extremely poor weapon for home defense. It is difficult to load, it is single action, it packs little stopping power and it carries only five rounds. Given its small size, a .22LR mini-revolver is designed for concealed carry, not for home security.

In preparation for trial, I bought a North American Arms .22LR five-shot mini-revolver, "stainless steel with the wooden grip." At this point in Robra's testimony, I showed her my gun as an illustrative exhibit. Robra agreed it was the same make and model as those she purchased.

I then "published" my gun to the jury. In this sense, the word "publish" meant obtaining Judge Bellows' permission to pass the gun around the jury box so the jurors could handle it. I wanted to impress on them how incredibly small this particular gun was. I wanted the jurors to see it could easily be hidden inside of an adult's closed fist.

Or within the sleeve of a loose-fitting coat.

****

Robra continued, explaining how she had bought the guns on the internet. She recounted the two trips to the Winchester gun shop to pick up the guns and the intervening journey, initiated by Severance, to a Leesburg gun store to purchase .22LR ammunition. Severance walked into the store with her and specified she buy "low velocity" rounds that came in a green and white box. I showed Robra a photograph of a box of Remington Subsonic ammunition; she agreed it was identical to the box she purchased at Severance's behest.

Any doubt as to what kind of ammo was purchased was removed by Severance's own handwriting on an internet receipt recovered from Robra's home office. After writing "2 .22 NAA revolvers" he had scribbled "1 box .22 Subsonic ammunition." He also noted that Robra should buy a gun-cleaning kit. The kit was subsequently recovered from Severance's Escort in West Virginia.

Severance showed Robra how to load the mini-revolvers. Loading this type of gun is a somewhat complicated task. It requires the user to remove the pin holding the cylinder to the gun frame. This causes the entire cylinder to detach from the frame. The user then must hand-load very small rounds of .22LR ammunition, replace the cylinder and screw the pin back in.

In an experiment before trial, I took the NAA mini-revolver I had purchased and practiced taking it apart and loading it. The quickest time I ever clocked was 14 seconds. That may not seem like a long time, but in the middle of an assassination attempt it would be an eternity. The lengthy reloading time explains why Severance did not stop to reload after firing five rounds during the Lodato murder. He did not have time to reload.

After Robra learned how to load the guns she placed each one in a different location on the second floor of her home. One remained in its gun box in a hallway closet. She kept the second inside of a small leather pouch inside a desk drawer in her study. Neither firearm was secured by a lock and the Subsonic ammunition was in the drawer with the second gun, also unsecured. I showed photos of the empty gun box and pouch to Robra and admitted them as evidence.

Robra practiced loading the guns once or twice in the summer of 2012 but then forgot about them. At some point in the fall of 2012 she came home from work and saw Severance cleaning one of the guns. She found this odd because, in her experience, it was only necessary to clean a gun after firing it. Severance said he was cleaning it because guns **"aren't always clean when they leave the factory."** This was an obvious lie and Robra admitted as much on the stand.

Robra testified she never saw the guns again. She only discovered the guns and Subsonic ammunition missing after Severance left her home in March of 2014, concurrently noting he had left her .38s behind. She agreed only she and Severance knew about the guns, she had not been the victim of a burglary during that time frame and that she did not have guests over who walked around her home unaccompanied. Taken together, these circumstances established Severance took the two NAA firearms and the box of ammunition with him when he fled from police in March 2014.

Throughout the pendency of the case the defense attorneys repeatedly argued I was misrepresenting the evidence by insisting Robra had bought the guns "for Severance." The defense repeatedly pointed out that Robra steadfastly maintained she bought the guns "for herself" and not for Severance.

This was an issue of semantics and not of substance. Yes, Robra subjectively believed she was buying the guns "for herself," but Severance subjectively believed

Robra was buying the guns "for him." Robra admitted she never would have purchased North American Arms revolvers had Severance not bade her to do so. Severance picked out the guns on the internet. He told Robra what ammo to buy. He taught her how to load the guns and test fired them himself. He took the guns with him when the police started closing in on him because he knew they could definitively link him to the murders.

No matter what she thought she was doing, Robra bought the guns for Charles Severance. They were his guns.

End of story.

**\*\*\*\***

It may be hard to accept, but Linda Robra was not a knowing participant in Severance's crimes. Charles Severance was intelligent and cunning and he used these attributes to manipulate Robra. He knew what buttons to press and what arguments to make. He played on her instinctive antipathy toward the government and her longstanding familiarity with firearms to goad her into buying his assassination kit.

Severance convinced Robra she was obtaining the guns for her own protection. She had no inkling he planned on using them to commit murder. She did not know Severance's plans and he never admitted his crimes to her. When she was first interviewed, she was clueless as to his propensity for active violence. As time went on and she started to piece it together, I think she realized Severance was guilty.

Robra did know Severance was a felon and not lawfully allowed to possess firearms. She did know he had handled the two revolvers and she willingly kept the guns in areas of her house to which he had entry. She found him cleaning the guns and was suspected he had fired them, so she was responsible for allowing a felon access to guns. While regrettable, her actions fall far short of being an accomplice to homicide.

The reader may question why Robra was not uneasy about Severance's repeated outbursts of anger and fondness for talking about murder. The answer lies in the fact the human psyche is complex and can often believe what it wants to believe.

Despite his antisocial personality and intense ire, Severance possessed charisma. Much in the same way Charles Manson and David Koresh were able to manipulate their followers, over the course of his life Severance was able to find kindred spirits and enthrall them, at least for a while. He was briefly married in the early 1990s. He had a group of oddball friends with whom he commiserated in Cumberland. In Robra, he found another willing acolyte.

Although she did not visit him in jail, Robra maintained an affinity for Severance even after he was charged with murder. She tried to gently shade her trial testimony in his favor. On the other hand, she appeared in court and testified truthfully, even admitting the things that worked against Severance when directly challenged. Her testimony about the firearms was a significant part of the prosecution's case.

****

I finished Robra's direct by shoring up two points. First, I established Robra was not at home in Ashburn on the days of the Kirby and Lodato murders. Her absence allowed Severance to act without her noticing, driving to

Alexandria and back after completing his assassination missions.

Robra worked part-time as a substitute teacher. I provided her a copy of her school work schedule for the relevant time frames and moved it into evidence. The schedule showed Robra was working and out of the house on both of the dates in question.

Finally, Robra testified about the events leading up to Severance packing up and leaving her home. She said she remembered seeing Detective Whelan's business card on her car's windshield on the afternoon of March 6. She thereafter called Whelan and talked to him briefly. Whelan said he wanted to speak to Severance at a time and place of his choosing. He did not tell her *why* he wanted to talk to Severance.

After speaking with Whelan, Robra asked Severance to call the detective. He angrily declined to do so. The next day he told her he had "decided to go camping" and started to pack his belongings. The day after that, Severance started up his Ford Escort and left, destination unknown.

Robra admitted Severance had said nothing about "going camping" before March 7. The first time he mentioned "camping" was the day after the concurrence of Chief Cook's press conference and Detective Whelan's visit to Robra's home.

The very same day he donned the tricorn hat and the poncho and was denied asylum at the Russian embassy.

**** 

A prosecutor builds her case by calling witnesses, and the sequence in which witnesses are called is just as crucial as the content of their testimony. The order of witnesses must present a logical, flowing story to the jury. Crucial testimony should be placed where it will be given emphasis, such as at the beginning of a day. Insignificant witnesses should be clustered in the middle of the trial where they will not be given undue emphasis. Scientific testimony, like our firearms experts, is harder for a defense attorney to successfully impeach on cross-examination. It also tends to reinforce the testimony of earlier fact witnesses. I always try to call expert witnesses near the end of the government's case.

Robra's testimony required the jury to pay close attention and the jurors needed a mental "break" after she was off the stand. We moved on from her testimony and dove into the execution of two search warrants related to the case, one of Robra's home and one of Severance's parents' house. Sean Casey was called to the stand to explain the execution of the search warrants.

Casey started by talking about the search of Robra's house, which occurred on March 12, 2014. He testified about the two spent .22LR Remington cartridge cases he located in Robra's garage. He discussed the empty North American Arms gun box he recovered from the second floor of her home as well as the two .38 revolvers. During Casey's testimony I moved several documents into evidence; these papers referred to the NAA mini-revolvers and had been discovered in Robra's office. Some of the documents had Severance's unmistakable handwriting on them, establishing his knowledge of the guns and specifically referring to Subsonic ammo.

Casey then pivoted to the search of Severance's parents' house, which occurred two days after that of Robra's home. He discussed the box of .22LR Remington Subsonic ammunition he seized from the parents' basement. Severance's father told Casey the ammunition was located in a part of the cellar where his son kept his things. The father confirmed he had not purchased the ammo.

I directed Casey through more details about the ammo. I presented him photos of the box as he explained it originally contained 50 rounds. When he opened it, only 40 rounds were left, leaving 10 rounds unaccounted for. A serial number located on the box allowed Remington to tell Casey the ammunition had been manufactured before Nancy Dunning's murder.

Trooper Murphy testified shortly after Casey. He related his encounter with and arrest of Severance in 2004, two months after Nancy Dunning's murder. He described the .22LR mini-revolver he seized from Severance's Escort that day. I showed him the gun I had purchased and admitted as an illustrative exhibit. Murphy agreed it was the exact make and model of the firearm he had discovered in Severance's car.

This testimony circumstantially proved Severance had access to three different .22LR NAA five-shot mini-revolvers and that his access to these guns jibed with the dates of our three murders. It also proved he had access to two different boxes of .22LR Remington Subsonic ammunition, one at the time of the Dunning murder and another during the time frame of the Lodato and Kirby offenses.

## CHAPTER FOURTEEN

*"Hollow point and below the speed of sound is sweet music and very very effective… because Tomahawking a Homestead in the backwoods of America is the second coming of the Lord Jesus Christ… Violence wins."*

On Thursday, October 15, we began with the search of Severance's station wagon in West Virginia. The FBI had assisted by having its Evidence Recovery Team (ERT) handle the vehicle search in Wheeling. As its name implies, the ERT is an elite group of FBI agents who are trained to locate, seize and document forensic evidence.

The FBI Agent who oversaw the ERT search of the Escort testified that his agents recovered several items of interest from the car. During the search, the ERT seized the two composite notebooks containing Severance's most private thoughts. About 500 pages of documentary evidence were recovered directly from Severance's vehicle.

In addition to the notebooks, ERT located and seized the gun-cleaning kit, a leather bomber jacket and a plastic bag filled with latex gloves. The bomber jacket looked very similar to the one worn by the man depicted in the Target video on the day of the Dunning murder. Subsequent forensic analysis of the jacket failed to provide definitive proof it had been worn during that crime but the physical similarity to the video was striking.

In another coincidence, a 2003 photo of Severance downloaded from his website depicted him wearing a leather jacket exactly like the one seized from his car. We had no way of proving it was the same jacket, but the resemblance was inescapable. What appeared to be the same jacket popped up on three different occasions: the Target video, the 2003 Severance photo and Severance's car.

The latex gloves were an interesting item. There were about 30 pairs of gloves, of the type used by thousands of doctors across the country, balled up and contained in a large Ziploc bag. The gloves were anomalous and no innocent explanation could be divined for their presence in the Escort.

****

I have cultivated a detached attitude about murder and loss as a way of coping with the misery my job requires me to experience. I have participated in far too many conversations with those grieving the violent death of a loved one. In my world, identifying too closely with a victim can cause me to lose perspective and to make trial decisions based on what is morally "right" as opposed to what can be supported by admissible evidence. I always keep some emotional distance from devastated families, if only to protect my own sanity.

Despite this, I found it impossible to avoid being affected by the character of the Dunning family, who had lived through indescribable torture. For years they had struggled with Nancy's horrific murder. The police had been unable to identify a suspect or establish a motive; for a decade the Dunnings feared that death might again descend on their family unexpectedly.

I was well aware of the heavy responsibility I carried with regards to the Dunnings. Not only had Nancy been murdered, the crime had been unsolved for over 10 years—an open wound in the heart of the community. Worse yet, investigators had considered Jim Dunning a person of interest and portions of the community suspected his guilt. If Severance were convicted of Nancy's murder the jury verdict would be an official determination that Jim Dunning was innocent.

Obtaining a conviction in the Dunning case was not going to be easy. Because of the "10-year gap" it would be the hardest murder to prove. Intensifying the drama was the defense team's intention of asserting Jim Dunning's guilt as part of their trial strategy.

While trying to blame an innocent man might seem distasteful, particularly so when he is deceased, a defense attorney cannot avoid an effective avenue of defending his client because it makes him feel bad to pursue it. The Severance defense team had a professional obligation to seek an acquittal on all counts and blaming Jim Dunning was an obvious strategy. That did not make it any easier on the Dunning family, who were horrified to learn they might have to sit through a courtroom exposition on Jim's supposed guilt.

I was direct with the Dunnings about how ugly the defense strategy would be. In a pretrial conference, I explained the defense attorneys had issued subpoenas to almost 20 witnesses. Even some friends of their family were under subpoena. While these people would never intentionally implicate Jim, their testimony would be used to paint him in an unflattering light. I asked whether the family wanted to sit through a trial in which the defense continuously called Jim Dunning a murderer. I suggested they might wish to step out of the courtroom when the topic arose.

I then left the conference room, allowing the Dunnings some space to privately discuss this development. A few minutes later, the door opened and Nancy's son, Chris, beckoned me back into the room. Chris looked directly into my eyes with resolve and said: "Bryan, we've lived with this for over a decade. If we have to live through two more weeks of this, we can do it. We have to see it through." I was moved by his quiet tenacity.

Throughout this trial the dignity and decency displayed by all three families served as an immense source of inspiration for me and my team.

****

On a personal level I did not want the defense attorneys to delve into the theory that Jim Dunning was responsible for his wife's murder. From a purely professional viewpoint, however, I felt the defense attorneys' decision to cast Jim as the guilty party could very well backfire on them.

Of one thing I was certain: there was absolutely no evidence implicating Jim Dunning in Nancy's death. Since there was zero evidence, any defense attempt to cast blame on Jim would allow us to claim the moral high ground. I could stand in front of the jury during summation and thunder about how the defense's attempt at darkening Jim's name illustrated the weakness of their case. I was ready with arguments that would resonate with the jurors.

For example: "The Dunning children had to live through their mother's cold-blooded assassination twelve years ago. Today, they have to live through the cold-blooded character assassination of their deceased father." Or: "How easy it is for the defense to disparage a dead man: a man who cannot take the stand and defend his own name." Or: "Can you imagine, ladies and gentlemen of the jury, how you would have reacted had Jim Dunning been charged on evidence this thin and then you had been asked to serve as his jury? I don't know if you would have laughed or cried at putting a man through that tribulation with absolutely nothing to back it up, but there is no doubt it would have taken you roughly three minutes to find him not guilty."

I would never get to use these arguments because the defense, mid-trial, decided not to use the "Jim Dunning did it" defense. Or, should I say, the defense was convinced that trying to pin the blame on Jim would prove to be disastrous.

I would like to claim the credit for convincing the defense Jim had nothing to do with Nancy's death, but I cannot.

One person was responsible for clearing Jim Dunning's name. In yet another example of what could be called providential pivots in the direction of the case, that person was Jim's son, Chris.

**** 

Given Jimmy Entas is not usually recognized for his sense of empathy, I was concerned he might not be the right person to lead Chris Dunning through a point-by-point recitation of the day of his mother's murder.

I could not have been more wrong. Jimmy's handled the situation with a cultivated sensitivity. His direct examination of Chris Dunning was subtle and incredibly detailed. He found a way to ask Chris the same question in different ways, allowing him to recount the horror of his mother's murder multiple times from slightly different angles. The effect was to focus and amplify the drama of the moment.

This focused drama was unusual given Chris' personality. Chris is a reticent person who does not seek the limelight. I doubt he would be comfortable giving a speech in front of an audience. On the witness stand, however, fueled by a decade of pain and rage, he was fearless. Chris recounted the most painful moment of his life in front of a courtroom full of strangers with aplomb and dignity.

No one who has a brain and a pulse could have watched Chris' trial testimony and thereafter believed Jim Dunning was guilty.

#### ****

Chris Dunning confidently strode into the courtroom with his head held high as Jimmy announced him as the next witness. Chris started by introducing himself and relating the unusual fact that the date of his testimony, October 15, 2015, just happened to be his 35th birthday.

Jimmy immediately directed Chris to the date of Nancy's death. Chris said the plan that morning was to meet his parents for lunch at a local restaurant not too far from their home. This was a regular date for the three of them. They set the time for 11:30 a.m.

Chris arrived at the shopping center where the restaurant was located at about 11:15 a.m. After walking around the for a minute, Chris bumped into his dad and the two of them went into the restaurant right about 11:30.

Nancy was always punctual and, after she was 10 minutes late, Chris grew worried and called her cellphone. The phone rang but no one answered. Chris said it was **"dawning on him"** something was wrong and he **"knew they needed to leave"** to go look for Nancy. Jim and Chris were aware Nancy had planned on going to Target that morning. Since they had driven to lunch separately, they decided to split up to look for her: Chris would drive to Target and Jim to the family home.

The route from the restaurant to Target took Chris directly past his parents' house. When he drove by, he noticed the door to the attached garage open and his mother's car parked inside, prominently displaying the "Dunning for Sheriff" bumper sticker. Reasoning she had made it back from Target, Chris parked out front and walked toward the house. Chris said that as he did so, he felt something was wrong and so he soon found himself **"jogging"** into the garage and then through the unlocked door leading into the house itself.

As Chris entered the home he noticed several shopping bags lying undisturbed on a table. He walked around a corner and into a hallway that led to the foyer. It was then he saw his mom lying on the ground just inside of the front door of the home. When he ran to his mother Chris could see blood on her face. Nancy was unresponsive, so Chris picked up the house phone and called 911. While he was on the phone with the dispatcher, his father arrived at the house and walked in the same door Chris had used to enter. When Jim Dunning saw his wife he took the phone and identified himself as the elected Sheriff.

At this point, in one of the most dramatic points in the entire trial, Jimmy stopped his questioning and asked Judge Bellows for permission to play the 911 call Chris and Jim had made the morning of Nancy's death. Seconds later, the 13-year-old recording started to play.

Chris' sobbing voice washed over a quiet courtroom.

On the recording the jury could hear Jim take the phone from Chris and start talking to the dispatcher. From beyond the grave, Jim Dunning manifested as a presence in the courtroom and the jurors could experience his anguish. Jim repeatedly implored the dispatcher to send help.

After speaking with the dispatcher Jim went to Nancy to check her pulse. Once he had confirmed her heart was not beating, Jim walked down the hallway back toward Chris' location. Chris said his father's **"legs were not really under him. He almost fell, really, when he was coming back."**

Jimmy asked Chris to come down off the stand and illustrate the manner in which his father had walked down the hallway. Recreating that moment was Chris' idea.

Chris stood before the jury. He took a moment to compose himself, which had the effect of heightening the tension. As Chris spoke, his voice crackled with emotion and he faltered. He briefly paused and began anew.

I looked to my right and was surprised to see Severance intently watching Chris' reenactment. For once he was not staring straight ahead.

Chris recreated his father's physical movements in the seconds after discovering Nancy lying lifeless on the floor. The reenactment, coupled with the 911 call, served as a time machine that transported the jurors back to the day of Nancy's murder.

Chris showed the jury how his father lost strength with every step. His movements emphasized Jim's collapse to the ground in a way that words alone would never have been able to. As he slowly fell to the floor, Chris continued to narrate for the jury. Soon his voice broke. Chris was on the verge of tears.

So was I.

Chris ended on his knees with the horror of his mother's murder laid bare. All movement in the courtroom had ceased. I noticed a juror shielding her face with her hands as she turned away.

All air had fled the courtroom.

And with it went the idea that Jim Dunning had anything to do with his wife's murder.

\*\*\*\*

When Nancy Dunning was murdered in 2003, I was a rookie prosecutor. I was far too junior to be asked to work on the case. In the decade before Ron Kirby's death, I had never really read the police reports associated with the Dunning case and I had never listened to the 911 recording. My only information about the investigation was obtained second-hand.

Several people who had listened to the 911 call related that Jim told the dispatcher his wife had been "murdered." Jim's use of this specific word was seen as possible evidence of his guilt. Since Nancy was found at the bottom of the stairs with no obvious gunshot wounds, why would Jim assume she had been murdered? Why not assume she had fallen down the stairs and that her death was accidental? Was Jim's use of the word "murder" an example of Poe's famous "Telltale Heart?"

Those who thought Jim's use of the word "murder" was evidence of his guilt failed to notice one glaring circumstance. That it was not noticed tells me something about human nature: seasoned professionals had fallen prey to what is known as "confirmation bias." These people believed Jim may have been guilty of the crime. They therefore subconsciously looked for "evidence" supporting that belief, disregarding anything tending to cast doubt upon it. Confirmation bias is a widespread problem and can pop up in many different disciplines. In a criminal investigation it can lead prosecutors and detectives down a dead-end street.

I'll give an unusual example of confirmation bias: "ancient alien" enthusiasts. I love watching television shows about the "ancient alien theory." I don't personally think aliens came to earth thousands of years ago and built Stonehenge or Machu Picchu. (As an aside, I have visited both sites and failed to detect evidence of extraterrestrial craftsmanship.) But the idea is provocative and I enjoy the hyperbolic claims put forward on these programs.

I once learned Bigfoot is really a criminal from an alien planet who is serving his sentence in Earth's Pacific Northwest. This is apparently why we don't find the bodies of deceased Sasquatch. Once the podiatrically-enhanced convicts have completed their intergalactic sentences, the Bigfoots—(Bigfeet?)—are transported back to their home planet through an interdimensional portal.

A simpler explanation is we don't find Bigfoot bodies because Bigfoot does not exist.

The ancient alien theorists are guilty of confirmation bias. They have already made up their minds to believe in the theory and cling fervently to any "evidence" that might support it, while ignoring the evidence refutes it. An oddly shaped piece of archaic jewelry establishes jet airplanes regularly flew above the Nazca Lines thousands of years ago. The absence of Bigfoot bodies becomes proof of trans-planet sentence completion instead of evidence Bigfoot does not exist.

Or perhaps the Bigfoot earned parole?

****

What was the glaring fact on the Dunning 911 tape that had been obscured by the specter of confirmation bias?

When Chris Dunning picked up the phone to call the police, almost the first words out of his mouth were: "someone came in and attacked my mom." That is a word-for-word quote from the recorded call. Just like Jim Dunning, Chris had also instinctively assumed his mother's death was an intentional act caused by another person—and not an accident. I had never heard anyone mention Chris' words on the tape. I was stunned when I listened to them for the first time because they so clearly caused a problem for the "Jim Dunning did it" theory.

That Chris also immediately assumed his mother was the victim of a crime meant one of two things: either this assumption was a perfectly reasonable inference based on the way the crime scene appeared or else Chris Dunning was in on a conspiracy with his father to murder his mother. These are the only two plausible explanations as to why Chris and Jim both initially assumed Nancy's injuries were not accidental.

To my knowledge, no one connected to the case ever suggested Chris was part of a complex murder conspiracy. If they had, their reasoning would have been totally divorced from reason, facts and logic.

Human intuition suggested to both Jim and Chris that Nancy was the victim of foul play. Both men made this subconscious assumption and both relayed it to the dispatcher.

The one piece of "evidence" that supposedly supported Jim's guilt turned out not to be evidence at all.

**** 

Even now, several years after the completion of the trial, I continue to have people come up to me at events and say things like "Don't you think Jim had something to do with it?"

Such questions make me cringe. One of the reasons I wrote this book was to answer them once and for all. I will make this as clear as I possibly can: Jim Dunning was completely innocent and had nothing to do with Nancy's death.

Chris even convinced Severance's attorneys Jim was not involved in the murder. The morning after Chris' stirring testimony Megan Thomas approached our table and revealed the defense was releasing all of the witnesses related to the "cast the blame on Jim Dunning" defense. Although she did not explicitly say the defense was abandoning this line of argument, the release of the witnesses tacitly admitted as much.

I felt a wave of relief course through me. I was not certain Severance was going to be convicted, but I was certain Chris Dunning's compelling testimony had cleared his father's name. The poetic justice was not lost on me.

That mattered to me then and it matters to me now.

**** 

We ended the Dunning phase of the case by calling a series of witnesses, starting with the medical examiner who conducted Nancy Dunning's autopsy. Nancy had been shot three times: twice in the chest and once right behind the left ear. The evidence suggested she was shot in the chest twice and then a third time behind the ear after she had collapsed to the floor.

Neither Ron Kirby nor Ruthanne Lodato were shot behind the ear. This difference in M.O. is easily explained. First, as previously noted, killing Nancy Dunning was more personal for Severance. He was practicing "aversion therapy" with regards to the Sheriff, with the message being: "You take my son, I'm going to take someone close to you—and I'll make sure she is taken permanently. How does it feel?"

Another explanation is that Severance did not have enough ammunition at hand for a *coup de grace*. In the Kirby shooting, Ron was able to retreat into his home after being shot in the foyer. As he fled, Severance continued to fire. Since Severance was using a five-shot revolver, he quickly ran out of ammunition and did not have another round to fire once Ron fell to the ground. Similarly, Ruthanne was shot three times and retreated into the living room before collapsing. Severance entered the house after her, probably to deliver a head shot as she lay on the floor, but Jeanette interrupted him. He fired two rounds at Jeanette for a total of five. He did not have any ammunition for another shot.

Several crime scene investigators were called to say nothing had been stolen from the Dunning home, eliminating robbery or theft as a motive. The CSI witnesses also noticed the killer had left a smear of blood on the storm door of the Dunning home. The blood smear was subsequently tested for DNA and identified as containing Nancy's DNA. No other person's DNA was found in the blood smear.

About 18 inches below this blood smear a foreign male DNA profile was located. This profile came from the door's locking mechanism and was nowhere near the blood smear containing Nancy's blood. No blood was recovered from the locking mechanism at all. This unknown "touch DNA"–called that because it was left behind when some unknown person touched the mechanism–was compared to Jim and Chris Dunning and both were eliminated. Once Severance was arrested, his DNA was obtained and compared to the touch DNA profile. He was also eliminated, meaning we had no idea who had left the DNA on the locking mechanism.

This information was divulged to the defense and I realized Severance's attorneys would make it one of the centerpieces of their strategy: "An unknown male DNA profile from the front door? That isn't our client? There is your real killer!"

The unidentified male DNA on the locking mechanism did not in any way prove Severance's innocence in any way. First of all, if Severance wore latex gloves during the attack he would not have left any DNA behind. This was illustrated by an uncontroverted fact: the blood smear higher up on the Dunning storm door was definitely left by the killer as he fled the scene and only Nancy's DNA was recovered from the blood smear. No foreign DNA—zero—was recovered from the smear and this strongly implied the killer was wearing gloves. Gloves like those recovered from Severance's Ford Escort.

There was no specific reason to suspect the foreign male DNA recovered from the locking mechanism belonged to the killer. It could have been left by any male visitor to the Dunning home or even by one of the dozens of police officers who arrived after the shooting. The police try to avoid contaminating crime scenes but are human and sometimes make mistakes.

If the killer had just shot Nancy and was fleeing the scene, there was no reason for him to touch the locking mechanism at all. The mechanism was well below the handle needed to open the door and it was implausible to think the killer knocked on the Dunning's front door and, before shooting Nancy, took the time to lock the storm door behind him. It was far more likely the shooter knocked and began firing right as Nancy answered the door, taking advantage of the element of surprise. And if the storm door wasn't locked, why would the killer touch the locking mechanism as he made good his escape?

The DNA profile recovered from the locking mechanism was the epitome of a "red herring." It meant absolutely nothing, a point I would emphasize in my summation.

****

As I explained earlier, I was a full-fledged member of the investigative team prior to Severance's arrest. The converse was also true: after he was locked up, the detectives became full-fledged members of the trial team. I regularly consulted with the detectives about strategy. Given the detectives' innate understanding of human nature, their ideas about the trial plan were extremely helpful.

We decided the prosecution's case would end with Dave Cutting highlighting specific portions of Severance's Manifesto of Hate. This strategy had two specific benefits: one, Severance's writings were impossible for the defense to cross-examine and two, we would end on a disturbing high note.

There were a couple of significant issues left to address prior to Cutting's testimony: the Target video and the firearms evidence. Because the firearms testimony tied all three murders together it made sense to present it after the Target video, which showed the Alexandria Assassin walking around the store in close proximity to Nancy Dunning right before she was murdered.

The CCTV system in use at the Target in 2003 was not up to 2015 standards. It did not record in high-definition and it stored footage on analog VHS tapes. Since the camera system was of poor quality the images it captured were of poor quality, too. Many of the stills taken from the video appeared distorted when we "freeze-framed" them and put them in digital format for presentation to the jury. FBI attempts to enhance the footage were of little utility. Analog tape is notoriously difficult to enhance.

One thing was certain: the man following Nancy around the store in 2003 looked very different than the Charles Severance sitting in the courtroom. Up until about 2005, Severance had maintained a neat appearance with no beard and short, close-cropped hair. In his younger days Severance was a relatively handsome man but the intervening years had not been kind. His beard and hair had grown into unkempt confusion. He had aged dramatically and now looked far older than his 55 years.

The jury could not look at Severance in the courtroom and compare his appearance to the man depicted in the distorted Target video. We therefore presented the jurors with photographs of the way Severance looked in 2003. Fortunately, Severance had made this easy for us by posting old photographs of himself on the unusual website he maintained. In one he was looking straight at the camera while wearing a leather jacket. This photo also captured an idiosyncratic feature of his appearance: the prominent widow's peak above his high forehead.

The black leather jacket and the widow's peak matched the man in the Target video exactly. In 2003, Severance was the same age, height and weight as the man following Nancy Dunning around the store. Although the poor quality of the Target tape made an absolute identification of the man impossible, the concurrence of similarities allowed me to make a powerful point to the jury: if a disinterested observer were asked to compare the Target video with a 2003 photo of Severance, they would conclude: "It looks a lot like Severance, but I can't be sure." However, when asked to consider all of the other circumstances presented by our evidence, the same observer would be convinced beyond a reasonable doubt that it was Severance on the video.

Our case confronted the jury with a man who looked very much like the younger, cleaner Charles Severance in the Target store on the day Nancy Dunning was murdered. Another man, who looked very much like the older, scruffier Charles Severance, killed Ruthanne Lodato 10 years later.

If the murders were connected—and the firearms evidence we were about to introduce would prove they were—over the decade between the Dunning and Lodato murders the Alexandria Assassin had aged in the *exact same way* and had changed appearance in the *exact same manner* as Charles Severance.

The chances of that being a coincidence were infinitesimal.

# CHAPTER FIFTEEN

*"Thou shalt not kill is a lie. No self-respecting, god-fearing patriarch would not kill me and women who delight in terrorizing his family."*

Though he has since retired after a distinguished career, at the time of the trial Julian "Jay" Mason was the supervisor of the firearms section at the Virginia Department of Forensic Science's Northern Laboratory. He had worked as a firearms examiner for 34 years during which he had conducted somewhere around 5,600 firearms examinations.

Jay and I had worked together on several prior violent cases. I knew he could teach the jury about firearms analysis because I had personally learned a great deal from him over the years. The firearms evidence was absolutely crucial and I needed a consummate professional on the stand to present it. Jay was up to the task.

After a series of questions recounting Jay's academic and professional accomplishments the court accepted him as an expert witness in the forensic examination of firearms and ammunition. I then asked Jay to explain to the components of a round of ammunition and how a firearm functions, to include a detailed exposition on the differences between semiautomatic pistols and revolvers. Jay agreed the absence of cartridge cases at the three crime scenes supported an inference that a revolver had been used. Jay held up the NAA .22LR revolver I had purchased and demonstrated how hard it was to reload.

Jay had done the initial examinations of the ammunition components from the Dunning murder back in

2003, so he started by recounting his work on that case. He told the jury three bullets had been recovered, one from the scene and two from Nancy's body. All three were identified as Remington .22LR plain lead, hollow point bullets exhibiting all of the characteristics of Subsonic ammunition. Jay was also able to observe rifling impressions and determined the pattern to be eight lands and grooves with a right twist—the same pattern created by a North American Arms .22LR mini-revolver.

We moved on to the Kirby murder. Jay had been asked to look at the five bullets that had been recovered, three from the autopsy and two from the scene. With regards to the three bullets recovered from Ron's body, Jay was able to identify them as Remington .22LR plain lead, hollow point bullets; consistent with Remington Subsonic ammunition. The two bullets recovered from the scene also appeared to be Remington Subsonic, establishing that a total of five Subsonic rounds had been fired. On four of the recovered bullets, Jay observed eight lands and grooves with a right twist; the fifth was too damaged to determine the number.

Next was the Lodato murder, in which five fired bullets were recovered. Ruthanne was shot three times and three bullets were recovered from her body. The assailant shot at Jeanette twice, hitting her once and missing once. The round that missed Jeanette fragmented and was unsuitable for comparison. However, the fragments were examined and nothing about them was inconsistent with a Remington Subsonic round.

Jay examined the other recovered bullets and determined all four were Remington .22LR plain lead, hollow-point ammunition consistent with Remington Subsonic rounds. He again observed the rifling impressions of a NAA firearm: eight lands and grooves with a right twist.

Mason continued, noting there was no national gun database that would allow a comparison of bullets recovered from a crime to all guns sold in the United States.

I was also concerned jurors may have heard about "composition testing" of ammunition from outdated television shows. Composition analysis was common in the 1980s. Given a bullet from a crime scene and a box of ammunition from a suspect's home, an expert would attempt to identify the chemical composition of both samples to determine whether the fired bullet originated from the recovered box of ammo. If the CSI effect caused a juror to remember this procedure, he might wonder why the police had not compared the recovered bullets from the Dunning scene to the box of Subsonic ammo found in the basement of Severance's parents.

Jay provided the explanation: by the 1990s composition analysis had fallen out of favor because it had proven to be unreliable and reputable labs no longer conducted such testing. Jay's employer, the Virginia Department of Forensic Science, had not conducted composition analysis for many years.

\*\*\*\*

Mason arrived at the crux of his testimony: although all of the recovered ammunition displayed eight lands and grooves with a right twist, the rifling impressions were sufficiently different to establish no one gun was used in any two of the murders. In Jay's expert opinion, it was likely three different, but very similar guns—indeed, the same make and model—had been used in our murders, with one gun being fired during each of the crimes.

This meshed with the evidence of Severance's gun ownership we had amassed. We had proven he possessed three different North American Arms .22LR mini-re-volvers: one at the time of Nancy Dunning's murder and two more during the time frame in which Ron Kirby and Ruthanne Lodato were murdered. We had established Severance was obsessed with Remington .22LR Subson-ic ammunition and had possessed two different boxes, one during the time frame of the Dunning murder and another a decade later.

Most significant was the following exchange:

PORTER: **"Mr. Mason, over your 34-year career, how many times have you seen Remington .22LR Subsonic ammunition used in a criminal offense?"**

MASON: **"Three times."**

PORTER: **"What were those three times?"**

MASON: **"The three cases we've discussed to-day."**

****

After Mason's stint on the stand I called two oth-er firearms experts, Anne Davis and Gary Arntsen. Both agreed with Jay Mason in all material respects, providing another example of my patented "Rule of Three:" if three firearms experts concurred in their findings, the defense attorneys would have a difficult time rebutting them.

Early in the trial process the defense attorneys had sought their own firearms expert to explore and attack our evidence. The defense identified Anne Davis as their preferred scientist and Judge Bellows appointed her. I was gratified to learn that Davis completely agreed with Jay Mason's opinions. She had conducted about 5,000 firearms examinations in her lengthy career and could not recall ever seeing Remington Subsonic .22LR ammunition used in any crime other than the three Alexandria murders. Even though she had been originally requested by the defense, we decided to call her as our witness.

Gary Arntsen was next. Gary worked in the state lab with Jay Mason and was an accomplished firearms examiner in his own right. Gary likewise supported Mason's conclusions and agreed that in over 3600 cases he had worked, he had not seen Remington Subsonic .22LR ammunition used in any crime other than the three murders at issue in our case.

We had presented the testimony of three forensic firearms examiners with over 80 years of collective experience. These experts had conducted over 14,000 firearms and ammunition examinations over the course of their careers.

The only cases in which they had ever seen this particular type of ammunition used were the three murders committed by the Alexandria Assassin.

There was absolutely no way these three crimes were not connected. Forensic science had provided the link.

\*\*\*\*

I am often asked whether I think Severance committed any other murders during the mysterious "10-year gap." We looked around the country to see if there were similar, unsolved murders in which Severance might be considered a suspect. No such crimes were ever identified and the answer to the question remains "probably not, but it's possible."

I don't think Severance killed during this time period. In my opinion, the Dunning murder was cathartic for him and provided a momentary release for his anger and hate. Like a volcano, it took some time for the vitriol to start building up to another eruption. For Severance, that pressure-building process took just about 10 years.

Severance was also completely obsessed with a particular gun and ammunition combination and would not kill without it. If he did not have access to his assassination kit, he was not capable of acting. It was the combination of his renewed access to the right type of gun and ammunition, courtesy of Linda Robra, along with the upcoming 10-year anniversary of the Dunning murder that spurred him to kill again.

****

Dave Cutting and I spent a lot of time figuring out which portions of the Manifesto of Hate to cast a spotlight on during his stint on the stand as our last witness. The obvious goal was to leave the jury with the unmistakable conviction Severance was an angry, unstable man who was particularly fixated on violence.

Once Cutting was seated, I displayed a letter Severance wrote in April 2005 on the courtroom monitors. Severance had helpfully dated many of the writings contained in the Manifesto and the emails and posts we retrieved from his computers contained date stamps. The references to the calendar helped us place his comments in chronological context and established his anger remained constant over a long period of time.

The letter was addressed to Severance's son, who would have been six in 2005, but it was not truly intended for the child. This letter, and numerous others like it, were probably meant for the boy's mother to read. Alternatively, since the letter was never mailed and remained in the composition notebook, Severance may have just garnered enjoyment by committing his innermost thoughts to paper, and then reading and re-reading them.

Cutting and I started slow, highlighting the following phrase from that 2005 letter:

**"Your father is having a very effective impact on the war. Many of the details are classified, confidential and will remain secret. "**

This letter was written about 16 months after Nancy Dunning was murdered. What grown man writes something like that to his six-year-old son?

\*\*\*\*

In addition to writing a great deal of disturbing notebook entries in shaky script, Charles Severance was a dedicated "troll." He spent a great deal of time reading and commenting on news stories he found on the internet.

The defense attorneys tried to explain the trolling as the disjointed ramblings of an eccentric gentleman. They argued the anonymity of the internet allowed trolls to feel comfortable posting violent ideas online. They emphasized many people leave disturbing commentary on websites, but very few resort to physical violence. While these points could not be denied, Severance's internet postings were exceptionally disturbing. His obsession with violence was illustrated by both the stridency of his tone and the frequency with which he wrote.

A sample of posts Severance composed in the summer of 2013—and which Cutting highlighted from the stand—include:

**"I feel like discharging a firearm."**

**"Scalping privileged members of the enforcement class, honoring family, settling old scores and tomahawking a homestead in the Backwoods of America is fun."**

**"Everything is personal. Family vendetta will settle the score after the kangaroo court."**

Cutting then went on to highlight several 2013 emails that had been obtained from Severance's computer pursuant to a search warrant:

**"All children of the illegitimate enforcement class must be murdered, kidnapped, molested or scalped by divine right. Treating adversaries without mercy is tradition. It makes perfect Biblical and historical sense."**

**"The miserable, lying cowards of the enforcement class are entitled to have their families publicly humiliated and plundered because tomahawking a homestead in the Backwoods of America is in the best interest of the child. Violence wins."**

By themselves, these musings did not prove Severance was a murderer. They did prove that, 12 years after the custody decision of an Alexandria judge, Severance was still exceptionally angry about the ruling. One only has to note his sarcastic references to the "kangaroo court" and the legal standard of "best interest of the child" to be convinced.

His solution to avenging the wrongs he perceived to have been committed against him? "Tomahawking a homestead," "murder" and "humiliating" the "families" of the "enforcement class."

The writings I had cited so far were just the warmup. They got 'better,' I guess, if you can call it that.

The last internet posting Cutting pointed out to the jury before moving on to the most damning, handwritten documents, said:

**"No self-respecting patriarch would not murder an adversary who crosses his family. It has nothing to do with diplomacy, religion, business or national security. Everything is personal. Viva le Vendetta. Vengeance and violence wins. Tomahawking a homestead in the backwoods of America is fun and in the best interest of the child. Violence wins. Let that be a lesson to all members of the enforcement class."**

Starting to get the picture? The jury was.

\*\*\*\*

Charles Severance was a student of history and was extremely well-read, particularly with regards to political theory. His writings exhibited more than a passing familiarity with the writings of Rousseau, Hobbes and Edmund Burke. He was very confident in his own genius, to the extent he disdained other's intelligence and considered himself far smarter than those with whom he interacted.

There is a recurring political theme running through Severance's Manifesto, loosely based on the political writings of Hobbes and Rosseau. Without going into great detail about the thinking of these historical authors, suffice it to say there is a striking disparity in their worldview that Severance somehow reconciled and assimilated into a half-baked political theory.

The French philosopher Rosseau praised what he termed the "noble savage," holding that before the institution of government man lived in a "noble" state and focused on satisfying his basic needs. In sum, the noble savage theory posits that man, before the corruptions of modern government, was innately good and lived a simple life focused on obtaining the necessities of life, such as food, water and shelter.

In contrast, Thomas Hobbes believed man's natural state was inherently cruel and noble savages were, as he famously wrote, destined to live a life that was "solitary, poor, nasty, brutish and short."

One does not have to be an academic to see the distinct differences in these two views of man's natural state. However, the dichotomy did not concern Charles Severance. He lifted the parts of each philosophy comporting with his worldview. From Rosseau, he took the ideas that government corrupts men and that those who lived before the advent of modern government were inherently "noble." These "noble savages" lived in small family groups in a state of natural grace, where the family "patriarch's" word was law and where the family was free from outside influences.

Severance thought that when modern governments tried to tame "noble savages" through the forcible institution of Western law, the angry, violent "Hobbesian" part of the savage was aroused and unleashed. "Proud patriarchs" became justified in lashing out through violent action. They were justified in "tomahawking the homesteads" of those bent on oppressing them.

In Severance's mind, *he* was the noble savage, a patriarch who had been wrongfully abused by a corrupted "law enforcement class." His Hobbesian nature had been aroused and he was justified in revolting against the "utopian elites" that had oppressed him. The revolt would necessarily be violent; after all, "political power comes out of the smoking barrel of a gun." And this justified violence would take the form used by the Native Americans with whom Severance identified: attacking the oppressors in their "homesteads."

The homesteads he would "tomahawk" just happened to be located in a neighborhood in which he had once lived. A neighborhood that, from Severance's viewpoint, represented everything wrong with the "elites" and "law enforcement class." A "backwoods" neighborhood exemplifying the decay of American culture.

One small detail needed to evolve with the times. Severance' tomahawk would be a "deadly" .22 North American Arms five-shot mini-revolver that was "small and easily concealed."

****

Anger at authority, intelligence and a sense of superiority all came together in a perfect wave of resentment and violent thinking. Severance believed he was an unappreciated savant. He saw himself as someone whose intellect was so advanced it could not be understood by the idiots he encountered in his daily life.

Imagine Severance's resentment, then, when he ran for mayor of Alexandria and was laughed at, garnering only a handful of votes. Imagine his indignation in 2004, when the government charged him with a felony and took away his "God-given right" to carry a firearm.

Severance was obsessed with his ability to possess firearms and was outraged when it was taken away. He saw firearms as a vehicle by which he could assert power over a world of morons who did not recognize his intellect. Firearms were the great "leveler." They could make an impotent man feel empowered. They gave Severance the ability, should he choose to act, to lash out against his "oppressors" and teach them a significant lesson. As Severance himself put it, quoting Mao, "political power comes out of the smoking barrel of a gun."

Severance seethed because he had made nothing of himself. He considered himself the smartest, strongest, most handsome, most glorious, most religious patriot in the country. Yet, no one else was smart enough to see it! Others mocked him or accused him of being mentally ill. He could not hold a job, a relationship with a woman or pay his bills. By the time he was in 40, he was an unemployed hermit.

The final straw for Severance, the point at which seething resentment turned to action, was when an Alexandria judge, considering the "best interest of the child," awarded full custody of Severance's son to the mother. Severance thought he had a moral and religious duty to raise his son in his image, just like the patriarchs of the Bible. Secular governmental authority had now immorally intervened in the father-son relationship and "kidnapped" his flesh and blood. The judge disparaged Severance's fitness as a father, insinuating he was mentally ill and ordering uniformed deputies to stand watch over his last goodbye with the child.

And yet the "idiots of the law enforcement class"— whom Severance could see from his small Alexandria condominium on the outskirts of their "safe and secure" Del Ray neighborhood—had all the things that he, in his genius, should have: a large home, stable employment, the approbation of friends, the love of family and the right to raise their children as they saw fit.

Charles Severance decided if he could not have the things enjoyed by his "elite" neighbors in the "safe and secure neighborhood" up the street, the "elites" should not be able to have them, either.

Patience was an excuse for cowardice.

\*\*\*\*

The phrase "patience is an excuse for cowardice" cropped up many times in Severance's writings. It illustrated Severance internally reassuring himself he had a moral obligation to resort to violence. If he displayed "patience" to his "adversaries," in reality he was guilty of "cowardice." Translated, the phrase was Severance's way of saying: "don't deceive yourself, Charles, if you don't avenge the injuries an unjust society has heaped on you, you're not being patient, you're just a coward."

Severance soon developed a complicated political theory justifying the ambush murders as acts of political resistance to a corrupt government. While his theory was not internally consistent or even logical to an outside reader, it made perfect sense to him.

The Manifesto of Hate provided a frightening look into the mind of a murderer:

**"Excessive deliberation is like patience an excuse for cowardice. No political society, no law enforcement authority. State of Nature. Death to the enforcement class and their bourgeois lackeys."**

**"Any man who claims to have authority over another man may be murdered."**

**"I am haunted by the past and being hunted in the present. I can no longer distinguish friend from foe."**

**"Violent change or revolution is necessary to rein in the excesses of government law and order. Effective coercion on the beneficiaries of a government that failed to protect. Innocence died on the cross**

**2000 years ago, the guilty is all that are left."**

**"Suffering father's scheme is rife with murder and greed. By right of might wins, because might does not always make right, but it assuredly makes government."**

**"Murder on my mind and my mind on murder."**

**"Attachments to government cease to be natural when they cease to be mutual. It is not he who dies with the most toys who wins... He who denies the most years of life to his adversary wins."**

**"Thou shalt murder and vengeance is mine."**

And then, perhaps the most chilling lines Severance ever wrote:

**"The last scream of a victim echoes through eternity. It is not dreadful to torture an adversary. It has nothing to do with business, everything is personal."**

**"They kidnap and they die."**

****

The Manifesto of Hate contained numerous references to the guns and the ammunition used in the murders. These documents also detailed Severance's conviction of the efficacy of his assassination kit:

**"I got an amigo who wants to buy a used North American firearm, .22 long rifle, five round cylinder, stainless steel, wooden grip mini revolver made in Utah. It should never have fired medium velocity or high velocity .22 cartridges, only low velocity Subsonic .22 ammunition. On the street or in the hollow, it is called a Mormon Death Squad."**

A "Mormon death squad" was a group of Mormon men who, in the 1850s, would kill Mormons who had committed sins so heinous they could not be saved through grace. Only one method could atone for these misdeeds: the spilling of the sinner's blood. Although some experts believe these groups are apocryphal, the legend is squads of men were authorized by religious leaders to seek out offenders and kill them, all in the name of the church.

In a chilling missive, addressed to the son he had not seen in 12 years, Severance wrote:

**"My son: Please purchase three North American Firearms, .22 mini-revolver and 500 rounds of Subsonic ammunition. The five-round stainless-steel revolver with the wooden grip is small and easily concealed. Thou shalt murder and vengeance is mine saith the Lord. Hollow-point and below the speed of sound is sweet music and very, very effective... Violence wins."**

And yet another specific reference to the guns and ammunition:

**"North American Arms out of Utah makes a beautiful, tiny and deadly .22 mini-revolver, five cartridge, stainless steel Mormon death squad special. Best to discharge Subsonic less-than-speed-of-sound ammunition."**

**"Thou shalt not kill is a lie. No self-respecting, God-fearing Patriarch would not kill men and women who delight in terrorizing his family."**

How on earth would Charles Severance know the "beautiful and tiny" North American Arms .22 mini-revolver was "deadly?"

\*\*\*\*

There was no mistaking it: Severance was a very angry person who had "murder on his mind." The question, however, was whether any of his writings were veiled references to the three Alexandria murders.

Whenever the opportunity arose the defense team forcefully maintained they were not. King and Thomas rammed home the fact none of the murder victims were specifically named: "if these writings constitute a confession to these murders, how come you never see the name Dunning, Kirby or Lodato in them?"

I could provide an explanation for this omission. Severance was extremely cautious. Unlike many deranged assassins he did not want to be caught. He wanted to go on killing those he considered oppressive members of the "law enforcement class" until he obtained "satisfaction." If a killer does not want to be caught it makes sense to be obscure when writing about the killings.

Another possible answer was more disturbing: perhaps he didn't even know the names of his victims.

****

Throughout the early stages of the investigation I had struggled with solving a vexing puzzle: why did Severance pick Nancy, Ron and Ruthanne?

It is clear Severance purposefully selected Nancy Dunning. The evidence suggested he had been waiting outside of her house on the morning of her death and had tailed her as she drove to Target. The video established that, after he grew impatient waiting for her to finish her shopping trip, he entered the store himself. Sheriff Dunning was an identifiable member of the "law enforcement class" whose deputies had booked Severance into the jail in 1997, served him with a protective order in 2000 and stood sentry over his last visit with his child in 2001. As previously mentioned, Nancy's status as Jim

Dunning's wife made her an inviting target for an exercise in "aversion therapy."

It was far more difficult to link Ron and Ruthanne to Severance. Ruthanne's father and brother were both judges, and this would at first blush seem to be a likely reason to target her. However, neither of the judges ever heard a case involving Severance. With regard to Ron, the only conceivable link was his work on the Wilson Bridge—a bridge Severance had taken issue with during his mayoral campaign.

Like most, I originally assumed Ron and Ruthanne had been intentionally selected. As I learned more about the twisted mind with which we were dealing, I became convinced Ron and Ruthanne were random victims who happened to live in the Del Ray neighborhood that was Severance's true target.

Del Ray was the tangible abode of the "enforcement class" and "law enforcement elites." All members of the "enforcement class" were guilty of oppressing Severance, whether or not they had personally participated in the oppression. All members of the "elite" were cogs in a corrupt system by which the government curtailed the personal liberty of "noble savages." Therefore, all Del Ray "homesteads" were fair game for "tomahawking."

Our trial witnesses established Severance had been present in the Lodato neighborhood in the weeks before the murder, presumably scoping out targets. He wanted to kill during daylight hours on a weekday, partly to recreate the Dunning crime, but also to impart the most terror and fear on the City of Alexandria. If pillars of the community could be assassinated in broad daylight by a ghost-like assassin, no one was safe. The terror among the elites would be heightened.

If the goal was to kill someone in an affluent neighborhood it was likely the victim would be affluent, too. Since the murders occurred during daylight hours on a workday, it followed the victim would also probably be retired. It stands to reason retired, affluent people who lived in Del Ray were likely to be well-known and connected to the Alexandria community.

Ron and Ruthanne had the unfortunate luck of living in a neighborhood Severance considered a metaphor for an unhinged political theory. Older, with flexible schedules, they happened to be at home on a weekday morning. Severance was watching through his golf rangefinder and, once he was convinced they both were alone and easy targets, he decided to strike. He waited for the right moment to approach their front doors, a moment when no cars could be seen and no one was on the nearby streets walking their dogs.

\*\*\*\*

Charles Severance never wrote about his specific crimes in detail. He didn't name the victims, list their addresses or expressly state: "I knocked on the door and shot them." However, in several incredible documents, Severance did admit his guilt. He also explained why and how the murders happened.

The first of these handwritten documents, recovered from the Ford Escort and circumstantially dated to 2013, said:

**"Introduce murder into a safe and secure neighborhood. It shudders with horror. Do it again and again and again... Add violence and increase uncertainty among status quo, Utopian-oppressive elites."**

These words, in which he clearly states the goal was

to introduce "horror" into a specific neighborhood, support my position Severance was not targeting particular people. Instead, he was engaging in a violent "reign of terror" that was "increasing uncertainty" among the residents of Del Ray—an area in which residents felt "self and secure." Severance took cruel pleasure in disrupting that sense of security.

As Severance acted "again and again and again"—note the explicit reference to three "murder(s)"—the "oppressive elites" were terrorized and uncertain if they were going to be targeted next. "Elites" might not "oppress God-fearing patriarchs" if they were afraid they could be murdered by an urban assassin. The randomness of the crimes increased the "terror" inflicted on the community.

Cutting proceeded, relating snippets of Severance's writings in a fusillade:

**"Violence on Utopians is the New World Order. Reverse role and become the enforcement class only by violent means, violent change, violent regime change... violent behavior and above all else, violence. Violence wins."**

"Violence wins" was one of Severance's favorite phrases. I would turn that phrase around on him and use it in the conclusion of my closing argument.

**"Murder is good. Court justice is bad. Kill authority. Listen to their screams."**

We ended our case with Severance's written blueprint for murder. In a full-page document resembling a demonic poem, the Alexandria Assassin wrote:

**"The Parable of the Knocker."**

**"The starting torque is 2.5 times the running torque. Therefore, it is better to be firm and decisive."**

**"Knock and the door will be answered."**
**"Seek and ye shall find."**
**"Knock and the door will open."**
**"Ask and ye shall know."**
**"Knock. Talk. Enter. Kill. Exit."**

I still get a chill up my spine when I read these words. It is frightening how dark of a place the human mind can be.

\*\*\*\*

Since the "Parable" was such an important part of the case—after all, it is the title of this book—and because it encapsulates Severance's world view, I will take the time to decipher it in some detail.

The "Parable of the Knocker" was found in one of two bound composition notebooks seized during the search of Severance's Ford Escort. The fact the notebooks were recovered from the car gave an indication of what they meant to Severance. He wanted them close to him as he fled from the police dragnet.

The poem was discovered in what we called the "Green" notebook, simply named for the color of its cover. The Green notebook contained many of the most disturbing and incriminating portions of the Manifesto. Given several handwritten references Severance made to current events, it was possible to circumstantially date the writings inside of the Green notebook to the time frame around 2012-2013, just about the time Ron Kirby was murdered.

After Robra had purchased the guns and ammunition, giving Severance unfettered access to his assassination kit, his writing proved he was explicitly thinking about murder.

****

There is no mention of Hobbes or Rosseau in the "Parable of the Knocker." The "Parable" does exhibit religious overtones with mysterious language evocative of the King James Bible. That is to be expected; Severance was fascinated by religion. When called as a witness by the defense, Severance's mother testified that, in his twenties, Severance joined a cult and started giving most of the little money he had to the "church."

There were numerous biblical references in the Manifesto, to include citations to the New Testament and even a number of Xeroxed pages of the Bible itself, replete with handwritten annotations. He invariably interpreted innocuous passages as justifying violence. In one of many similar writings, Severance corrupted one of the Ten Commandments to read:

**"Thou shalt not kill is a lie... Thou shalt <u>kill</u>, saith the God of Vengeance."**

****

Charles Severance was fixated on the Bible and, as a legion of killers has over the course of history, he found justification for his actions in the words contained in the "Good Book." In his view, both political philosophy and religion required him to respond violently against a government that had attacked him. Severance made this clear when he wrote:

**"What God-fearing Patriarch would not murder men and women who delight in terrorizing his family?"**

The Parable of the Knocker is a dark twist on a real biblical passage known either as "the Parable of the Midnight Knocker" or the "Parable of the Friend at Night" and found in the Gospel of Luke. In the original, a person who needs bread knocks on the door of a neighbor. The neighbor tells the knocker to go away. However, the knocker is persistent and finally convinces his neighbor to give him the bread he seeks. The passage is usually interpreted as emphasizing persistence in prayer.

Immediately following the parable, at Luke 11:9-10, the following words appear: "And I say to you, ask and it shall be given you; seek and you shall find; knock and it—the door—shall be opened to you."

From roughly 1995 to 2001, Severance lived on the outskirts of the neighborhood that would later be the focus of his anger. Nancy Dunning, Ron Kirby and Ruthanne Lodato qualified, at least in his mind, as his "neighbors," and thus the "Parable of Knocker" applied to them.

By repeatedly killing his "neighbors," Severance was being persistent in "knocking" on the doors of his peers and trying to convince them to give him what he craved: freedom from the "oppression" of the "law enforcement class."

**** 

In several of his writings, Severance engaged in an internal debate over whether he should resort to murder. These written debates suggest there was a shred of humanity left in this monster of a man and that Severance struggled with the morality of assassinating innocent victims in their homes. In one document Severance wrote:

**"Can you forgive someone for kidnapping your child? Can you murder someone for kidnapping your child? Forgive or murder?"**

The beginning and end of the Parable of the Knocker contained additional examples of this internal struggle. The very first line said:

**"The starting torque of a motor is 2.5 times the running torque. It is therefore better to be firm and decisive."**

During the trial the defense pointed to these lines as meaningless gibberish, but their meaning was not lost on me: Severance was struggling to find the nerve to kill. He held a degree in mechanical engineering and it was not surprising for him to reach for an engineering metaphor. A quick Google search revealed Severance was stating a physical fact: it takes approximately 2.5 times more energy to start a motor than to keep it running.

As the 10-year anniversary of Nancy Dunning's murder approached, Severance began to feel he had not accomplished his original aims and needed to complete some unfinished business. He found it difficult to start killing again and the reluctance made him ashamed. The engineering metaphor at the beginning of the "Parable" was Severance's way of reassuring himself: "once you kill your first victim, the next ones will be easier."

To reinforce the need to act, he reminded himself at the end of the "Parable" that "patience is an excuse for cowardice." Severance was, in effect, saying to the man in the mirror: "hey, if you wait any longer to start assassinating elites, you aren't a noble savage, you're a coward."

Severance could not stand being a coward. So, he killed again, thinking that by committing murder he was being brave. Ironically, these crimes proved otherwise. It does not take bravery to knock on someone's door and ambush them when they open it.

I left the Parable up on the jurors' monitors for an extra couple of seconds. I wanted those words burned into their retinas.

One thing the movies do get right is what the prosecution says when it is done with its evidence. It was time for me to use that line as Cutting slowly alighted from the witness stand.

"The prosecution rests, your honor."

# CHAPTER SIXTEEN

*"Violence on Utopians is the New World Order. Reverse role and become the enforcement class only by violent means, violent change, violent regime change... violent behavior and above all else, violence. Violence wins."*

With the government's evidence concluded, the trial now moved to the defense case. Severance's attorneys had two enormous tasks at hand. First, they had to convince the jury Severance was obsessed with writing about violent acts but would not turn his musings into action. Second, they had to give a plausible alternative explanation for several damaging facts: why Severance had wanted the two North American Arms revolvers, why he had apparently disposed of them, why he had driven to the Russian Embassy and why he had written so many troubling things in his journal.

The defense attorneys would have to proffer their explanations without their client's testimony because they decided not to put him on the witness stand. The Constitution provides criminal defendants with a slew of due process rights, one of which is the absolute right not to testify. The prosecution cannot force a defendant to take the stand. Most people are aware of this right against self-incrimination through the familiar phrase "taking the Fifth," a reference to the Fifth Amendment to the Bill of Rights.

If the defendant chooses not to testify the government is prohibited from commenting on the decision. A prosecutor cannot argue along the lines of "wouldn't an innocent man accused of murder take the stand and deny it? Isn't a refusal to testify exactly what you would expect from a guilty murderer?" To the contrary, the judge instructs the jury the defendant has an absolute right not to testify and that no negative inference should be made from his decision.

It would have been an egregious mistake to call an unpredictable Severance to the stand and the seasoned defense team was not prone to unforced errors. There were far too many inconvenient facts for Severance to try to personally explain. With his angry demeanor, his proclivity to say outlandish things and his mental health problems, calling Severance as a witness would certainly have proven to be a disaster for the defense.

Severance himself must have understood how dangerous testifying would have been because he acquiesced in the decision. The defendant has the power to decide whether to take the stand and can disregard the advice of his lawyers. Given Severance's belief in his intellectual superiority, there was a slight chance he might turn "maverick" and elect to give his version of events. In the end, his ability to rationally gauge the efficacy of testifying was additional proof he was not "crazy" as that term is often understood.

The defense team was under no obligation to tell us whether Severance would take the stand and I was not certain if we would hear from Severance until the defense rested its case without calling him. *Ex ante,* I had to be prepared in the event he elected to testify; this translated to hours of preparation for a cross-examination that was almost certainly not going to happen.

Even though Severance's was unlikely to testify, I relished the prospect of him doing so. Severance's testimony would have been a dramatic crucible—a battle of wits I was confident I could win. I did not expect a "Perry Mason moment" in which Severance tearfully admitted his guilt. However, I was convinced he would not be able to cogently answer the multiple lines of inquiry I had devised. I also thought I could goad him into displays of intense anger, establishing for the jurors his capability for violence. In the event, I never got the chance to cross him.

\*\*\*\*

Over the course of the trial it became evident Severance was no longer communicating with his attorneys in any meaningful fashion. He was sullen toward them and on a number of occasions told Judge Bellows he no longer desired their representation. He seemed particularly upset about the defense team's injection of his mental health into the case.

Severance's disdain for his defense team had to be frustrating for the three dedicated lawyers representing him. Thomas, Leibig and King worked extremely hard on the case. They fought the Commonwealth's evidence, filing an extraordinary number of pretrial motions. They planned a well-reasoned and coherent defense strategy. They called dozens of witnesses to bolster their arguments and they devised intelligent stratagems to explain some of our most damaging evidence. The defense's collective brilliance made an acquittal a distinct possibility.

Citizens often question how defense attorneys can defend someone like Charles Severance. Negative impressions about "mouthpieces" are reinforced by a defense lawyer's ethical obligation to seek an acquittal at almost any cost and because of the astronomical fees high-profile defense work can harness. In reality, dedicated lawyers defend difficult cases because they believe everyone deserves a champion and because the system only works when the government is put through the paces.

Severance's lawyers were motivated by a professional desire to test the quality of the police investigation and to hold the prosecution to its lofty burden of proving its case "beyond a reasonable doubt."

****

The core of the defense strategy was that, while Charles Severance was an extremely odd person and prone to writing angry screeds, these traits were functions of a mental disorder from which he suffered and did not mean he was capable of violent acts. Severance, in his attorneys' opinion, was all bark and no bite.

Establishing this was the ostensible purpose for introducing mental health evidence in the defense case. I think a secondary reason was to diminish the jury's opinion of Severance's moral culpability in case the jury believed he was guilty of one or more of the crimes. I took to calling this the "insanity lite" defense.

I note my "insanity lite" theory is just an educated guess on my part. The defense team was under no obligation to explain their reasoning to anyone and, to this day, the lawyers have never discussed their trial plan with me. But such a strategy would give the defense three successive fallback positions: "let's seek an acquittal on the theory their case is largely circumstantial. If that doesn't work, maybe we can convince just one juror he is mentally ill but not violent and get a mistrial. In the worst-case scenario, if he is convicted and we convince the jury he is mentally ill, perhaps they will be sympathetic at sentencing."

While the decision to introduce mental health testimony into the case was probably necessary, it was a choice with a marked downside for the defense. It could easily work to our benefit, convincing the jury Severance was unhinged and capable of murder.

As has been discussed, the defense attorneys were not raising the classic insanity defense. Instead, their initial position was Severance was completely innocent. Mental health testimony was introduced to support this position in two specific ways. First, it might explain why Severance would write such alarming, violent missives without intending to act on them. Second, if Severance was irrationally afraid of law enforcement, his mental diagnosis could explain why he sought asylum from the Russians when the police wanted to talk with him. In a nutshell, the defense posited Severance's paranoia accounted for his Manifesto and his attempts to escape the police.

****

Before putting their mental health testimony before the jury, the defense attorneys called Severance's parents, his sister and one of his brothers as witnesses. They also called several people who knew him when he lived in Cumberland, Maryland.

All of these witnesses agreed Severance was sarcastic and angry; they even conceded he was a little unstable. Each also averred that, in their opinion, "Charlie" was incapable of transforming his anger into violent actions. Each was shown still photographs from the Target video and expressed an opinion the man depicted therein was not Charles Severance. Finally, they concurred Severance was fascinated with the playing and creation of role-playing board games and had a "very active imagination," thus advancing a different defense theory: Severance's violent writings were just clumsy attempts at creating role-playing simulations.

I was not impressed with a series of relatives and acquaintances giving an opinion "Charlie" was not the man shown in the Target video. What would one expect his family members to say? Their testimony on this point was inherently biased. As contrast, would it have mattered had I called six police detectives to the stand to say they were convinced the man depicted in the Target video was Severance?

The answer is no, for the obvious reason the detectives were biased against Severance. They were convinced beyond any doubt he was a murderer. Their testimony about the video would have been colored by this implicit antipathy toward the defendant. Both prosecution and defense witnesses were susceptible to the specter of "confirmation bias." Severance's relatives would never believe it was him on the video and the detectives would never believe otherwise.

Whether or not the man in the Target footage was Severance was not a question for an interested witness, it was a question for the jury to decide based on the totality of the evidence.

A series of defense witnesses telling the jury Charles Severance was eccentric and argumentative—maybe, in layman's terms, that he was an unmitigated asshole— but not physically violent was more concerning to me. This supported the Severance team's contention we had charged the wrong man. It also set the stage for the defense to call its most important witness, Dr. William Stejskal, to discuss Severance's mental health.

Dr. Stejskal was an extremely experienced and well-respected forensic psychiatrist. I had encountered him in previous cases and I personally held him in high regard. He would make a compelling witness. He was the defense's best shot at convincing the jury Severance was a just a misunderstood man suffering from mental illness.

I had to poke holes in this "eccentric gentleman" argument. My problem was I would be cross-examining a true expert who had testified in a litany of very serious cases. To make the task more difficult, I would be questioning him about his field of expertise. I was fighting a battle with the doctor on a battleground of his choosing.

There was no denying I was nervous. I felt the case may hang in the balance.

\*\*\*\*

The defense attorneys might have been concerned Stejskal's testimony would backfire. The doctor was a man of integrity and would answer my questions honestly. If I could probe the right areas on cross, Stejskal's testimony might become helpful for the prosecution. It appeared the defense strategy was to get the doctor on and then quickly off of the stand. In the trial transcript, excepting the questions the defense attorney asked about his expert qualifications, Stejskal's direct questioning spans about 35 pages. My cross-exam comprises 74.

Chris Leibig started by recounting Stejskal's impressive resume. Stejskal possessed a master's degree in psychology as well as a Ph.D. He had over 30 years of experience as a forensic psychologist and had previously testified as a mental health expert between 100 and 175 times. It was undeniable; Dr. Stejskal was an expert outstanding in his field.

Leibig moved into the doctor's diagnosis of Severance. Stejskal opined Severance suffered from a "personality disorder with mixed paranoid and schizotypal features." The doctor admitted he could not diagnose Severance with schizophrenia and there was no evidence he suffered from auditory or visual hallucinations. He agreed Severance's speech and thought processes were organized and that he never complained about thoughts being inserted into or withdrawn from his brain, hallmarks of the schizophrenic mind.

Stejskal explained people who suffer from personality disorders lack "adaptive flexibility" when dealing with others. Because they are **"rigid"** in their ways of dealing with others they have **"problems getting along in life."** Stejskal opined Severance had a **"very suspicious, mistrusting attitude toward life in general."** Severance was "schizotypal,"—while he could not be diagnosed as schizophrenic, he displayed certain "schizo"-type behaviors such as "odd thinking."

Leibig went through some of Severance's violent writings with the doctor, having the doctor read them aloud. Stejskal said that, although Severance's ruminations were disturbing, in his expert opinion none of them constituted "homicidal ideation," a point to which I would return on cross. This opinion allowed the defense to maintain the Manifesto was just Severance's way of working out some anger on paper.

Leibig then moved into the final area of significance to the defense, asking a convoluted question about whether an innocent person suffering from paranoia might flee the police and seek asylum at the Russian embassy. Stejskal replied a person with Severance's personality disorder was **"more likely"** than a normal person to flee from the police, given that police knocking on their front door would directly play into their paranoia.

Having obtained the necessary ammunition for arguing the writings were harmless, Leibig sat down.

I rose to start my cross-examination.

\*\*\*\*

Stejskal's diagnosis of Severance was limited by a glaring omission: Severance had refused to meet with him and, therefore, the doctor had never spoken with him. On cross, Stejskal agreed that never conducting an evaluation on a patient was an impediment to rendering an opinion, but he added he was still comfortable with his diagnosis.

I explored the fact that forensic psychology is more of an art than an exact science. There are no rigid formulae by which a psychologist can reach a mental health diagnosis. The field is malleable, with diagnostic criteria changing over time and with doctors relying more on their experience and intuition than in other medical specialties. This is not to disparage psychology; the discipline has an increasingly significant impact on the modern world. It was not the doctor's fault that the complexities of the human mind were not susceptible to algorithmic analysis.

However, given the vagaries of forensic psychology, different doctors may examine the same patient, observe the same behaviors and reach different diagnoses. A doctor's diagnosis of a patient can also change over time as more, or different, behavior is exhibited or as new information is gained. The thrust of my position was diagnosing a mental disorder was far more difficult than diagnosing cancer.

I moved on to Stejskal's opinion of Severance, getting him to recount the symptoms Severance exhibited: a distrust of others, a belief people were exploiting him, a reluctance to confide in associates, an inclination to bear grudges and a tendency to quickly counter-attack when threatened. As I would note in my summation, these are exactly the traits one might expect in a serial killer.

The conclusion of my cross-examination was structured around a point of contention I thought might break my way: whether or not Severance's most violent writings constituted "homicidal ideation." When prompted, Stejskal explained this phrase is a psychiatric term of art that refers to entertaining thoughts of personally killing another human being. To a mental health professional, thinking obsessively *about* murder is not necessarily "homicidal ideation." What matters is whether the person is obsessively thinking about personally *committing* murder.

Severance's writings—such as "Can you murder someone for kidnapping your son?" or "The only good cop is a dead cop"—did not constitute "homicidal ideation" in Stejskal's expert opinion. While I am sure Dr. Stejskal was correct these musings did not meet the textbook definition of "homicidal ideation," this hairsplitting did not comport with common sense. I was convinced I could win what amounted to a battle of semantics.

In effect, Stejskal was telling the jury that, despite hundreds of references to murder, Severance had never engaged in "homicidal ideation." I used the opportunity to confront Stejskal with a dozen of Severance's rants.

The doctor repeatedly denied that phrases like: "They kidnap and they die" constituted homicidal ideation. With every denial I felt the pendulum swinging in our favor.

I asked Stejskal whether the phrase "Murder on my mind and my mind on murder" constituted homicidal ideation. Unwilling to concede the point, the doctor paused and pursed his lips. He then allowed this particular phrase was **"within the ballpark"** of the textbook definition.

Unknown to Dr. Stejskal, I had discovered a Manifesto passage in which Severance did talk about killing people in the first-person tense. I decided to save it, effectively keeping my powder dry and not giving the good doctor an opportunity to explain it away.

Dr. Stejskal was the high point of the defense case. Soon after he left the stand the defense rested. It was time for closing argument.

\*\*\*\*

Closing argument—or summation as it is called in some jurisdictions—is the emotional focal point of any trial. Courtroom rules allow the attorneys substantial leeway to summarize their case. As the name suggests, at this final stage of trial the lawyers are free to recount the evidence supportive of their respective positions.

Closing gives the lawyers their best chance of revealing their personality and skill. Because the purpose of the exercise is to sway the jury, closing lends itself to dramatics and lawyers with a bit of flair find themselves in their element. The ability to present a compelling argument is what earns an attorney the respect of her peers.

To an extent closing argument is a theatrical soliloquy. One person stands before twelve others, attempting to convince them of the righteousness of his position through sheer force of will. An attorney must be confident and cogent, appealing to both the jurors' intellect and emotions. In a murder case closing arguments are lengthy and must be structured in a way that piques the curiosity of the jury. A seasoned trial lawyer will vary tempo and intonation, taking on different personas as required. The kinship with acting is obvious and makes closing argument the part of a trial most frequently presented in movies.

There are actually three separate closing arguments in a criminal trial. The prosecution goes first, providing the jury with its summary of the case. The defense is then given an opportunity to put its slant on the evidence. Finally, the prosecution get another chance to address the jury panel and rebut the defense's contentions. Our opportunity to have the last word is a function of the fact we bear the burden of proving the case.

David Lord gave a spirited and masterful closing argument before Megan Thomas provided the defense's version. David's acuity and quick mind were on display as he reiterated the themes first presented in his opening statement. As much of David's task was recounting the testimony of our witnesses, I have chosen to elide his comments for the sake of brevity.

Attorneys place too much credit on the theory that closing argument is where a case is won or lost. Jurors are intelligent and are usually capable of putting the pieces together themselves. Some may have made up their minds before closing arguments even begin. Nevertheless, the drama involved with summation lends this phase of a criminal trial an aura of heightened significance.

The significance is trebled when a case is as lengthy and complicated. I realized I would be presenting my closing argument almost a full month after the first testimony had been presented. It would be difficult for the jury to remember what our early witnesses had said, let alone recall it in detail. I had a monumental task ahead of me: providing an hours-long summation that kept the attention of a dozen weary jurors, refuted the contentions of the opposing lawyers and meshed a plethora of evidence into a compelling narrative.

****

Megan Thomas began her closing argument with an appeal to the sympathy of the jurors: **"Everyone is suspicious of the middle-aged man with no place to call home."** She had gleaned this sentence from one of Severance's writings and used it as a thematic linchpin. In effect, Thomas admitted Severance was a horrible person. She maintained, however, that anger and vitriol did not prove Severance's guilt. She insisted the police, under pressure to make an arrest, had focused their attention on the first eccentric, "middle-aged man" they encountered. When they learned he resembled the composite sketch, they rushed to judgment and arrested the wrong person, letting the real killer go free in the bargain.

After saying most of the Commonwealth's witnesses had subconsciously become **"helpers"** to the police by shading their testimony, Thomas turned to one of the most incriminating pieces of evidence we had introduced: the surveillance video of Severance's car leaving the scene.

The defense attorneys had spent quite a bit of energy

fighting against the video's admission during the trial. After Judge Bellows ruled it would be admitted, the defense must have realized the jurors would be convinced the video depicted their client's car. The similarities were too numerous to be mere coincidence. Thus, the defense attorneys apparently concluded they had to provide an explanation as to why Severance may have been in the Del Ray neighborhood on the day of the murder.

Megan Thomas provided that explanation. She first opined we had not proven the car on the video was Severance's. She then quickly changed gears, probably because she knew we *had* established it was his car, and suggested that, if the jury agreed it was Severance's Escort, there could be an innocent explanation. Perhaps it was just an unfortunate coincidence? Thomas reiterated Severance's avidity for colonial history, particularly General Braddock's foray into the Ohio River valley in the 1740s.

Perhaps Severance was in Alexandria visiting the historical memorial to his beloved General Braddock on the exact day and at the exact time of Ruthanne's murder?

The memorial with one of Braddock's original cannons, located at the foot of Braddock Hill, in the heart of Del Ray. The memorial situated in the middle of a triangle described by the Dunning, Kirby and Lodato homes.

**\*\*\*\***

As bizarre as it seems, my work on this case leads me to an inescapable conclusion: Severance's fascination with a British general who lived 250 years before him led him to select the neighborhood in which to begin a killing spree.

Severance's obsession with the Ohio Valley during colonial times physically manifested in the way he lived his life. In Alexandria, Severance resided on Gunston Road and referred to his home as "Gunston Manor." Gunston Road was named after Gunston Hall, the still-standing home of founding father George Mason. Mason was an equity partner in the Ohio Company, an organization invested in land in the Ohio River Valley. When Severance left Alexandria he moved to Cumberland, Maryland, the site of Fort Cumberland, the revolutionary-era fort at which General Braddock stayed during his 1755 campaign.

The fact the Braddock memorial is right in the middle of a triangle encompassing the three murder scenes is not a coincidence, nor is the fact that Braddock Road bisects the neighborhood where the murders took place. I don't know the exact manner in which Braddock's ghost played into Severance's murderous plans but I am certain it did. Severance associated the Del Ray neighborhood with General Braddock. Braddock symbolized the white man's efforts to bring "civilization" to the "noble savages" of the Ohio River Valley. Better yet, those native Americans "tomahawked" Braddock during a protracted siege and thus avenged their brethren by spilling Braddock's blood.

Severance used to live in Del Ray. Indeed, he resided there when the "Alexandria elites" decided to take his son away from him. Severance, the "noble savage," had been "a proud patriarch" before the "law enforcement class" interfered in his way of life. Since Alexandria was the starting point of Braddock's foray to civilize the native Americans, perhaps Severance believed that introducing murder into a safe and secure Del Ray was a metaphorical way of battling the origins of Western government.

Del Ray was Severance's Ohio River Valley. The homesteads of the elite deserved to be "tomahawked." Severance had a "duty" to his "class." The duty required violence, because "violence wins."

"Patience was an excuse for cowardice."

For these inscrutable reasons, three people had to die.

\*\*\*\*

Megan Thomas said: **"being in Alexandria isn't a crime.... We know Severance talked about General Braddock.... We know that Mr. Severance liked to visit the same historical sites over and over again.... We know there is this historical site right on Braddock Road.... Even if you believe it was his vehicle on February 6th, it isn't a crime."**

I understand why Thomas offered this argument. It was one she had to make when confronted with a video that indisputably put her client's car in close proximity to a murder. I can imagine the defense team debating this issue and finally deciding they had to say something, to provide some alternate explanation a credulous juror might latch onto.

A criminal trial is not a zero-sum game, with each side trying to convince the jury the evidence is slightly in their favor. The government must clear the high bar of "beyond a reasonable doubt." If a defense attorney can sway a single juror into indecision she might obtain a "winning" result. A guilty verdict must be unanimous, so just one "not guilty" vote results in no verdict being returned at all. This phenomenon is referred to as a "hung jury" and forces the judge to declare a mistrial.

A mistrial ends the case as though no trial had been held at all. The court schedules a new trial date and holds another trial in its entirety, in front of a different jury. Mistrials are commonly perceived as defense victories because the defense has seen the prosecution's entire case and can adapt its tactics in the second trial. Thomas' argument about Severance visiting the Braddock memorial was a 'Hail Mary,' a risky play that might cause one juror to reasonably doubt our evidence and thus secure a mistrial.

The necessity of making the argument did not diminish the opportunity I had just been presented with. As the words escaped Thomas' mouth, I was thinking to myself the defense had just made a major concession, one that ripped a hole in the "somebody else did it" defense.

Severance's lawyers had conceded that he may have been in Alexandria, near the scene of the Lodato murder, on the date of and at the exact time of the murder. If the jurors believed this was just a series of coincidences, all was lost.

**** 

Megan Thomas then moved on the crux of her argument: the government's case was weak and the prosecution had not proven Charles Severance was the killer beyond a reasonable doubt.

Thomas noted the composite sketch was a tool made for and used by law enforcement officers, implying that if the police used the sketch for investigative purposes, it must be a pretty reliable depiction of the murderer. She surmised the sketch constituted **"the best evidence (the**

**prosecutors) have of how"** the murderer looked. She told the jurors the defense had poked holes in Jeanette's in-court identification of Severance as the killer because Jeanette had **"always been consistent that the beard and the hair (in the sketch) are wrong."**

While her argument about the composite was well-constructed, there were two points Thomas could not effectively rebut. First, a composite sketch is not a photographic representation of a suspect; it is an imperfect tool used to generate leads. Second, there were logical explanations for any difference in the beard's appearance between the composite and Jeanette's description. I would provide them in my rebuttal.

Thomas dove into the defense team's take on the firearms evidence. She suggested Jay Mason had developed a **"rooting interest"** in the case and might have subconsciously shaded his testimony to help the prosecution. She emphasized North American Arms was not the only manufacturer that produced a firearm with eight lands and grooves and a right twist. This was technically true, but of no consequence because North American Arms produced the only five-shot, mini-revolver in .22LR caliber. If the jury understood the firearms evidence, this argument would easily be dismissed.

Thomas emphasized Remington Subsonic ammunition was extremely common, with several million rounds produced over the years. In effect, she was attempting to downplay the significance of Severance's obsession with this ammo. If there were millions of boxes of this stuff floating around, was it really such a coincidence that Severance had access to two boxes?

This overlooked a robust counter-argument: if Subsonic ammunition was extremely popular and easily available, shouldn't the firearms experts have seen it frequently used in crimes? If it was ubiquitous, why weren't there hundreds, if not thousands, of violent crimes in which Subsonic ammo was recovered?

With Subsonic ammo so widely produced and sold, that our firearms experts had only seen it used in ***these three murders***, committed within one mile of each other, was even more striking. With millions of rounds in existence, the fact Subsonic ammunition was never used in any crime other than our Alexandria offenses was extremely idiosyncratic.

****

The next part of the defense closing focused on "insanity lite." Thomas conceded Severance fled because detectives came to the house but attempted to explain away the flight through Dr. Stejskal's testimony. She said someone **"with grave and persistent and pathological paranoia… (was) going to do something strange and extreme"** when police wanted to speak with him. Severance hated the police, so he naturally wanted to avoid them when they arrived at his front door.

Thomas minimized the thousands of disturbing writings that had been moved into evidence by relying on Stejskal's diagnosis; it wasn't surprising someone with a personality disorder compiled a disturbing Manifesto.

She admitted Severance's handwritten screeds were **"repugnant (and) awful."** She said it was easy for the Commonwealth to **"pick very bad language"** from the large body of writings, but this **"out of context"** sampling was unfair to her client. She engaged in an impressive oratorical sleight of hand: the writings didn't **"mean what they said they mean"** and should be disregarded.

**\*\*\*\***

Thomas ended her argument as she should have: by arguing that most of the Commonwealth's evidence was circumstantial, by emphasizing the prosecution bore the burden of proof and by reminding the jury Charles Severance was cloaked with the presumption of innocence. She did an admirable job of making these points, finishing in a crescendo of powerful rhetoric:

**"Presumed to be innocent. There are some places in the world where that isn't true. There are some places where the defense has to prove someone didn't do it. That's not here, in this courtroom, in this building in Fairfax, Virginia. Proving Mr. Severance guilty means the Commonwealth has proven their case beyond a reasonable doubt. Anything short of that... means you must find him not guilty. Remember, everyone is suspicious of the middle-aged man with no place to call home, but suspicion of guilt is not enough."**

With that, Thomas abruptly sat down. The defense team had said its last words to the jury.

# CHAPTER SEVENTEEN

*"Knock, talk, enter, kill, exit."*
*"Patience is an excuse for cowardice."*

One thing never shown on T.V. is the immense amount of time prosecutors spend preparing a murder case. While a prosecutor cannot control the outcome of a trial, he can control the amount of preparation he puts into it. I personally dedicated about 50 hours to writing and practicing my rebuttal argument. Late nights and weekends at work naturally followed. It is not an exaggeration to say that, between the police detectives and the lawyers, literally thousands of hours were spent in preparation for this trial.

As the lead prosecutor, I had the responsibility of presenting the government's rebuttal argument. It ran over 100 pages on paper and would take almost two hours to present. The evidence was too complicated and the matter too grave for me to truncate my comments. I had to forcefully rebut every defense argument and emphasize how our evidence pieced together. Nor could I rely on memory; there was too much evidence. While I could not dryly read prepared remarks in open court, I did place them on a lectern as I spoke to make sure I did not omit anything.

I never viewed the trial as a personal battle against the defense attorneys. It was never about notching a career-boosting win. It was about holding Charles Severance accountable for his actions. It was about honoring the memory of the victims and hopefully bringing some solace to their grieving loved ones. It was about publicly clearing Jim Dunning's name. It was about protecting my beloved hometown. It was about stopping the killing.

I had never prosecuted a more important case or presented a more important summation. The weight of the responsibility was tangible; I felt it pushing down on my shoulders as I stood to begin my rebuttal.

But there I stood.

I could do no other.

\*\*\*\*

Vincent Bugliosi was a remarkable man. He is best known as the prosecutor who put Charles Manson away and as the author of a book about the Manson trial, *Helter Skelter*. An outstanding prosecutor, he won 105 of the 106 jury trials he prosecuted and all 21 murder cases he took to trial.

In the wake of the success of his first book Bugliosi wrote a number of others about his experiences. Later in life, he was sought out by the media for his opinions on legal issues. One book he authored, *Outrage*, was Bugliosi's take on the O.J. Simpson prosecution. Oddly enough, that book played a significant role in the Severance case almost two decades after it was written.

My little brother, Scott, is an attorney who currently works for the Department of Justice. In 2014, Scott was a prosecutor in Arlington County, Virginia. He had previously served as a prosecutor in the Bronx and, during his foray in New York, had read *Outrage*. Soon after Severance was indicted, Scott gave me a copy and said it would help me attack the Severance case. He was absolutely right.

At first glance it would appear the book's title, *Outrage*, referred to the crimes Bugliosi was convinced

Simpson committed. In a *double entendre*, the title also reflected his view on the manner in which the Simpson case was prosecuted.

While he placed much of the blame on the defense team, the police investigators and Judge Ito, Bugliosi directed the majority of his ire toward the prosecution. Bugliosi believed Marcia Clark and Jonathan Darden had been distracted by the media circus that came along with prosecuting a celebrity. He was criticizing the very office in which he had built his career and I assume this was difficult for him. Yet he pulled no punches, arguing the prosecutors did not establish confidence in their case and lost sight of what should have been their only focus: the victims of Simpson's terrible crimes.

*Outrage* is Bugliosi's blueprint for how a case should be prosecuted. He emphasizes that, when a person has been "brutally murdered" and is "decomposing in (his) grave," a prosecutor has a solemn obligation to effectively and energetically prosecute her case. He forcefully contends a murder is not just a crime against the victim, but also a crime against the entire community. Bugliosi posited that a prosecutor trying a murder must always remember the victim and their family and use their memory as a motivation to excel.

This attitude infuses Bugliosi's book and reading it had the immediate effect of changing my mode of thinking. Instead of focusing on the stress I was under, I realized I had a moral obligation to focus on bringing an end to the killing. Instead of viewing the case, with its attendant media attention and pressure, as an albatross around my neck, I needed to see it as an opportunity to serve my hometown and the memories of the victims.

The case was not about me. It never had been and it

never would be.

Severance's crimes were an outrage.

It was my job—my sacred obligation—to make sure the Severance prosecution was not.

**** 

Bugliosi's book influenced me in another way. At many points he set out in bold print the exact words he would have argued had he been in charge of the Simpson prosecution. These arguments were clear, forceful and impassioned. Bugliosi had a way of getting beyond the nuts and bolts of a trial and reaching jurors on a more visceral level. His arguments cut through mundane ground interference as though they emanated from a higher plane.

To say Bugliosi's book influenced my rebuttal argument would not do it justice. I borrowed liberally from his rhetoric and directly incorporated it into my summation. But going into the trial, I wondered if I had the ability to follow his lead.

I have played guitar for over 20 years. One of my favorite bands is Buffalo Tom, a trio out of Boston that reached their zenith of popularity in the mid-1990s after producing a series of outstanding albums. Buffalo Tom is still playing and releasing new music. I recently traveled to Boston to watch them play and was happy to see them put on an energetic and entertaining show.

Over the years, I spent a lot of time learning Buffalo Tom songs. I now can recreate a decent version of about a half-dozen BT compositions. While I'd like to think the group's talented lead singer and guitarist, Bill Janovitz, would recognize my cover versions, there is no doubt he would grow angry as he watched my clumsy fingers butcher his work. My attempt to "cover" Bugliosi might likewise fall flat.

Bugliosi wanted *Outrage* to serve as a repository of his theory on trying a murder case. He wrote the book as a game plan for murder prosecutors. In effect, he was saying to members of my profession: "Don't make the mistakes of the Simpson prosecutors. Here are my thoughts: they worked for me, they would have worked in the Simpson case and they can work for you, too." Bugliosi's publisher, W.W. Norton, has given me permission to use excerpts from *Outrage* and I appreciate the privilege. If you enjoy the true crime genre, all of his works are worth a read.

Vincent Bugliosi died in June 2015, about four months before I made my rebuttal argument. I never had the chance to thank him for his unwitting help on the Severance case. The paragraphs above are my attempt to do so.

\*\*\*\*

I stood and walked toward the podium in the center of the courtroom. I paused and looked at the jury, allowing silence to dominate the room for several seconds. The empty air caused the tension to momentarily build. I was no longer nervous and when I began, I did so in a measured, confident tone.

**"I'd like to make an observation. You folks have been sitting here for almost four weeks. You've heard about a hundred witnesses. Because of the complexity and length of this trial, it could be natural for you to think there is a real issue as to whether or not the defendant is guilty."**

**"Well, let me assure you that you have not been**

**here for over a month because there is any real issue of guilt. Mr. Severance's guilt could not be any clearer. We are here because that's how the system works. The Commonwealth brings charges and bears the burden of proof. The defendant concocts a desperate defense, as any criminal would when he realizes that when he is convicted, he is about to become intimately familiar with the inside of a penitentiary."**

**"Based on the mountain of evidence that has been adduced—instead of Mount Everest, I call it Mount Evidence—it is untenable to believe he is *not* the person who committed all three murders."**

Most of this—save the Mount Evidence line—was a vintage Bugliosi argument, intended to provide a powerful start to my rebuttal. It would indeed be reasonable for a juror who had been sitting through a month-long trial to assume there was a real question about the defendant's guilt. I needed to disabuse the jurors of the notion and to assure them that, in a case of this magnitude, a lengthy trial was just par for the course.

I also sought to establish my absolute, unshakeable faith in the defendant's guilt. If the jury sensed I did not believe in Severance's culpability, they would not believe in it either. This was one of Bugliosi's most forceful criticisms of the Simpson prosecutors: they presented their case to the jury in a cautious manner, often seeming apologetic for having to prosecute a famous athlete and thereby telegraphing they were not convinced of Simpson's guilt.

I would not make the same mistake. From the beginning of my rebuttal argument until the final word, I intended to exude confidence in the strength of our case. This was easy, because I knew Severance was guilty.

Notwithstanding what is routinely shown on television, a prosecutor is prohibited from overtly arguing his personal opinions. The evidence is what matters, not the prosecutor's subjective viewpoint. Arguments like: "I've been a prosecutor for 30 years and I am telling you, I've never seen a stronger case" are strictly prohibited and in extreme situations could result in a mistrial.

A prosecutor must engage in subtlety, establishing his conviction in the strength of the evidence through a confident demeanor that does not allow the possibility the defendant is innocent.

**\*\*\*\***

What experience jurors have with the criminal justice system usually comes, to the detriment of prosecutors everywhere, from television shows and movies. Media portrayals of criminal trials always, always, always get it wrong. Sometimes this is done out of ignorance. Sometimes it is because the writers are intentionally trying to make a point about a particular case. Most of the time it is because the plot needs to be broken down to the 44 minutes of screen time contained in a weekly episode.

There is always the chance a jury will be subconsciously influenced by these "fast food" media depictions and expect the case to be easily resolved within a short period of time. Jurors may forget they are involved in a real-life tragedy with real-world consequences—and that in the real world, things are often messy.

A fact present in every single murder trial causes another unavoidable problem: the victim is dead and cannot testify. A jury can easily conceive of the victim as a disembodied abstraction as opposed to a flesh and blood person. Defense attorneys seek to humanize their client;

the prudent prosecutor does the same with the victim.

With this in mind, I transitioned into my next "big idea" argument:

**"The defense in this case is clear: someone else did it. The police, in light of their incompetence and the need for an arrest have wrongfully accused a gentle soul, an eccentric gentleman."**

**"I want to make a point. This is not a movie. This is not a television show. This is not Law and Order or CSI:Miami. This is the real world."**

I put a photograph of the three victims up on the courtroom monitors and continued:

**"I ask each of you to remember that in this case, three real, flesh and blood human beings were murdered for absolutely no reason, gunned down in their homes as they did no more than answer a knock at the door."**

I clicked the remote control in my hand, revealing the next slide. For the first time the jury saw the handwritten "Parable of the Knocker" in its entirety. We had alluded to it and shown parts of it at earlier junctures in the trial, and these glimpses had whetted the jurors' appetite. I watched as their eyes scanned back and forth, reading the haunting words of the Alexandria Assassin:

**"Knock, Talk, Enter, Kill, Exit."**

\*\*\*\*

I displayed another writing from the Manifesto. Severance had helpfully written the date "January 2005" on the top of the page, proving he had composed it about a year after Nancy Dunning was murdered. After railing against the military, the CIA and law enforcement officers, Severance wrote the following passage:

**"Local law enforcement lunatics parade around as though they are exempt from family violence. They are not exempt. They are weak and prone to attack. An effective predator knows."**

While the document did not explicitly refer to the Dunning murder the import of Severance's words was clear: Jim Dunning was the "local law enforcement lunatic." Jim wasn't careful about his safety or the safety of his family and so was "not exempt" from violence to his "family." Jim was "weak and prone to attack." Severance was the "effective predator."

Why would Severance brag about being an "effective predator?" How did he "know" Dunning's "family" was "prone to attack?"

****

I next attacked one of the defense's main contentions: the police, under pressure to make an arrest and thereby calm the fears of the community, "rushed to judgment" and arrested the first unusual man they could find who resembled the composite sketch.

I told the jurors the defense was **"insulting their intelligence"** by telling them another man—one **"who happens to look just like the defendant, who has a hatred for the City of Alexandria like the defendant and who is obsessed with the same gun and ammunition as the defendant"**—had committed the murders. I submitted this might make sense if the crimes at issue were more mundane; my analogy was the universe of people capable of robbing a 7-11 is unfortunately very large but the number capable of committing assassinations in broad daylight was thankfully very small. It was more difficult to argue "the police got the wrong man" when the universe of potential culprits was infinitesimal.

Raising my voice and, with just a hint of sarcasm, I said:

**"What were the police supposed to do? Pretend the evidence pointed toward someone else? Wait to make an arrest just so they couldn't be accused of "rushing to judgment?"**

I pointed out the police had been in no "rush" at all. Nancy Dunning was murdered 11 years before Severance was arrested. Could that conceivably be considered a rush to judgment? Severance was arrested in March 2014, but not indicted for murder until September, after we had spent six months carefully amassing and assessing the evidence. Was that a "rush?"

Once the police were convinced Severance was the killer they had a moral duty to arrest him lest someone else be murdered:

**"How could these officers live with themselves if they just sat back and did nothing and the killer struck again?"**

The nail in the coffin of the "rush to judgment" defense was so definitive I could not wait to hammer it home.

**"Imagine if the police had made an arrest and the murders had continued. The community would have been outraged, the police chief would have been fired and the detectives would have been demoted and forced to walk a foot beat. Contrary to the defense "rush to judgment" argument, the police had a huge incentive to make sure they had the right guy before they arrested him."**

**"To arrest the wrong man would have been unthinkable."**

I also noted an inescapable fact: after Charles Severance was arrested, the murders stopped—proof positive he was responsible.

****

Severance's attorneys had repeatedly emphasized our case relied heavily on circumstantial evidence. Since the phrase "circumstantial evidence" has become synonymous with "weak case" in the public's mind, the defense attorneys were absolutely right to pound it into the collective head of the jury.

I had to convince the jurors there was nothing wrong with our evidence. My voice brimming with confidence, I said: **"My intention right here, right now, is to give circumstantial evidence a public relations makeover."**

Before I explored that topic, I pointed out our case contained a substantial amount of direct evidence. Eyewitnesses had identified Severance as being in the Lodato neighborhood both before and after Ruthanne's murder. Jeanette had directly and repeatedly identified Severance as the person who shot Ruthanne. Many of Severance's writings, most prominently the Parable of the Knocker, could be characterized as partial confessions in that he admitted to owning the right gun and ammo and made cryptic statements consistent with our M.O.

But there was no denying we relied heavily on circumstantial evidence. I hit the matter head on, citing a legal instruction the judge had read to the jurors just before closing arguments commenced: "the combined force of many concurrent and related circumstances, each insufficient in itself, may lead a reasonable mind irresistibly to a conclusion."

The instruction perfectly described the case we had

presented. The Commonwealth had methodically introduced hundreds of related facts and circumstances that
irresistibly led the jurors to one reasonable conclusion:
Charles Severance was a serial killer.

I employed a Bugliosi metaphor, explaining circumstantial evidence was: **"Best thought of not as a chain,
where the breaking of one link causes the entire chain
to fail, but as a rope. A rope is constructed out of hundreds of intertwined threads. Each individual thread
is weak but when bundled with hundreds of others it
forms part of a robust rope. Even if one of the threads
fails and snaps, the rope itself is barely affected because of the combined strength of hundreds of other
intertwined threads."**

Given the imperfect lens of T.V., lay people do not
understand what circumstantial evidence is. Most citizens have no real idea what is meant by the phrase. It
evokes a superficial response—if the prosecution is relying on circumstantial proof, they must not have any
"real proof."

This is a blatant misperception. In reality, prosecutors are forced to rely on circumstantial evidence in almost every murder case they try. I faced the difficult task
of explaining this to the twelve citizens seated before me.

**"DNA is circumstantial evidence! Fingerprints
are circumstantial evidence! Shocking but true!"**

**"Let me explain. The fact someone's DNA was
left at a crime scene does not directly establish they
committed the offense. There are other ways to explain how someone's DNA could have been deposited; perhaps they had innocently visited the scene, by
mere coincidence, the day before the crime was committed. There is no doubt, however, the presence of**

**a suspect's DNA at a crime scene is a circumstance a jury could consider in rendering a verdict. Depending on the case, it may be an extremely powerful circumstance, but it is circumstantial evidence nonetheless."**

Because most people don't understand what the phrase "direct evidence" means they are surprised to learn it does not encompass DNA and fingerprints. DNA and fingerprints may suggest a person committed the crime, but they usually do not directly establish guilt. Inferences must be made from the circumstances.

Really, the only types of "direct" evidence are a defendant's confession, a video of the murder being committed or an eyewitness identifying the defendant as the perpetrator. All directly link the defendant to the crime and require no intervening inferences. Defense attorneys tasked with securing an acquittal have methods for attacking direct evidence: witnesses can be mistaken and videos doctored. Even a videotaped admission to a crime may be suspect: defense attorneys frequently attempt to introduce expert testimony about "false confessions."

Almost every murder case is built upon circumstantial evidence. In a homicide, the best witness—the victim—is dead and therefore cannot testify. In a premeditated assassination like those at issue with Severance the killer is, by design, likely the only other eyewitness. He has a constitutional right to not testify and cannot be compelled to take the stand. In my experience, cold-blooded killers are usually smart enough to avoid confessing; I have only had one homicide in which the suspect admitted his guilt. While camera footage is now frequently amassed and analyzed, I have yet to handle a case in which the killing itself was caught on tape.

Put another way, a prosecutor handling a murder is

usually forced to rely on circumstantial evidence. That is a "real world" fact of my job never discussed or explained on T.V.

Imagine a world in which police detectives and prosecutors were too cowardly to bring murder cases in the absence of direct evidence. Since most murder investigations reveal absolutely nothing directly implicating the suspect, in this hypothetical universe the vast majority of murderers would never be held accountable.

Every murder investigation I have personally been involved with relied to some extent on circumstantial evidence. It follows that, if direct evidence were required before a murderer could be charged, I would never have charged a murder in my career. In every single situation I would have been required to tell a grieving family: "I'm sorry, I am convinced the suspect murdered your loved one in cold blood and I agree we have a very strong case—but it's all circumstantial evidence. He was clever enough to avoid eyewitnesses and did not confess. I'm afraid we cannot bring charges. I wouldn't want to lose."

Spineless jellyfish make poor prosecutors. Someone has to be willing to stand up and do the right thing.

I am proud to say that, when it is done correctly, my profession boils down to doing the right thing. Protecting the citizenry. Protecting our country. Protecting the rule of law. Providing a voice to victims who cannot use their own: children, the elderly and the victims of violent crime. Holding killers accountable so they cannot hurt anyone else.

The media frequently places a microscope on the misdeeds of the very few prosecutors fail to live up to the high ethical and professional standards inherent in the job. I can live with that; district attorneys hold a huge amount of power and should be mindful they will be held accountable if they wield it capriciously or unethically. But the public should rest assured there are thousands of D.A.s fighting the good fight every day on behalf of those who cannot fight it themselves. These dedicated professionals attend to their task with diligence and with respect for the rules of ethics. They uphold the law and the Constitution.

They do so for little fame and less fortune. They are the paradigm of what public servants should be.

\*\*\*\*

I walked closer to the jury box:

**"If, as the defense attorney has argued, the prosecution needs multiple eyewitnesses, the firearms and the killer's DNA at the scene in order to obtain a conviction, in effect we are telling prospective assassins 'just make sure no one is watching, wear gloves and get rid of the gun before the police are on to you and you are home free.'"**

**"This is not and cannot be the law without reducing our society to a state of mortal peril. It's not that easy to get away with murder and when you folks come back into this courtroom with your guilty verdicts, you're going to be telling this defendant, sorry, it's not that easy."**

Having made a series of broad thematic points, I spent a significant amount of time recounting the testimony and putting it together for the jury. I have already explained the evidence, such as the firearms, Jeanette's identification, the Target video, the surveillance video and the Manifesto of Hate in great detail throughout this book, so I won't recount it here.

After 90 minutes of talking, my voice was getting hoarse.

****

I started the final portion of my argument by dissecting Severance's favorite phrase, "Tomahawking a Homestead in the Backwoods of America."

Noting Severance identified with Native Americans and was fixated on the time frame in the 1700s during which Western settlers moved into the Ohio River valley provided context. Portions of the Manifesto quoting Hobbes and Rosseau established Severance's complicated political theory.

When pressed about the "tomahawking" phrase, Linda Robra had admitted Severance used it to discuss Native Americans attacking and killing white settlers in their homes. She agreed Severance thought these tactics were justified.

The totality of these related circumstances established Severance **"lashed out and tomahawked the homesteads of the nefarious, utopian, status quo elites in an effort to defend his class, his socialization, his way of life."**

I knew Severance was defending his "class" when he committed murder because, hidden in one writing from the green notebook, he had explicitly said so. I displayed it as I argued, highlighting the specific quote:

**"I can forgive an affront to myself. I cannot forgive an affront to my class."**

**"I killed as a matter of duty to my class."**

When I first read this document, I was struck with how straightforward Severance was about his motivation. I also immediately noticed he had used the first-person tense when composing these lines.

Dr. Stejskal had repeatedly denied Severance's writings constituted "homicidal ideation" because none of his references to murder were written in the first-person. These particular lines avoided the doctor's very specific objection. I had saved them for this very moment, near the end of my summation, to heighten their effect:

**"I killed as a matter of duty to my class.... Even Dr. Stejskal would have to admit that's homicidal ideation."**

## CHAPTER EIGHTEEN

*"I've been nudging and trolling for over a decade and nobody has noticed. Violence wins. Assassinate because it is in the best interest of the child."*

Just like the end of a fireworks display, it was time for the grand finale. A cascade of powerful rhetoric designed to leave the jury convinced of Severance's guilt. Echoes of Bugliosi's ghost caromed off the walls of the courtroom as I spoke:

**"Now, may I ask a question, one I hazard the defense cannot answer? At what point do all of these facts stop being a coincidence, ladies and gentlemen? When has the moment been reached in which you folks, as intelligent, commonsense people say to yourselves 'oh, come on, you've got to be kidding?'"**

**"When a person is innocent of a crime, chances are there isn't going to be any evidence pointing toward his guilt. Now and then, because of the very nature of life and the absurdity of existence, maybe one thing may point toward a person even though he is innocent. In unheard of situations, it is unlikely but possible that two circumstances may point toward an innocent person as a murderer."**

**"But in this case, everything—every fact, every circumstance, every inference—points directly toward this man's guilt. All of the evidence leads your reasonable minds to the conclusion he is guilty. The conclusion is irresistible. The Commonwealth has set forth for you a staggering number of pieces of evidence that point to this man, and this man alone, as the assassin responsible for robbing this Earth of**

three precious human beings."

"In light of this mountain of evidence, it is simply not humanly possible he is innocent."

****

Prior to starting my rebuttal, I had asked Judge Bellows for permission to stage a dramatic moment. I wanted to cross the courtroom during my oration, stand in front of Severance and look directly at him as I called him a murderer.

Judge Bellows, probably fearing an outburst, gave me some leeway without granting my request in its entirety. Bellows agreed I could walk toward Severance but ordered that I stop at an invisible line running across the courtroom several feet from Severance's wheelchair. The imaginary line was close enough that the drama of the moment would not be lost on the jurors.

I summoned a metaphor directly from Vincent Bugliosi. As I commit it to the pages of this book, it has a certain anachronistic air to it, but it definitely worked inside of the courtroom:

"Back in the 1860's, Victor Hugo, the author of *Les Miserables*, wrote a story about the octopus. In the story, he told of how an octopus is different than most animals. It doesn't have talons to defend itself. It doesn't have claws like a lion or teeth like an alligator, but it does have what an ink bag and, to protect itself when it is attacked, the octopus lets out a dark fluid, thus making all of the surrounding water murky. In this manner, the octopus may escape into the darkness."

"Now, I ask you folks, is there any similarity between the octopus' ink bag and the defense in this case?"

**"Have they shown you any real, valid, legitimate defense, reasonably based on the evidence that has been adduced, or have they sought to employ the ink bag of the octopus and, by trying to make everything dark and murky around Mr. Severance, allow him to avoid accountability and escape into the darkness."**

**"I intend to clear up that water."**

I strode across the courtroom to the Bellows line. I bladed my body at a 45-degree angle to the jury box so I could look at both the jury and Severance without moving my entire body. Severance sat stoically, staring straight ahead without blinking.

At the outset of the case, I suffered from a lack of confidence. I doubted whether I had the necessary skill to steer it to a positive conclusion. I lamented the fact I had caught my "career case" one month into my first term. The inherent stress directly affected my life and that of my loved ones.

With the help of many I had regained my confidence. I now realized I had signed up for the job. I had a solemn obligation to the victims, their families and my hometown community. Emotion crackled inside of me. I was now extremely close to the end of an incredible journey in which I had grown as a lawyer and a person.

I got as close to Severance as Judge Bellows would allow and, with a strident voice and welling confidence, boomed:

**"Behold the octopus!"**

**"The water has cleared from around him. No more murk, no more mud! Exposed for what he truly is: a murderer!"**

**"A clever murderer perhaps—but also a coward-**

ly one. Running around shooting people when they answered a knock on their doors."

"He got away with it for twelve years. It's time those twelve years came to an end."

****

I ended by breaking out of the microcosm of the case and speaking to the jury openly about the timeless struggle of good versus evil. I felt the words made an impact because they spoke to the human condition. Since I have failed to find a way to accurately synopsize the tenor of my conclusory remarks, I will reproduce them in their entirety:

"For thousands of years, theologians and philosophers have struggled with an inherent problem posed by the construct of a divine creator. It is known as the problem of evil: If the world is created by some benevolent, omnipotent being, why does evil exist at all?"

"Mainstream religions come up with complicated theological systems in which evil is allowed to exist because of free will or our inability to walk the true path. These systems evolve so there can continue to be an internally consistent theory that has a single benevolent creator at its core."

"Unfortunately—and perhaps I am jaded by the world of violence and retribution in which I live and work—but the world I see is different. The world I see around me is better explained by a completely different system, one in which two polar opposites—call them what you will: positive and negative, yin and yang, light and dark, good and evil—are constantly fighting and struggling for supremacy."

**"Sometimes it seems the evil is winning. Sometimes, I question whether man is inherently good at all. But then I realize something. If the evil of mankind outweighed the good, we wouldn't be here at all. If the evil outweighs the good, then mankind would have been doomed to the darkness of despair eons ago and none of us would be right now in this courtroom, deciding this extremely grave case."**

**"By a slim margin, by a razor's breadth perhaps, nonetheless the good outweighs the evil. It has to be that way."**

Giving a speech in front of dozens of strangers with television and newspaper reporters recording your every word is a difficult proposition. The difficulty is compounded when the speech involves you opening your heart and telling those strangers your innermost thoughts about religion and love, good and evil. Yet, as I stood before the jury and explained my deepest philosophical ruminations, I felt liberated.

****

I lowered my voice so it lost the tone I had adopted for much of my remarks. Once again, I paused. Just for a second, I savored the moment.

**"Over two hundred times in his writings, Severance uses the phrase 'violence wins.' Over and over again: "violence wins, violence wins, violence wins."**

**"The 12 of you have the power to tell the defendant he's wrong. The 12 of you have the power to tell the defendant that violence does not win in the end. You have the power to tell the defendant loudly and clearly as the conscience of the community that the love these three beautiful, precious human souls**

showed during their lives far outweighs the evil and horror he has wrought."

"Love wins in the end."

I finished with words I have used in every jury trial I have ever tried. I came up with these words as a very young attorney and I am amazed that, all these years later, they still seem appropriate:

"Nancy Dunning's voice was stilled 12 years ago. Ron Kirby's was stilled 20 months ago. Ruthanne Lodato's was stilled just over a year ago."

"The defense has had their say and, in a minute, my voice will be silent, too."

"Then there will only be one voice left."

"That's your voice—the 12 of you speaking collectively as the conscience of the community, telling the defendant he is wrong about violence winning and doing so by confidently speaking one word ten different times."

"You know what that word is."

\*\*\*\*

I will always remember the moment. I felt electric. I stood, erect, silent and with my hands outstretched, for several seconds. I slowly made eye contact with each juror.

Having surveyed the souls who now had the responsibility of rendering a verdict, I dropped my gaze, quietly turned and returned to my seat. Judge Bellows addressed the jurors for a minute, thanking them for their service. He identified and excused the four alternate jurors who had previously been randomly selected, leaving the final, 12-member jury. Bellows then dismissed the jury to begin their deliberations.

I closed my eyes and once again thanked God for how well the trial had gone for us.

There are no atheists in train tunnels.

\*\*\*\*

I recall in vivid detail what I was thinking as the jury filed out of the courtroom. I was very proud of the investigative and trial teams. The detectives had handed us a professional and thorough investigation. A group of dedicated police professionals had worked countless hours to identify a serial killer.

My team had translated the investigation into a comprehensive trial plan. I was exceptionally pleased with the manner in which the plan was executed. All of the evidence we had sought to admit into the case was before the jury. We had dealt with a plethora of gremlins, none of which had caused significant damage. We had put a huge amount of time and effort into the case, preparing every aspect in excruciating detail. It had paid off. We had left it all on the field of battle and done everything within our power to secure a conviction.

No matter how hard we had worked, no matter how well our trial plan had been implemented, a conviction was not guaranteed. In our country, the outcome of a criminal trial is not preordained and, given the heavy burden placed on the prosecution and the presumption of innocence, there is always a significant chance of an acquittal.

I believed in the hard work of the detectives and my trial team. I wanted Severance to be held accountable for his actions. I wanted him to be publicly exposed as a cowardly murderer.

Given the abject cruelty surrounding these three homicides, my desire for a just result was exponentially heightened. Whenever I thought of the horror Nancy, Ron and Ruthanne experienced in their last minutes, I experienced a physical reaction. I felt a sense of moral outrage and an obligation to the memories of the victims themselves.

There were other victims who deserved a just result. Jeanette, understandably, was terrified Severance would come after her. She was on the edge of tears as she related the chronic nightmares she experienced. A conviction would mean she need not worry about Severance targeting her in the future.

I counted Jim Dunning as the fifth victim in this case. By charging Severance with Nancy's murder, I had partially cleared Jim's name. For those watching the trial, Chris Dunning had evaporated any lingering cloud of suspicion, but an acquittal would allow the whispers and innuendoes to slowly return like an incoming tide. Securing a conviction in Nancy's death would exonerate Jim in the eyes of the wider public, a goal I now believed was imperative to achieve.

I also felt duty-bound to the surviving family members of all three victims. David, Jimmy, Marc and I had fostered a close relationship with these amazing people. I wanted them to have a sense of finality and to know the man who had ripped their lives apart in a flurry of violence could no longer harm them.

I wanted a conviction for the Alexandria community. I wanted the City to know its police department had put countless hours into the most complex case it had ever been tasked with investigating and, through the hard work of countless public servants, had risen to the task. I wanted Alexandrians to be able to slumber peacefully, confident the right man had been identified, prosecuted and convicted. I dreamed of helping to restore the aura of small-town sensibility to the city I was sworn to protect.

I wanted people to feel safe answering a knock at their front doors.

Most of all, I wanted a conviction so Charles Severance would be unable to kill anyone else.

But the longer the jury deliberated, the less confident I was in the outcome. Every second that ticked away made a conviction seem more distant. My mind raced, imagining apocalyptic situations with Severance walking free and retrieving his "five-shot mini-revolvers, stainless steel with the wooden grip."

****

At about 9:45 on Monday, November 2, Judy Holl came rushing into the "War Room" in which we were nervously biding our time. "There's a verdict!" she shouted. Just as quickly she flew out of the room to gather the families who were waiting nearby. I felt a quick wave of nausea, much like the one imparted by the initial drop of a roller coaster, as I stood to begin my trek upstairs.

As our team walked in, the courtroom was a beehive of activity. Reporters were busy typing on their mobile devices so they could quickly tweet "Guilty!" or "Not Guilty!" The victims' families were huddled together, quietly talking, in the first two rows of courtroom pews. The defense attorneys were clustered on their side of the courtroom.

Given the electricity in the room, a gaggle of people greeted me and tried to engage me in small talk. I was not in the mood. I was consumed with a feeling equal parts dread and anticipation; it hung over me like a wool blanket. To make it clear I did not want to chat I entered the "well" of the courtroom, walked over to the empty jury box and leaned against it, my chin in my hand. A news photographer snapped a picture of me that can still be found on the internet. When I look at that photo, I am immediately transported back in time and remember the line I was repeating in my head: "Let's get this over with."

Soon thereafter Judge Bellows took the bench. I returned to the prosecution table to await the verdicts, casting my eyes at a random point behind Bellows and burning a hole in the courtroom wall. I did not look at the jurors as they filed into the courtroom. I was afraid of what I might read on their faces.

The manner in which the verdict in a criminal case is announced was apparently designed by some 1600s functionary to heighten the drama in the courtroom. Judge Bellows asked the foreperson whether the jury had reached a unanimous verdict on all 10 counts of the indictment. Receiving an affirmative reply, Bellows asked for those verdicts, which had been reduced to writing on several pieces of paper. The foreperson handed the documents to the bailiff, who handed them to the courtroom clerk. She quickly scanned them and handed them in turn to Judge Bellows. Bellows, returning to his sphinxlike form, studied the documents intently for what seemed an eternity. Meanwhile, all in attendance held their collective breath and watched the spectacle.

I felt like I was about to pass out.

Bellows then handed the verdict forms back to his clerk and asked her to announce the verdicts.

\*\*\*\*

"On Count One, the jury finds the defendant, Charles Stanard Severance... guilty of the capital murder of Ruthanne Lodato."

One down, nine to go. An immense wave of relief rushed over me. Even if the jury found him "not guilty" on all other charges, a capital murder conviction meant Severance would never again see the outside of a prison.

"On Count Two, the jury finds the defendant, Charles Stanard Severance... guilty of using a firearm in the murder of Ruthanne Lodato."

"On Count Three, the jury finds the defendant, Charles Stanard Severance... guilty of the capital murder of Ronald Kirby."

"On Count Four, the jury finds the defendant, Charles Stanard Severance... guilty of using a firearm in the murder of Ronald Kirby."

Four counts, four convictions. Obtaining a conviction in the Kirby case was a huge victory. The jury agreed the same person was responsible for murdering Ron and Ruthanne.

The only question left was whether we had secured a conviction in the Dunning case. Going into the trial I rationalized that I could live with an acquittal in Nancy's murder as long as we obtained convictions on the other charges. I was personally convinced Severance was guilty, of course, but I realized the "10-year gap" made a clean sweep of all three murders more difficult.

My willingness to accept an acquittal on the Dunning murder had abated during the trial. Our case had proceeded exactly as planned—or perhaps even better, given the emotional impact of Chris Dunning's testimony. The evidence of Severance's culpability in the Dunning murder was overwhelming. Anyone who had watched the entire trial had to be convinced Severance killed Nancy.

I sat facing forward and totally immobile. I remember thinking it ironic I was reacting to the jury verdicts in the same manner as Severance. He, too, sat staring straight ahead as the verdicts were read. I don't think it was lost on him that he was going to spend the rest of his days slowly wasting away in a prison cell.

****

The clerk had reached Count Five, the murder of Nancy Dunning.

"The jury finds the defendant, Charles Stanard Severance.... guilty of murdering Nancy Dunning in the first degree."

Another wave of emotion broke over me as these words were read. Tears welled in my eyes. All of the hard work, all of the sleepless nights, all of the collective decisions the trial team made—all had been rewarded.

My personal journey was likewise complete. Despite my doubts and fears, and with the help of countless others, I had risen to the challenge.

The reign of the Alexandria Assassin was over.

****

The verdicts on the remaining five counts followed quickly. Severance was found guilty of shooting Jeanette and of various related firearms offenses. I had indicted 10 charges. The jury convicted on all of them.

Virginia is one of a few states that engages in jury sentencing. After returning a guilty verdict, another hearing is held in which evidence related to the appropriate punishment is adduced. The jury then meets again to deliberate on the appropriate sentence.

After a brief interlude, the jury unanimously sentenced Charles Severance to the maximum penalties allowed by law: three life sentences, plus 48 years in prison and a fine of $400,000.

Three life sentences with no possibility of parole.

And, as these words are written, Charles Severance wallows in the anger and self-pity that marked his wretched existence. Severance resides in Wallens Ridge State Prison, a facility in southwest Virginia designed to hold the "worst of the worst." Every day, each and every facet of his life is monitored and directed by members of the "oppressive law enforcement class" he so desperately despises. For Charles Severance, this is a fate far worse than death.

Severance fervently believed that violence wins.

Jeanette, Chris Dunning and twelve jurors, good and true, proved him wrong.

# AFTERWORD – LESSONS LEARNED

In the years that have passed since the trial I have frequently been asked what could have been done to stop Severance before he started killing. Unfortunately, there are no easy answers to this difficult question.

Charles Severance's anger and sense of alienation are shared by many others who resort to violence. The thinking of those who engage in public mass shootings is similar to Severance's. So is the ideation of terrorists. In these situations, the perpetrator feels alienated from mainstream society. They perceive an "enemy" who has insulted them and deserves to be chastised, whether the enemy be "law enforcement elites" or a religious minority. Violent action is cloaked in a quasi-political or religious veneer and a fervent belief that violence will change the world. Furthermore, a person who feels unappreciated by his fellow man may suddenly "matter" if he is "brave" enough to act.

Mass shooting events have become so frequent in the United States I fear we are becoming inured. Over 300 mass shooting events were reported in 2018, almost one a day on average. It is undeniable we have a crisis on our hands.

My experience in this case—and many other violent crimes—has provided a unique vantagepoint from which to consider the intersection of violence and mental health in America. This afterword is my attempt to address several difficult realities Americans would rather ignore as well as proffer some specific ideas that could improve the situation.

## Difficult Realities

Society has to be realistic. While their numbers are small, other Charles Severances do walk among us. It is disturbing to consider there are hundreds of potential serial murderers scattered throughout the United States as this very moment—people who perceive slights, nurse grudges and dream of harming others.

I want to stress that studies prove the majority of those who suffer from mental health issues would never commit a crime, let alone an act of violence. To the contrary, people who suffer from mental health disorders are far more likely to be a victim of crime than an offender. But a very small percentage of those suffering from mental illness do pose a direct threat to others.

In the six years I have served as the elected prosecutor for a medium-sized city, my office has prosecuted a litany of violent cases directly related to mental disorders. The list includes a mentally ill person who killed and sexually assaulted a complete stranger and was determined to be criminally insane, a mentally ill person who escaped from a non-secure mental health facility and tried to rape a woman and another who waited on the elevator of an office building until someone got on and then told the victim—a total stranger—she had been waiting "to kill" him before attacking him with a knife. I could easily add more frightening examples.

Unless the future proves "Minority Report" prescient, law enforcement will never be able to stop all killers before they act. The best they can do is minimize the frequency of violence. Even this cannot be achieved without being honest about the problem and, right now, society is not being honest. There is a distinct tendency for our leaders to blame the mental health system in the aftermath of a mass killing. I heard the usual bromide in the run up to our trial: "Severance was deranged! Off his rocker! Why didn't the mental health system figure it out and stop him?!"

Our country is operating under a delusion that future Severances can be easily identified and stopped by mental health professionals. There is a common assumption the mass shootings we experience with stunning frequency are the result of the criminally insane perpetrators who can easily be identified and hospitalized.

Politicians perpetuate this myth. In the aftermath of violence, our leaders hold press conferences, offer their hopes and prayers and repeat the myth that mass killings are the product of systemic failures of the "system."

The idea the "mental health system" is capable of stopping every mass murderer is a fantasy designed to make the citizenry feel safe. By offering up vague notions of "fixing the system," politicians avoid discussing politically riskier ideas that could hurt their chances of winning an election.

Politicians talk about the "mental health system" as though it were a monolithic federal agency. To the contrary, the "system" is comprised of a hodgepodge of state and local agencies as well as a network of private mental health professionals. The numerous "silos" mean the quality, quantity and availability of mental health services varies significantly across the nation.

The mental health system does have a role to play in addressing our national crisis of violence. However, there are a number of significant restrictions on what the system can achieve.

For instance, people who suffer from anti-personality disorders present a dilemma of detection. Persons with personality disorders are often sufficiently rational to mask their symptoms and may never be identified as needing treatment.

Even those persons who are identified cannot be hospitalized against their will unless there is evidence they present an imminent danger to themselves or others. Frequently, the person will be aware enough to avoid providing a doctor with evidence he constitutes a danger.

Consider Charles Severance. Was the "mental health system" at fault for his crimes, failing to recognize a serial killer? Severance suffered from several personality disorders but was not schizophrenic. He eked out a marginal existence in society. He was not in a catatonic state. He did not talk to unseen voices. He did not tell his friends and family about his inner rage, at least not in detail. He did not tell his parents he was going to drive to Alexandria and commit murder. He wrote his disturbing thoughts down in his notebook until the hate boiled over and he felt he had to kill.

It is axiomatic that if a person suffering from mental health issues is never brought to the attention of a doctor, the mental health system cannot intervene.

So how is it the Severances of the world are not brought to the attention of the mental health system?

First, those most likely to notice a person is having mental health issues are the person's closest friends and family who often do not want to believe a loved one needs help. Severance's parents did not think their son was angry enough to kill. They tried to get him mental health treatment only once, in the early 1990s. Severance went to an appointment and received some medication. He took one dose, disliked the side effects and said he was never going back. Our investigation determined he received no other psychological treatment—ever.

There are a host of reasons why friends and family

might be unwilling to push mental health treatment on a loved one. They may feel they are guilty of "betrayal" if they try to push treatment. Since a mental health diagnosis brings with it a negative stigma, family members are reluctant to press the issue for fear of branding a family member as "crazy." A parent could feel as if they are somehow admitting a defect in themselves if they agree their child needs help or could fear provoking an angry response. The path of least resistance is to do nothing.

It is even more absurd to expect those suffering from mental illness to proactively seek treatment themselves. Those in crisis often have no insight about their illness. Most vehemently deny being mentally ill at all. The paranoid are likely to see mental health treatment as a governmental effort to control them.

In those cases where a person in crisis is identified it is extremely difficult to hospitalize them without their consent. Placing someone into a mental hospital against their will is an enormous intrusion into their liberty and a host of due process guarantees are rightfully built into the commitment process. Under the current regime, the state cannot commit someone for treatment unless the person is suffering from a severe mental illness **and** is currently an active threat of engaging in acts of violence. There must be credible evidence that the person constitutes an imminent danger of violence before commitment proceedings can be initiated.

This requirement of imminent danger poses a significant problem when dealing with offenders like Charles Severance. Had a mental health professional ever screened him for his risk of violence, Severance was sufficiently in control of his faculties to answer in a way that would have made him seem benign. If a professional asked: "are you having thoughts of killing someone?"

Severance would have understood the consequences of a truthful answer and would have dissembled: "Doctor, I would never dream of hurting anyone."

The chances Severance could have been identified by "the system" and hospitalized against his will are exceedingly slim.

**** 

Even in the rare case where someone is deemed a danger and is committed to a hospital, they are usually released from the hospital relatively quickly.

Roughly a hundred years ago, the American system of treating mental illness primarily relied on large, secure mental health hospitals run by the states. People who were in the throes of a mental crisis would be institutionalized without a showing they constituted a danger. They would languish in Byzantine hospitals, unable to challenge their continued detention in court.

As our views of mental health evolved, so did our practices with regard to the mentally ill. Hospitals were closed, the requirement of active danger was imposed before involuntary commitment would lie and mental health doctors became more empathetic to their patients. Commitment rates were drastically reduced throughout the country. When a person was involuntarily committed, the goal of the treatment team morphed into trying to stabilize the patient and expeditiously return them to society.

These reforms were overdue and a huge improvement. I do not advocate for the return of mass hospitalization of persons undergoing a mental health crisis. The right call is always the least-intrusive intervention necessary and outpatient treatment usually is appropriate.

Nevertheless, a comprehensive review of how we identify, treat and consider mental health disorders—and how we deal with them inside of the courtroom— is part of a holistic attempt to address the acts of mass violence afflicting our country.

****

If, by some lucky accident, Charles Severance had been identified as a risk before he started killing, it is unlikely he could have been successfully treated. I am not a mental health professional, but my understanding is it is extremely difficult to treat personality disorders and almost impossible to "cure" those suffering from this unfortunate malady.

The necessary ingredients for a series of assassinations were all present inside of Charles Severance: anger, obsessiveness, a heightened sense of being wronged, wicked intelligence, a fascination with firearms and a conviction that violence was the correct method of imposing "justice" on an unjust world. In an earlier age he may have just been called "evil."

The violent and angry mindset exhibited by Severance is not unique to him. It is the same motivation behind any number of modern tragedies. Every mass shooter is motivated by a similar mindset, as are suicide bombers in Afghanistan. So too, Charles Manson and the Unabomber. In all of these examples, obsessive anger, fueled by a sense of resentment and ignited by a lack of empathy, results in a sociopathic attempt to "change" things. Yet the change never comes. September 11th did not lead to the downfall of the United States, Manson's "Helter Skelter" never materialized and Severance's "revolution" against the "elites" existed solely in the frightening confines of his own disturbed mind.

****

Charles Severance bears many similarities to the

Unabomber, Theodore Kaczynski. There is a passing physical similarity between them, particularly with regard to their beards. Those who suffer from antisocial personality disorders, as both Kaczynski and Severance do, often inadequately attend to personal grooming. Perhaps this is a conscious attempt to flaunt society's norms. The young Charles Severance was a handsome man who often caught the attention of women. As he aged and his illness festered, his grooming deteriorated, leading to the disheveled and outlandish appearance he presented in the courtroom.

Both the Unabomber and Severance were recluses, although Kaczynski took this to a higher level, living by himself in a cabin in the woods. While Severance did have limited social interactions, residing with Robra and occasionally visiting his parents, he spent almost a decade by himself, driving around the United States and living out of his Ford Escort. He would occasionally disappear for several days without warning.

Kaczynski and Severance were highly intelligent and well-read, earning degrees from prestigious universities. Both were prolific writers, producing a corpus of work that could be rightfully called a Manifesto. Kaczynski's was more organized and explicit in its aims, but both incorporated a twisted political theory into a written corpus outlining their worldview.

I find it striking both men despised modern society and wished to return to an earlier, simpler age. Severance's adherence to the "noble savage" theory perfectly illustrated this commonality, as did Kaczynski's assertion the "Industrial Revolution" was a "disaster" for the human race. Severance longed to be a colonial "patriarch" wearing a tricorn hat and tending to his homestead.

Kaczynski sought the downfall of "modern technology," suggesting a "revolution" against technology and modern government was necessary. Twisted minds think alike.

Both men suffered from abnormal thought processes. They suffered from ideas of reference; i.e., attaching strong personal significance to occurrences which were, in reality, innocuous events or coincidences. There is no evidence either was actively psychotic or suffered from the other harbingers of severe schizophrenia: thought insertion, thought deletion or bizarre delusions.

Another commonality is neither Severance nor Kaczynski wanted to be caught. They were convinced they were clever enough to outsmart law enforcement and get away with their crimes, free to kill again whenever the urge to do so overcame them.

This desire to avoid being captured is a substantial difference from those who engage in mass shootings. Yet there remain similarities between Severance and mass shooters. Both types of killer want to make an impression on a world that has failed to recognize them. If a person can dominate the news cycle and terrorize huge swaths of the citizenry, in a twisted sense, they "matter." Mass shooters want their names plastered all over the news. Severance anomalously wished to remain anonymous—but he likely reveled in seeing the news coverage of his crimes.

While it is facile to expect the "mental health" system to be the sole solution to the crisis of mass murders, I turn now to several concrete proposals that could make a difference. I do not assert that they would completely solve the crisis. I set them forth as a beginning point for deliberation and discussion.

## Mental Health Treatment

**One:** A concerted effort should be made to facilitate communication between the myriad of public and private mental health professionals constituting our fragmented "mental health system." Real concerns exist about the confidentiality of patient information but, in certain situations, mental health professionals must be required to alert law enforcement about patients who may be about to resort to violence. The rules surrounding such notifications can be debated and tweaked but once decided upon should be made universal across the country. Uniformity of requirements facilitates compliance.

Psychologists are ethically bound to consider the needs of the patient above all else. This does not mean, however, they must disregard public safety. While assessing the future threat a person poses is a difficult foray into the unknowable, a new emphasis on trying to calculate threats to public safety is vital. Once a person is determined to pose such a threat that information must be shared with police.

Given the fractured network of treatment providers, each with different legal or professional restrictions on the dissemination of patient information, any real reform in this area will require congressional involvement.

**Two:** We must continue to lessen the stigma attached to mental disorders. The unfortunate negativity attributed to people who are experiencing mental illness is a roadblock to progress. It causes those who suffer to be reluctant to seek treatment for fear of being branded "crazy." Perhaps more to the point, the stigma associated with mental illness is often a barrier to a healthy person intervening with a family member or friend in the throes of a crisis. In many cases, family members are going to see disturbing behavior from a loved one well before they resort to violence. Therefore, they may serve as an "early warning system" for disturbing behavior. They should be encouraged to report it–not fearful of stigmatizing their loved one with a pejorative label.

Society does not normally take a negative view of those suffering from a physical ailment. A person who has a severe mental illness is as much a victim of circumstance as a person with a diagnosis of cancer. Neither asked for the disease and both must live with it. An inference there is some defect in character in a person suffering from mental illness is morally wrong and a significant impediment to early intervention.

The way to reduce this negative stigma is to educate people. The citizenry needs to hear that mentally ill people are far more likely to be a victim of crime than to commit one. Education has the beneficial effects of lessening fear and dispelling ignorance.

**Three:** There should be a concerted public service campaign to explain what personality disorders are and what symptoms characterize them.

Unless you or a family member has been afflicted by one, it is probable you have had almost no exposure to the causes, symptoms and effects of personality disorders. Most lay people have a binary view of mental illness: either you're "crazy" and "mumbling to yourself," or you're not. Few understand the significant spectrum upon which mental health disorders exist. Personality disorders are even more arcane, but a significant number of those who resort to mass killings have been diagnosed with them.

Personality disorders are rarely discussed outside of

the mental health profession and are almost unknown to the greater community. Suffice it to say that if personality disorders present symptoms outside of the traditional understanding of what "mental illness" should look like, society would be well-served by a populace better trained to look for their warning signs.

**Four:** Federal, state and local governments must increase funding for mental health services. While I maintain the mental health system is not the only answer to the crisis, it is undeniably plays a substantial role. We have far too few in-patient beds in Virginia and struggle to find treatment for those who could benefit from out-patient programs. Money must be spent on training for mental health professionals, particularly with regard to personality disorders. If intervention, outpatient treatment and inpatient beds are not available, it is obvious intervention and treatment will not occur.

More money should be expended on mental health wings in correctional facilities. While I believe Charles Severance must remain locked up to avoid him murdering another human being, I would have no issue with him serving his sentence in a secure hospital as opposed to a mainstream prison.

Where treatment options are underfunded or non-existent, it is often police officers and prosecutors who are left to deal with those suffering a mental crisis. This is what happened in the Severance case: on two separate occasions, he was arrested for firearms offenses after displaying disturbing behavior. However, the only consequences of these arrests were a short stay in jail and a subsequent felony conviction. In neither case did he receive supervised probation or mental health treatment.

As a prosecutor, I have no desire to be left "holding the bag" and acting as the mental health provider of last resort—a job for which I am not trained. Prosecutors are a blunt tool, seeking to encourage compliance with societal norms through pressures such as probation and suspended jail time. A person suffering from severe mental illness often is incapable of adapting their behavior to conform with what society expects and, where this is the case, the regular approach cannot work. I strongly advocate for more funding for mental health treatment, hopefully to intervene before a person is arrested, but also to provide prosecutors with an avenue by which a non-violent criminal defendant may be diverted for treatment. My office's innovative Mental Health Initiative and Treatment Court programs are two examples of programs for which we could use substantial additional funding.

**Five:** We must create more options for mandating treatment for those suffering from severe mental illness. As it stands now, a person experiencing a mental health crisis may volunteer to undergo treatment. If the person refuses to volunteer—as many do—the only way the government can force him to see a doctor is if there is probable cause to believe he is an "imminent danger to himself or others." Even if a person is suffering from an extremely serious mental health crisis, it is almost impossible to require him to receive mental health treatment unless he is actively threatening to harm someone.

I do not support expansive government power to sweep up the mentally ill. I do support creating a mechanism by which a judge could order a person to be taken into custody for a mental health evaluation and/or treatment if, based on the credible testimony of the person's next-of-kin or his treating mental health professional, the judge finds the custody is in the person's best interest and that the person is incapable of making an informed or rational decision about seeking mental health treatment. In many such cases, the person will be quickly released after a mental health professional determines outpatient treatment will suffice. In more serious cases, this mechanism would hopefully allow the system to intervene before a tragedy occurs. Of course, I propose that a host of due process be baked in; the right to an attorney, the right to appeal a judge's decision and the right to a jury trial on the question of involuntary treatment if it is ordered by a judge.

This is a defensible idea which could end up benefiting both the person suffering from a crisis and society. Such "win-win" strategies must be explored.

**Six:** Adopt more stringent measures designed to prevent those in crisis from accessing firearms. Over the past decade a number of states have enacted what are known as "Extreme Risk Protective Order(ERPO)" laws. An ERPO bill recently passed in gun-friendly Florida.

These statutes allow family members and law enforcement officers to petition state courts for an order to seize firearms from people suffering a mental health crisis. ERPOs apply only in circumstances where a person is an active risk for violence and are designed to balance public safety with the constitutional rights of the person who is the subject of the petition. The person is given notice of court hearings, the right to present evidence and the right to appeal a decision of a trial court.

## Firearms

Before I begin my discussion of firearms, I need to

make something clear: I understand the ownership of firearms is constitutionally protected, a fact recently emphasized by the Supreme Court in the *Heller* case.

On the other hand, as former Supreme Court Justice Robert Jackson famously noted, the Constitution is not a suicide pact. The Supreme Court has agreed the government can impose reasonable restrictions on the Second Amendment right to keep and bear arms. In a similar way, it may impose reasonable restrictions on the First Amendment right to free speech. For example, it is illegal to falsely yell "fire!" in a crowded movie theater because of the dangerous panic such speech may cause.

Right now it is impossible to have an informed debate about any proposed gun law. This particular issue is so polarizing it forces a tribalism in which a person must choose a side and toe the party line in all respects. Any weakness or willingness to negotiate—or even to have conversation!— is seen as an abject capitulation.

This situation is lamentable and not conducive to public safety. Reasonable people can differ on what constitutes an acceptable restriction on the right to possess a gun. The process of determining which restrictions should be imposed requires those on opposite sides to intelligently discuss proposals with a willingness to at least listen to the other party. We must work together, in a spirit of public discourse and civic-mindedness, to protect society from violence.

To that end, I offer several ideas about firearms.

**One:** Congress should adequately fund and update the National Integrated Ballistics Information Network (NIBIN). NIBIN is the primary means by which law enforcement officers link recovered firearms and ammunition to other crimes. As currently constituted, NIBIN is bedeviled by several glaring inadequacies. There should be nationwide, standardized requirements for the timely entry of information into the system and more money for data entry so backlogs can be eliminated. Just as pressing, more data needs to be entered. While NIBIN has the capability of storing and comparing images of both spent cartridge cases and bullets, the reality is almost 90% of the images in the system are of spent cartridge cases. Images of fired bullets require more time and specialized equipment to upload and are usually not entered. This lack of data hampers the ability of the system to produce "hits." If a revolver is used in a crime NIBIN will likely be of no use, since revolvers do not eject cartridge cases.

More funding for the inclusion of images of test-fired bullets from recovered firearms and from spent bullets recovered from violent crime scenes is imperative. More data means a more comprehensive system and one capable of producing many more "hits" for follow-up investigation. Had a well-funded system containing a significant number of images of spent bullets been in place at the time of Severance's 2004 arrest in Rockingham County, it is possible the Dunning case would have been solved far earlier.

Additionally, all states should adopt legislation requiring state and local law-enforcement officers to upload data into NIBIN. As I write these words, only two states mandate the submission of firearms evidence, Delaware and New Jersey. Given 48 states do not require submission, nationwide compliance with providing data to NIBIN is spotty and limited. In 10 states, the state crime lab does not submit evidence to NIBIN at all.

If every police department and sheriff's office immediately uploaded images of cartridge cases and fired projectiles, all sorts of connections with other violent crimes could be made. This would allow many shootings to be solved and it would have the salubrious effect of stopping some shootings before they are committed by helping to get violent offenders off the street. Like so many initiatives, significantly increasing NIBIN submissions would require new outlays of money. Given this is one proven way to immediately start solving cases, it would be money well spent.

**Two:** State and federal agencies must ensure all persons prohibited from possessing a firearm are entered into the National Instant Criminal Background Check(NICS) database. All states and the federal government restrict the right of convicted felons to purchase firearms. This system of prohibition, however, is only as good as the data entered into it.

A recent case from my jurisdiction illustrates the problem. In 2014, the suspect observed a stranger walking down a street in Old Town Alexandria and decided that he wanted to assault her. In preparation, he bought a firearm at a local gun store and drove to his intended victim's place of employment. She observed him outside of the store and, fearful of him, locked the door and called the police.

When officers arrived on the scene the suspect drove away. Soon, an Alexandria Police motorcycle officer located the suspect's car and pulled it over. Without warning, the suspect jumped out of the car and shot the officer once in the head, almost killing him and causing significant brain damage. The suspect was arrested after leading other officers on a high-speed chase and charged with Attempted Capital Murder of a Law Enforcement Officer. While I agree he was schizophrenic, the shooting of an officer and the subsequent attempt at escape implied that he knew what he was doing was wrong.

The suspect's attorneys raised the insanity defense. Two psychologists testified that he was schizophrenic and thought he was living in "the Matrix" at the time of the offense. The suspect told his doctors he thought the police officer was a computer program that could spontaneously regenerate after being shot. In light of the mental health testimony, the trial judge found him not guilty by reason of insanity and sent him to a state hospital for treatment.

Less than four years after that verdict, the suspect's treatment team opined that he was no longer a danger to the community and his attorney asked that he be allowed to return to the community. The judge agreed and the suspect walked out of the hospital.

Just eight months after his release the suspect was rearrested for attempted arson of a residence—a residence selected because of his anger toward the occupant. A search warrant was later executed on the suspect's apartment and two firearms located. It was determined he had purchased the guns at a gun store despite being legally disqualified to do so by the insanity verdict.

Investigation revealed that this information "slipped through the cracks" and was not entered into NICS. Since the suspect was not in the system, he was able to walk into a gun store and buy a firearm. Although thankfully no one was hurt, this second arrest involved an intentional effort on the suspect's part to harm a particular person.

A review of this purchase revealed inadequacies in the process used to enter data into NICS. In 2018, Virginia determined something like 750,000 felony convictions had not been entered into the database, to include more than 300 murders and over 1300 rapes. The issue is not limited to Virginia. The most common explanation is the agencies tasked with entering the data are under-staffed and underfunded.

The solution is twofold: first, every state should conduct a thorough review of their background check databases to determine the extent of the problem. The review should include felony convictions as well as those who have been acquitted by reason of insanity. Once the review is complete, legislatures must robustly fund the agencies responsible for entry of such information both to enter the missing data and to keep up with such entries in the future.

There are cases in which a legally-prohibited person was able to purchase a gun and use it to commit a mass shooting. In February 2019, a disgruntled employee and convicted felon shot and killed five co-workers in Aurora, Illinois, wounding several police officers in the attack. It was determined the man's felony conviction had not been entered into NICS, allowing him to purchase the gun used in the crime from a gun store. It is lamentable this tragedy could have been averted.

**Three:** Universal background checks should be mandated. An increase in the data entered into NICS will exponentially increase its efficacy. However, current federal law only requires background checks for sales made by a federally licensed firearms dealer. Private citizens not engaged in the business of selling guns are free to conclude transactions without any check at all and almost a quarter of legitimate guns sales involve no background check. Sales made at gun shows make up a significant portion of this tally

The solution is to require background checks for all

firearms transactions to include private, personal sales. What is rare about this proposal is not just its simplicity—it is its overwhelming public support. While most gun proposals reveal a polarized electorate, polls have consistently shown universal background checks to have the support of about 90% of the population. One poll revealed over 70% of NRA members were in support.

As with many of these proposals, relying on a piecemeal process of each state adopting universal background checks will be ineffective. Firearms move in interstate commerce and, therefore, this proposal demands a change to federal law.

**Four:** Require all American firearms manufacturers to test fire a round of every firearm they manufacture and take a forensic image of the test-fired round. These images could either be maintained by the manufacturer or uploaded into a new NIBIN-style database for subsequent comparison to recovered ammunition components from violent crime scenes. When coupled with the current ATF eTrace program, which helps establish who originally purchased a particular firearm, this system could help provide leads in a number of serious, violent crimes each year.

If such a system had been in place during the Severance case, it is at least possible the recovered bullets from the Dunning murder would have been matched to the mini-revolver Severance purchased in 2003. While the system would not have prevented Nancy's death, it may have allowed police to identify Severance soon after the crime.

**Five:** Make it easier to prosecute "straw purchases" of firearms. Currently, a straw purchase prosecution is difficult to maintain because the government has to prove the purchaser actually intended to buy a firearm for a person they knew was prohibited from possessing one. For example, had I charged Linda Robra for a straw purchase the case against her would have been tough to prove because of her adamant position that she bought the guns "for herself." Indeed it is quite likely she would have been acquitted despite buying the guns at Severance's behest and thereafter allowing him unfettered access to them.

A new legal standard requiring evidence the buyer "knew *or reasonably should have known*" the firearm was being purchased for a prohibited person would make prosecutions easier and increase the deterrent effect of the statute. In addition, a new law should be adopted that makes it a felony to purchase a firearm and to thereafter negligently allow a prohibited person access to it.

**Six:** State legislatures must consider and debate other statutory restrictions on firearms. I am well aware this is a political "third-rail," but I have little use for grandstanding and posturing—my objective is to protect the community. If a new law may help achieve that end, I want to talk about it.

I advocate for a free, thoughtful debate about potential gun legislation. Both sides should discuss ideas with an understanding not all ideas are good ones. It may be that, at the end of the debate, no consensus on measures can be reached and no new laws enacted, but our republic was founded on the hope that discussion and debate would inure to the public good. If guns remain a "third rail" topic that cannot even be discussed, our society will be rendered less safe.

Topics for discussion could include small measures like banning bump stocks, intermediate measures such as outlawing extended magazines and significant measures like restricting assault rifles or requiring a national registry of firearms sales, searchable by buyer. A registry with even a limited amount of information could help identify those who are amassing an arsenal prior to an explosion of violence. I understand this last idea is the most politically fraught, but it should at least be debated.

I am under no illusion these proposals, even in the unlikely event all were adopted, would erase any chance of another Charles Severance getting his hands on a firearm. Yet we cannot afford to do nothing. We must be willing to engage in an intellectually honest debate about what should be done. If we do not, we will certainly accomplish nothing.


## CONCLUSION

One of the poverties of prosecuting murders is I am necessarily deprived of meeting the victims. So it was in the Severance case. Having grown up in Alexandria, I had a passing acquaintance with Ruthanne Lodato and I met Nancy Dunning once as a young man. I had never spoken to Ron Kirby. I did not know any of them well.

After Severance was indicted I scheduled regular meetings with the victims' families. Their recollections of Nancy, Ron and Ruthanne helped me understand what wonderful people they were. I learned about Nancy's philanthropic bent, about Ron's commitment to COG and about Ruthanne's impact on generations of Alexandria's children. I heard about the wisdom and humor they had shared with those who knew them and how much they loved their children.

This book may be written from my viewpoint, but the case was about the anguish of the Lodato, Kirby and

Dunning families.

Police officers are rarely praised for their hard work and I am proud to commend the detectives who worked this case. Detectives Cutting, Kochis, Casey and Oakley and the others who assisted them are the paradigm of what police officers should be. It was my privilege to work with them.

The attorneys and support personnel who formed my trial team are a credit to our profession. I am extremely proud of the fact our team prosecuted the case with a fierce tenacity and did a professional job of marshalling one of the most lengthy and complicated trials in recent Virginia history. Obviously, I am thankful Severance cannot hurt anyone else.

But these are not the things of which I am most proud.

On September 8, 2014, the day Charles Severance was indicted, I met with the victims' families in a conference room at the Alexandria Police Department. I told them the only thing I could promise was that I would fight the case with whatever ability God had given me. I promised I would stand with them every step of the way and see the case through to the end.

I kept those promises.

****

The Severance case was recently highlighted on a "true crime" television show. I was interviewed in preparation and was asked whether I thought the guilty verdicts constituted "justice" for the families. While I think the outcome of the case was just and the best that an imperfect human being could obtain, it did not, does not and could never constitute justice.

Securing justice for the Dunning, Kirby and Lodato families was impossible. An outstanding police investigation or a courtroom victory could never atone for the tragedy inflicted by Charles Severance's murderous rage.

It was and will always remain beyond my ability to do the one thing that could possibly make things "right"— because I could not give the families a chance to see Ruthanne, Ron and Nancy again. From day one, I was destined to fail in obtaining true "justice." The best I could do was bring the families a modicum of solace and the security of knowing Severance could never hurt anyone else. I pray I accomplished these aims.

The only entity that could provide justice to an unjust world is our Creator. Perhaps it is surprising for me to note that my experience in this case, and the amazing humanity I witnessed in so many different people, has brought me a little closer to believing in Him.

But it has. And I am thankful for that.

Fifty years from now, if anyone remembers this case or, by some miracle, is even reading these words, I hope they pause to consider the lives of Ruthanne Lodato, Ron Kirby and Nancy Dunning. Three beautiful people who spent their lives giving to and loving others.

May they rest in peace.

Their light outweighs the darkness. Their good outweighs the evil.

All of the false prophets throughout the ages–the countless, writhing multitude, those who have been and those who are to come–all of them are wrong.

Patience is not an excuse for cowardice.

Power does not come from the barrel of a smoking gun.

Thou shalt not kill is not a lie...

And violence does not win.

Love wins in the end.

CPSIA information can be obtained
at www.ICGtesting.com
Printed in the USA
FFHW021248051119
55996508-61836FF